The Mechanism of Speech

The Mechanism of Speech

Wolfgang von Kempelen

EDITED WITH AN INTRODUCTION BY
Bert Vaux, Cambridge University
Rivka Hyland, Oxford University
Amanda McHugh, Cambridge University

BASED ON A TRANSLATION BY
Shushan M. Teager

RESOURCE *Publications* · Eugene, Oregon

THE MECHANISM OF SPEECH

Copyright © 2022 Bert Vaux. All rights reserved. Except for brief quotations in critical publications or reviews, no part of this book may be reproduced in any manner without prior written permission from the publisher. Write: Permissions, Wipf and Stock Publishers, 199 W. 8th Ave., Suite 3, Eugene, OR 97401.

Resource Publications
An Imprint of Wipf and Stock Publishers
199 W. 8th Ave., Suite 3
Eugene, OR 97401

www.wipfandstock.com

PAPERBACK ISBN: 978-1-7252-6184-6
HARDCOVER ISBN: 978-1-7252-6185-3
EBOOK ISBN: 978-1-7252-6186-0

05/18/22

Contents

Translator's Preface | vii
Editors' Preface | ix
von Kempelen's Preface to the French edition | xv

1: On speech or language | 1
2: Reflections on the questions of whether speech or language are innate, or invented by man himself; and whether all languages draw their origin from a single fundamental language | 11
3: The organs of speech and their functions | 25
4: On the sounds and letters of European languages | 75
5: On the speaking machine | 164

References | 197
Contributors | 201

Translator's Preface

My translation of von Kempelen's *Mechanism of Speech* came about as a direct consequence of my late husband Herbert M. Teager's work on speech production and mapping air flow in the vocal tract during phonation. Many of the sources he consulted in the course of his research referred to von Kempelen's book, long out of print and difficult to find. With the help of our good friend Robert Chambolle, we were finally able to obtain a photocopy of the French edition held at the Bibliothèque nationale de France in Paris.

The first edition of von Kempelen's work was published in German (von Kempelen 1791a); a French translation (on which the present English translation is based) was published in the same year (Kempelen 1791b). A facsimile of the German original appeared in 1970 (Kempelen 1970).

I wish to thank Robert Chambolle for his help in this endeavor; Janet Martin, Associate Professor of Classics Emeritus at Princeton University, for translating the Latin passages in the book; Bert Vaux, Professor of Linguistics at Cambridge University, for writing the introduction and for his help with the publication of the book; my friends Monique Huvos, M.D., and Carolyn Payne, who checked the accuracy of my translation and edited the manuscript, and finally my family, for their unfailing interest and support.

Shushan Yeni-Komshian Teager
Belmont, MA
July 2013

Editors' Preface

"In order to invent instruments that produce sounds similar to the human voice, it is necessary to follow the plan nature had enjoined as our guide."

—Wolfgang von Kempelen, *The Mechanism of Speech*

In a recent piece in the *New York Times*, screenwriter Alex Garland describes his dismay on learning that the script he had been working on—for the 2015 film *Ex Machina*, in which the founder of a search engine asks one of his company's coders to test the success of the robot he has built in terms of its (her) artificial intelligence—would arrive in good company. When he began writing the script, Garland thought he would be the first to deal with the tensions between man and machine since Steven Spielberg's 2011 *A.I.*; instead, Garland watched as plot after plot of recent movies, both blockbusters and independent films, turned on what Peter Weibel describes, in his preface to the 2007 translation of *Mensch in der Maschine*, as "the ascent of the machine as rival and companion to man." Garland sees the many recent films concerned with this rivalry between man and machine—including *Her* (2013), *Transcendence* (2014), *Automata* (2014), *Chappie* (2015), and *Avengers: Age of Ultron* (2015)—as a sign of renewed interest in and paranoia about human dependence on technology. These films and the culture they represent are often concerned with machines that have already left humans behind in computation, and are threatening to leave humans behind in the last realm, it seems, that humans can still lay claim to: humanity. In *Her* and *Ex Machina* especially this existential threat centers on the machine's uncanny ability to communicate with her (and it is often a her, suggesting that we have not left Shaw's *Pygmalion* behind) human counterpart so well that the creator begins to doubt either her artificiality or his own humanity. No story of artificial intelligence on the big screen has been complete without the central scene of a human in dialogue with a machine; the current preoccupation with the relationship between man and machine must center on their ability to communicate in the same language.

Today's machines rely on an ever-expanding digital database of recordings and vocabulary patterns to simulate human speech, but this point of connection between man and machine—language coming from something built by a human—dates back to Wolfgang von Kempelen (1734-1804), the first human to create a speaking machine. Von Kempelen was many things in his time—scholar, engineer, son of generals and father to the infamous chess machine known as "The Turk"—but today he can also be understood as the man who made the first steps towards inventions that have changed the world, such as Apple's Siri (2011), Amazon's Alexa (2017), and systems like the one that allowed Stephen Hawking to communicate despite his vocal and general paralysis[1]. In this book, von Kempelen details the theory behind his speaking machine, in the hopes that future engineers might be able to take it "to the fullest extent of its perfection"; one wonders what he would have thought of the many inventors who have followed in his footsteps.

Von Kempelen was born to Engelbert von Kempelen and Anna von Kempelen (née Spindler). It was 1734 in the Habsburg Empire, and von Kempelen was baptized Wolfgang Franciscus de Paula Johannes Elemosinaius in the parish of St. Martin's in Pozsony (in present-day Slovakia). Little is known about his early education, but he likely attended the local grammar school, and was later schooled at Győr, one of the four boarding academies in the Kingdom of Hungary. Győr was an elite training college intended for students with a future in civil service. Here, we know von Kempelen was educated in grammar, poetics, rhetoric, religion, Latin, geography (including astronomy, physical geography, and regional geography), secular and ecclesiastical history, and arithmetic. His philosophical track meant that von Kempelen was also taught logic, ethics, civil and military architecture, and music. Like his godfather, Wolfgang Andreas Valentinschiez, and several of his ancestors, von Kempelen went on to pursue a career as a Major General at the Imperial Court of Maria Theresa in Vienna.

While there, von Kempelen entered the salt business, before turning to the engineering and inventing work that would define his legacy. He built steam engines, water pumps, and a pontoon bridge in Pressburg, his birthplace, around 1770. He patented a typewriter for the blind Viennese pianist Maria Theresia von Paradis (named after the empress Maria Theresa) in 1772, and a steam turbine for use in mills in 1788-9. He designed a theater and helped with the reconstruction of a demolished palace in Buda (present-day Budapest) in 1790, and he was one of several engineers to work on the famous fountains at Schönbrunn in Vienna. To this talent for

---

1. The components of which are described by Hawking at http://www.hawking.org.uk/the-computer.html (accessed 17 November 2017).

design and construction, von Kempelen added skill in drawing, etching, and poetry, and a multilinguism that was remarkable even for the cosmopolitan Austro-Hungarian empire: by the end of his life, von Kempelen was fluent in German, Hungarian, Latin, French, Italian, and English. He makes use of all of these languages (as well as Polish) in this book as examples for his explanations of linguistic theory.

Von Kempelen is perhaps best known for "The Turk," his chess-playing automaton famously described by Edgar Allan Poe in "Maelzel's Chess Player" (1836). After von Kempelen's death in 1804, Johannes Nepomuk Maelsel, a mechanical engineer, purchased the automaton and took it on tour in Europe and in the United States, where, in 1854, the machine met its end in a fire. While on tour, however, the chess-playing automaton famously competed against Napoleon (Vienna, 1809), Benjamin Franklin (Paris, date unknown), and Charles Babbage (London, 1819). Peter Weibel (2007) writes that, "In the history of the automaton, it is particularly two kinds of machines that have inspired people's fear and imagination: there are those capable of imitating human activities and those considered especially intelligent and as the singular achievement of the human species representing his anthropological monopoly, in other words, 'thinking machines' that can play chess and that can talk." Although the Turk inspired such fear in much of its audience, its reputation turned out to be only half-deserved. The machine concealed a human chess player; the automaton was only a semi-functional machine. For much of its life, and that of its creator, however, the automaton brought machines to the forefront of the European consciousness, inspiring enthusiasm and curiosity wherever it travelled. Although the secret of the machine has been discovered, the chess-playing automaton is still discussed today in the context of mechanical and artificial intelligence.

After the success of the Turk, von Kempelen began designing his speaking machine in 1769. He examined musical instruments with the aim of finding one that most closely resembled human speech. While most of his experiments (with trumpets, horns, Jew's harps, and reed instruments) did not bear fruit, von Kempelen continued to listen for an instrument that could approximate the human voice. He recounts in *The Mechanism of Speech* an incident that changed his approach to automated speech: passing by a tavern one night, von Kempelen heard a sound like a child singing. As he approached, he realized that the sound was coming from a bagpipe. Von Kempelen attempted to buy the bagpipe, but no amount of money offered was enough for its owner, for whom the instrument was his livelihood. The bagpipe player did, however, give von Kempelen the name of the man who had made his instrument, as well as a small reed flute on which von Kempelen experimented until he was able to acquire a bagpipe.

Von Kempelen writes that he was so excited about his discovery that he returned to his home in the city that evening and began working. He took a leather bellows from his kitchen fireplace and attached it to the flute, generating sound by forcing air through the instrument. He then attached the bellows-flute contraption to another, larger, flute. Covering the larger flute's three holes with one hand and operating the bellows with another, von Kempelen discovered that he could produce higher or lower sounds by lifting his fingers slightly, but could not alter the tone of the sound enough to produce distinct vowel sounds. With the thought of imitating the human mouth, von Kempelen then removed the larger flute from his contraption and fitted the funnel-shaped lower end of an oboe over it instead. While experimenting and continuing to operate the bellows, von Kempelen was able to produce different vowel sounds by rapidly moving his hand and fingers, partially covering the wooden funnel opening of the oboe. He found after some time that the most commonly audible vowel sound was an "a," and that if he left his hand and fingers in any one position long enough, this was the vowel that would sound. He theorizes in his writings that this means that vowels are only audibly distinct from each other in the way they relate to one another, presaging the proposals of structuralists and speech perception scholars by more than a hundred years (see Miller 1989 for a review of the speech perception literature on this topic).

The next day, as von Kempelen continued to experiment, his wife and children came to the room in which he was working, convinced that they had heard a human voice, but could not distinguish the language in which it was speaking. The misunderstanding is one of many examples of the encouragement von Kempelen drew from his family throughout the project.

Von Kempelen's research in connection with the speaking machine focused on speech theory in addition to mechanical engineering. He writes that he soon discovered the necessity of the movement of air for making any sound. By studying the movement of air in the human lungs, the modulation of the air by the glottis, and the manipulation of this air by the mouth and tongue, von Kempelen was able to confirm the mathematical certainty, as he describes it, of speech consisting of air moving through different openings. His experiments then moved toward replicating human lungs, glottis, mouth, and tongue, of which the lungs and glottis were already accounted for in the bellows and small flute. The search for a working tongue proved to be a long one, taking von Kempelen several months of experimentation. He describes substituting his thumb for a tongue, for example, splitting the current of air from the bellows in an effort to mimic the letter "L".

A breakthrough for the speaking machine came when von Kempelen visited an organ manufacturer to replace his leather bellows with a more powerful organ bellows. There, he found the partially-constructed machine that would propel his efforts forward. The machine, called the "human voice" by the organ manufacturer, was meant to imitate a human singing voice. It worked similarly to the machine von Kempelen had been constructing, but included thirteen reed pipes and a wind trunk with working valves. There was still much work to be done on the machine, which von Kempelen describes in great detail, but this discovery renewed von Kempelen's excitement for the project, and gave him a new outlet for experimentation.

Much of von Kempelen's book explains this theory alongside detailed tables and charts of his machine. The scholarly references to other early linguists and inventors suggest both traditional academic rigor of the time and an originality in reinterpreting his colleagues, which stemmed from his willingness to think differently in his quest to perfect his machine.

On the 26th of March 1804, Wolfgang von Kempelen died in his apartment in the Vienna suburb of Alser of debilitation, according to the coroner's report. He was buried in Währing Cemetery on March 28. Today there no longer exists a grave marking for von Kempelen; engraved words have proven ephemeral, whereas those spoken by von Kempelen's machine long outlived their creator.

Shushan Teager translated von Kempelen's text from the French version (Le mécanisme de la parole "The mechanism of speech"), which appeared shortly after the German original (Mechanismus der menschlichen Sprache "Mechanism of human speech") in 1791, together with a new preface by the author himself, suggesting that he may have played a significant role in the production of this translation. We hope that this translation of the French version will suitably complement the translation of the German text that appeared as our book was nearing completion (Brackhane, Sproat, and Trouvain 2017). We would like to thank Emma Brown and Isla Tyrrell for their assistance in editing this text and preparing it for publication.

Bert Vaux, King's College, Cambridge
Rivka Hyland, University College, Oxford
Amanda McHugh, King's College, Cambridge

The Mechanism of Speech
followed by a description of a
Speaking Machine

and Enriched with XXVII Plates

By Mr. DE KEMPELEN, *Present Aulic Councilor
to his Majesty The Emperor King*

---

*When therefore we press out these voices from
the innermost part of our body, and send them forth
straight through the mouth, the quickly-moving tongue,
cunning fashioner of words, joins and molds the sounds,
and the shaping of the lips does its part in giving them form.*

Lucretius *De Rerum Natura*, Book IV, line 549[1]

VIENNA,
Printed at B. Bauer's,
and available at
J. V. DEGEN, 1791.

von Kempelen's title page for the French edition

---

1. Translation by Rouse (1924).

von Kempelen's Preface to the French edition

Although it is after long and arduous toil that I finally find myself able to submit the fruit of my labors to the eyes of the public, nevertheless I dare not delude myself into believing that I am bestowing a precious gift upon it. The utility and merit of my discoveries may be limited to simplifying the teaching of speech to the deaf and mute, and in correcting the pronunciation errors that some people acquire when they neglect the proper use of the organs of speech. If this work, considered from the aspect of its utility, is of no great value, nevertheless its originality cannot displease some curious minds and naturalists.

Regarding the theory of speech in general, or rather the mechanism of speech, which forms the largest part of this book, I am far from believing that I have exhausted every subject belonging to this matter; I am only indicating the discoveries I have made through my experience. I draw principles and results from my experience, and I look to rectify what I have found to be incorrect amongst various authors on the subject, and through this I aim to shed some light on this part of our physiology. What I have said in the second part of this book regarding the origin of language has nothing to do with either the title of this book or the mechanism of speech, and could have been cut out, especially since research on this shows that the subject is much larger than can be enclosed within the narrow boundaries of a single volume. However, having studied and thought about this subject greatly, and believing myself to have made some novel observations, I could not help but to share them with my readers so that they can take advantage of them, if they deem it appropriate; this is all the importance that I attach to the ideas that luck has borne.

I also do not present the speaking machine, described at the end of my book, as a finished work that imitates speech perfectly, but dare to flatter myself, without too much conceit, that imperfect as it is, it at least provides sound principles for the construction of a more perfect version. I have brought it to the point where I can make it pronounce, forthwith and with no exception, all the Latin, French and Italian words that were proposed to me, some better than others, it is true, but several hundred words at least, clearly and distinctly. For example, *Papa, Mama, Marianna, Roma, Maladie, Santé, Astronomie, Anatomie, Chapeau, Racine, Soupé, Charmante, Opera, Comédie, Pantomime*, etc., also long and difficult words such as *Constantinople, Monomotapa, Mississippi, Astrakhan, Anastasius*, etc. Why and where the machine is still defective will be evident from my description, but since the initial difficulties of building such a machine have been surmounted, it is a matter of trying to perfect it with additions and corrections. It is for this purpose and with this hope that I have described it as clearly and as accurately as I can. Might it be possible, by the end of this century so fertile in discoveries, to find a master's hand that could carry this discovery, thought impossible until now, to the highest degree of perfection?

It remains for me to ask my readers to suspend their judgment on isolated propositions and not to reject the principles adopted and the remarks on speech, which at first glance may seem far-fetched and absolutely false, until they have read everything carefully. Some practice is necessary to isolate one's own manner of articulating a single and separate letter and to verify experimentally what I have said. Knowing the properties of one letter, or one sound, leads to understanding the properties of others, and so it follows. Those who do not know the German language should note that the German 'u', which is often discussed in this work, is pronounced like a [French] 'ou', the 'sch' as a 'ch' before a vowel in the French language, and that the German 'ch' is only a more strongly aspirated 'h' that is produced by bringing the posterior portion of the tongue closer to the palate. When the German 'u' is to be pronounced as the French 'u', two dots are added to it— 'ü'—or it is followed by an 'i' and written as 'ui'.

I must also warn my readers not to dwell on the spelling of the words I cite, but to consider them according to their pronunciation and usage in each nation. I was careful to add clarifying notes where they seemed necessary.

Finally, if clarity of style has been neglected, it should be kept in mind that the translation of this work was done in Germany and that in a treatise on physics, one is more committed to rendering a clear presentation than to the purity of language.

The Author

1: On speech or language

§ 1

Speech, or language in its broadest sense, is the faculty of communicating one's feelings and ideas through signs to one's fellow creatures. It can be simple or compound. The first, common to all animals and taught by Nature herself, is limited to a few ideas, whereas the second must be learned and has no limit.

§ 2

It seems beyond doubt that, in general, animals have their own language as well as their own ideas and a sort of reasoning.[1] However, as their needs and consequently their ideas are also very limited in comparison with those of man, their language cannot be very extensive. They cry, howl, hiss, bark, bray, neigh, bleat, and produce all sorts of sounds, often accompanied by signs that they simultaneously make with different parts of their bodies, just as we might add gestures to speech. This type of language may serve to do no more than express passion, desire, and internal agitation in general. Pain, joy, love, hate, affection, anger, desire, compassion, courage, awe, and fear are the sensations animals express best.

A short time spent studying the habits of animals will soon make their language as intelligible as if they used actual articulated words to communicate with us. I will cite some domestic animals known to everyone and dwell briefly on their language.

---

1. Reimarus [1762] does not wish to grant them the power of reasoning as such, but does admit nevertheless "that the imagination of animals relative to its purpose, has a certain analogy with ours. That is to say, by their vague perceptions, they can, in a certain manner, achieve the same objectives we can by our thoughts, our ideas, our reasoning, our spirit, and even by our free choice." §16. Moreover, are we not understanding something other than this analogy for the word "reasoning"? Because, for our purpose, it is immaterial whether the animal formally thinks like us or has vague perceptions as Reimarus believes. It is sufficient that he endeavors to manifest his feelings of the moment, or what is affecting his imagination, with his voice or with external signs.

§ 3

Among the quadrupeds the dog is the most adroit, the most alert, and the most perceptive. One of his primary characteristics is vigilance, and there is no doubt that he uses a sort of language to express it in different degrees. Let us observe him in the countryside on a quiet night: if he hears a noise, like footfalls, in the distance, his attention is aroused, and he begins by expressing his discontent with a muffled growl. If the noise continues, he will growl more loudly, then he will bark, but only at intervals, briefly and in a muffled manner. That is to say, he will emit a little explosion of sound every three or four seconds. The closer the object of his discontent advances, the louder and faster he will bark. Finally, he will increase his barking to such a point that he will hardly give himself time to breathe. Let us suppose that it is a man approaching and he threatens the dog with his cane. Feeling too weak to resist his adversary, the dog will retreat with each menacing gesture, but at the same time he will bark in a completely different manner and will make the same sounds he would if he were actually feeling blows. If the man retreats, the dog will continue with renewed courage and will bark with all his strength until the man is out of sight. Even then, his barking will only decrease by degrees. For a time, he will retain the rancor he feels for what he has suffered and for the stranger's disregard for him. Just when one might think that he has stopped barking, he will begin again, repeatedly, mixing his barking with a sort of cry that indicates that he is not yet at ease.

What does the dog mean by these different cries? He must have an objective. One could be to overawe the approaching man and force him to retreat. Another could be to warn his master of approaching danger and possible robbery. He seems to want to say,[2] "You, whoever you are, stay away because I am on guard here. I will not allow you to enter the house. Stop—Stop—or I will bite you. What? You are threatening me with blows? Here, where I am guardian? This is too much, this is insufferable—but I will not surrender to you. I am ready to risk everything. Ha! You are leaving—finally I forced you to retreat. Ha! If only I could have bitten you in the leg. Threaten me with blows? How could you, impudent man! I am getting angry. Beat a dog like me? Ha! I was a coward for thinking that you could."

Or he may wish to say: "I hear someone at a distance. I am only waiting for his arrival. Here he comes. Here he is, already at the door. Come master, come to my aid! He wants to hit me. I am too weak—I can no longer resist. Just the same, I have succeeded. There, he is leaving! Oh master, stay calm,

---

2. Although we may be far from actually assuming such a sequence of ideas in a dog, nevertheless we cannot deny him all manner of reasoning and we have to think that these different types of barks mean what follows, or at least something similar.

I chased him away by myself—Ah! if only I had bitten his leg—Ah! how ashamed I am of my lack of courage—wretch that I was! And that insolent man—threatening to hit me!"

Anyone who has ever paid attention to his dog will understand its language very well, even when the animal is out of sight. He will be able to judge the whereabouts of the intruder approaching his house by the variation, intensity, and frequency of the barks. He will know the instant the man places his foot on the threshold of his property, when he lifts his stick, the moment he leaves, and what distance he has retreated, etc.

On a hunt, when a dog comes upon the tracks of another animal, his barks are completely different from his barks at home. These are bursts of excitement and anticipation that mark his eagerness to reach his prey. At the same time, they express his fear of losing it, as if he wanted to call us to his aid. He uses yet another bark to express joy. If, for example, his master is getting ready to go out and the dog is given permission to go along—what contortions, what cries of great joy, what noise! If he has lost his master, or has been confined somewhere, the dog will make his distress known with miserable howls, to which he will add a final cry of despair. He will howl in the same manner when he hears animal cries or other sounds like singing, music, or ringing bells. There are many dogs that can be made to cry at will simply by someone pretending to cry. Couldn't this be a sign or an expression indicating compassion?[3]

§ 4

The rooster in the barnyard changes his tone at every turn: when he announces dawn with his crowing; later, when he chases his flock out of the coop; when he finds some grain and calls his females to the feast; when, seeing a vulture over the barnyard, he alerts his troop to the danger; when one of his hens is being chased or has been caught. All of these events are distinguished by different cries.

The sound a pigeon makes as he fights a rival is quite unlike his cooing when, with his tail sweeping the ground, he circles the female and

---

3. I have a small dog that invariably complains to me every time he has been mistreated. If, for example, during my absence one of my servants washed and combed him, clipped him or tormented him in some other manner, he will complain to me upon my return even three or four hours later. The moment he sees me come in, he rushes toward me with a cry, then he suddenly throws himself against his tormentor as he barks loudly; he then returns to me and repeats the whole process until I have placated him. Sometimes I have him tricked on purpose in order to later demonstrate his game to my friends and to ask them if this is not a type of language.

declares his love. When he calls her to the nest, his tone is completely different from the tone he uses to greet her when she comes to relieve him during the incubation of an egg. Pigeons also make distinct sounds when they are afraid of something or they have been frightened.

§ 5

In addition to the voice signals animals give each other, they gesture with different parts of their bodies as well. Continuing our observations of the dog, he makes no gestures whose meaning cannot be interpreted with a bit of attention. When two dogs of approximately the same size meet, their demeanor will immediately indicate their intentions. If both are courageous and snarling, they will raise their heads, backs, and tails, and circle each other as they growl and bare their teeth. From this we can conclude that at any moment they may begin to fight one another. If, on the other hand, one of them is deferential, he will lower his head, ears, and tail, and sometimes he may even throw himself on the ground as if to say to the other, "I surrender—I acknowledge your superiority. See my submission? It should calm your anger. You are too noble to mistreat a prostrated enemy." The winner will understand this language and spare the vanquished. Proud of his triumph, he will abandon the unfortunate wretch.

When we enter an unfamiliar house with a large dog at the gate, if the frightening mastiff greets us with his head and ears lowered as he moves his tail in arcs, we understand him so well that we do not even pause for a moment to pet him, convinced that he is welcoming us.

The docked tail of the sleeping dog is, so to speak, the hunter's compass, by which he is warned the moment the dog is on the trail of some game. Coming upon a partridge, the dog suddenly stops, does not move his tail, or intermittently moves it almost imperceptibly. Sometimes he even holds his paw up in midair as if he wishes to say, "Here I am, so close to the thing that if I make the slightest movement, if I so much as place my paw on the ground, I will frighten the partridge and it will get away."

The rooster lowers his wings as he bends over the hen, and the pigeon trails his rigid tail along the ground and, contrary to his usual behavior, jumps towards the female as he coos and lowers his head until his beak touches the ground, then suddenly straightens up. What do these animals mean by their gestures? The results leave no doubt that the hen, the female pigeon, and even the observer understand it all very well.[4]

---

4. Bougeant [1739] said many valid things, and among them he notes that animals are very truthful. "If animals could hear us converse, gossip, lie, beg, exaggerate, would

§ 6

Man, so superior to animals in his intellectual faculties and his talent for imitation, which is the basis of language,[5] should have this language developed to a higher degree than animals. This language, taught by Nature herself, must be universal and intelligible to everyone. A thousand examples confirm that such a language exists and is effective. Many travelers who have crossed immense oceans on their voyages of discovery certainly did not find interpreters in all the countries where fortune led them, yet they spoke to the inhabitants of barbarian countries. Their entire language consisted of hand and head signs, sometimes accompanied by sounds, by which they could make themselves understood as needed.

§ 7

This is what we would do if we wished to make ourselves understood in another language. We would point to physical things with our finger, or we would imitate the cries of specific animals. We would then make gestures that expressed the action we wished to attribute to these things. Instead of adverbs, many signs would express modification, and in this manner, we would make sentences that are very intelligible to all sorts of people. It is true that if we wish to point to something it has to be at hand. However, when it comes to animals, the task is always easier, because we can imitate the cries of so many of them. For example, we can imitate a cow by *mououou*, a sheep by *maiaiai*, a dog by *aou-aou-aou*, a pigeon by *coucouroucou*, a frog by *quoiquoiquoi*, etc.

If we wish to express an action, we can quite effectively pretend to carry it out. If we wish to speak of eating or drinking, we may chew as if we have something in our mouths or we may drink from our cupped hand. In this manner we could express many verbs: running, falling, sleeping, cutting, fighting, piercing, going, coming, staying, giving, taking, carrying, breaking, fearing, loving, hating, and weeping, among many others. As to adjectives, it is not difficult to express large, small, thick, thin, wide, narrow, beautiful, ugly, strong, weak, heavy, etc.

---

they have reason to envy our use of language? They do not have our superiority, but they also do not have our shortcomings. They speak little, but they only speak to the point and from knowledge. They always utter the truth and never cheat, not even in love."

5. Court de Gébelin [1773-82] said "We began with the same principle, *imitation*. Man had one model for speech, *nature and ideas*."

§ 8

In this universal language, anyone can tell an Indian, or a member of a newly discovered people, "My men and I, as you can see, are hungry. Go find two small sheep. If you bring them, I will make you a gift of this mirror. We will kill them and eat them. You will bring us some drinking water in this jug and for your reward you will have this hatchet."

§ 9

A deaf mute we have never seen can, upon letting us in the house, inform us that his master has gone riding, that he has gone hunting, that he will return in the evening to rest, that we should wait for him, that he will give us something to eat and drink, that while we wait we can be indoors, that he will immediately start to make the necessary arrangements, and that his master will be with us shortly. The better the education of such a mute person, the better he will be able to use signs. From this it should follow that this universal language is possible to perfect. It can doubtless attain the same elaborate level of refinement as our articulated language. However, it will then cease to be purely natural, that is to say, taught by nature, and will become a conventional language. The students of Abbot de L'Epée in Paris and those of Father Storch in Vienna speak in this conventional language and express the most abstract ideas with astonishing rapidity. In my opinion, the available evidence proves that it was not absolutely necessary for speech to be innate in man, but rather that he could have invented it himself. For if he could invent a manual signed language for the eye, why not a spoken language for the ear? We shall return to this question later.

§ 10

During my stay in Paris in the year 1783, I visited Abbot de L'Epée one day and met many of his deaf and mute students, and several visitors who had come to see them. By chance I stood near a window next to a rather pretty girl of about twenty, who for quite some time I took to be a curious visitor like myself. Suddenly she pointed to a chair and indicated that I should be seated. I thanked her, accepted, and asked her to be seated also. I continued to talk to her, but you can imagine my surprise when she informed me, by sign language, that she was deaf. I then realized what I had to do and responded to her, sign for sign. Noting that I could understand her easily, she became quite the chatterbox, so that our pantomime lasted more than half an hour. She told me about her life and explained that she had been coming to the Abbot for several years, that she had finished her courses, that she was no longer a student but continued to come out of habit, that she had been tested in the presence of the Emperor, who had been in Paris some time ago, that he had sent her a gift that she had carefully saved in a box, and that she would guard this precious memento for the rest of her life. Our universal language would not be adequate to express all this. It would instead have to be developed to a certain point before it could describe all of these ideas.

§ 11

In addition to this already developed and refined natural language, the students of Abbot de L'Epée and Father Storch have yet another language that they learn methodically, which is a technical language of their own. When they use it among themselves, I can understand nothing. It consists of agreed-upon hand signals that the Abbot claims are drawn from nature but which seem too arbitrary to me, and at times even far-fetched. Suffice it to say that this language of the hands is as rich as our articulated language, and that it can express even the most abstract ideas. However, it must be noted that these hand and finger signs do not stand for letters, which would make them equivalent to a writing system, but for whole words with all of their derivations and modifications: for example, verbs with a past, present, and future tense, adjectives and adverbs and their comparatives, etc. Not content with teaching these unfortunate people to speak this language fluently, the Abbot has also taught them to write with the same letters and words we ourselves use.

§ 12

Here I am reminded of the universal written language proposed several years ago by a Hungarian named Kalmar. I found his goal realized at this school, admittedly with a small group, but one large enough to convince me of the feasibility of writing a similar conventional language by substituting written characters for hand signals in such a manner that anyone who studied them could read them in his own language.

The writing of music is the same in all of Europe: what an Italian composer writes in Naples, the Russian singer can sing in St. Petersburg. One can compare the various instruments used to produce that music to so many mother tongues, in which everyone can express what the foreign composer, who probably would not know how to produce a single note on a similar instrument, had prescribed for the musician by notes arrayed on five lines.

§ 13

Before we leave the deaf and mute, we should note yet another detail that is important to the objective of this book. Some among them can understand everything said to them through lip movement and tongue position alone, especially when they are addressed slowly. In order to convince me of this, Abbot de L'Epée allowed me to select any book from his extensive library, open it at random and select a line. He then called one of his mutes, a boy of about twelve, and placed the boy in front of him in such a way that the lad could not see the text. He then read the line I had designated without making any sound, that is to say with mouth movement alone, and very slowly at that. On the spot, the young man took a piece of chalk and wrote the line on the board, word for word. From this we can see that our organs of speech behave in a constant manner according to fixed laws; that one sound is only differentiated from the other by the position of the organs, and that serious study of ourselves and others will give us an accurate knowledge of the means nature uses to produce such a great variety of intonations that are, basically, only the same single tone, as we shall show below.

Through practice and without much attention, we slowly and imperceptibly learn to recognize the play of these organs to such a point that we can often understand from a distance, by lip movement alone, what others are whispering to each other. This results from our habit of always looking at the speaker's mouth, as if we wanted to take in his words through our eyes and ears simultaneously, so that if the first of these senses did not grasp the entire discourse, the second could supplement it. This practice is of great help to those with poor hearing.[6]

§ 14

In the course of this book we will no longer dwell on the language of animals, rather only on the language of humans, for which we must give a definition. To do this, we have only to recall the definition we have already given for speech or language in general. If we define the word *sign* in a more precise manner, we will have an exact definition for human speech: speech, or human language, is the ability to communicate sentiments and ideas to one's fellow man through different intonations of the voice. These

---

6. One of my friends knows my organs of speech so well that when we find ourselves seated across a table from each other, he can understand everything I say to him in a very low voice, that is to say without the slightest burst of sound, only by the movement my lips, and this in several languages. We have tried it frequently.

intonations are called letters, syllables, and words. The first inventors of languages must have agreed among themselves as to the meaning of each of these 'signs of the voice'. However, this convention was not adopted by formal accord. In the beginning it was usage with which no one disagreed and which gradually became the rule.

§ 15

The principal objective of this book is the study of the mechanism by which all of these different intonations are formed. We will consider each intonation or letter by itself, examining the structure, position, and movements of each organ that contributes to its formation, and if all of this proves to be insufficient to establish a complete system for human speech, we can at least congratulate ourselves for having furnished a good deal of material relative to its establishment in the future. After classifying all possible sounds or tones, (at least all those in European languages), noting their almost imperceptible variations, discovering certain constant laws, and finally establishing immutable principles, the fabric of speech will unfold before our eyes. We shall be astonished at how simply we can build the foundation upon which man's happiness, to a great extent, depends, and the one that principally distinguishes him from animals.

§ 16

A small amount of air pushed by the lungs through the narrow slit of the glottis (the opening at the upper part of the larynx, between the vocal cords) produces the voice. The many obstacles which the tongue, teeth, and lips set up against this resonating air cause inflection and a variety of sounds, each with its own significance. This, then, is what the grand art of speech can be reduced to, this priceless gift of the Creator, this principal link of society. To it we owe the transmission of the rich heritage of our ancestors and the discoveries and inventions of centuries. It will retransmit that heritage, together with our own contributions, to the most distant of future generations. Whence does the eloquence that enchants our spirit draw power? How does divine poetry, animated by song, charm if not by speech? Alas! What would our spiritual state be today without speech and tradition? How would we be superior to animals? Consider how someone born mute, who never learned any sort of sign language, would languish without knowledge, like a plant under a harsh sky. He could form roots and branches but would never be able to produce flowers or develop its more noble or distinguished aspects. However, let us not digress any longer in praise of speech, the many benefits of which are known to all.

Allow me only to include a spirited passage from Mr. Herder, who said [in 1784]: "It is only through speech that man's torpid soul was awakened, that his idle and dormant faculty for thought and contemplation was animated and put into action. One can think of the organs of speech as the helm of our reason, or a spark from heaven to give light to our senses and life to our spirit. It is only with the capacity for speech that man obtained Divine inspiration, the germ of intelligence and infinite perfectibility, an echo of the Creator's voice to rule the earth, in a word, the Divine art of ideas, mother of all art."

2: Reflections on the questions of whether speech or language are innate, or invented by man himself; and whether all languages draw their origin from a single fundamental language

§ 17

Scholars are not as yet in accord regarding these questions, which are so interesting in the study of man. Although we are now more seriously dedicated to discovering the origin of languages, much relevant information remains in obscurity. The details of the various opinions on this topic will not be the subject of our research. They would divert us too far from our objective and would furnish enough material to fill a separate book.

A German author by the name of Zobel wrote more amply on this subject [in 1773]. I will limit myself to citing a few observations upon which I base my own opinion.

Sussmilch [1766] and many others maintain that language is innate in man. Their principal argument is that man could have never achieved the development of his reason without language.

If this proposition is proven, naturally all of its consequences must be accepted as true. Without reason or understanding, no language could be invented, and so it was absolutely necessary that the Creator grant man language before developing his intellect. However, what does it mean to have language without intellect? Would it not be speaking first and only then thinking and reasoning, pronouncing words without any sense, like a parrot? I admit that the book quoted above often seemed odd to me. At times I would read three or four pages filled with premises that led to the immediate conclusion that man himself must have invented language. Then, to my great surprise, the author would make a small detour and conclude the contrary. He was entirely convinced that he had completely destroyed all opposing opinion; however, I was not convinced. He claimed that man had to have a language in order to have reason, and, conversely, that man had to have reason in order to invent a language. To my imagination his two assertions seemed like an endless spiral, and I no longer knew what to hold onto. I did not know if the chicken had to come before the egg, or the egg before the chicken. Finally, Herder explained the enigma, as we shall see later.

Court de Gébelin endeavored to convince us, with striking eloquence, that it was not only the capacity for speech that we received from the Creator, but language itself. He asserted that man, with all his faculties, could have never been in a state to invent language, and furthermore that all languages sprang from one primitive language, like branches growing from a single tree. Even later generations of man did not depend on their own intellects, but were constrained to draw new words from the nature of things, and that consequently each word had to have a definite and exclusive sound.

With a mastery of etymology based on an extensive knowledge of languages, this celebrated author gave clarifications on numerous things. Unfortunately, many of his other explanations are unconvincing.[1]

§ 18

I am not convinced by the argument that because many of the same monosyllables are found in several languages, they must all come from the same source. Since we have only sixteen principal sounds[2] from which to form a vast number of words to express a prodigious number of ideas, chance alone could very well have made some of them similar.

By considering only a few of these similar words, we may easily conclude that they draw their origin from a primitive word. An extensive etymological study can very well show us that some words were transferred from one language to another. However, these examples, although very frequent, do not prove that entire languages, which are so different from one another, must always be branches of the same tree.

---

1. [See the section on the] Origin of Language [in Court de Gébelin 1773-1782].

2. If we eliminate the superfluous letters c, q, x, and y from the alphabet, and combine the analogous letters b and p, d and t, g and k, f and z, etc., which are constantly confounded in European languages, hardly more than sixteen will be left.

§ 19

What is this small number of primitive words that Gébelin[3] gives us in comparison to the innumerable cases for which no etymology can be found?

If we base our judgment only on the languages of people crowded into the smallest part of the globe for a great number of years, for the most part either at war or in commerce with each other, one group subjugating the other and giving part of its language and laws to the other group, then it is only natural that we find a surprising mix in their languages.

I myself identified more than six hundred completely Latin words in the German language. For example, *Körper—corpus, Namen—nomen, Fluss—fluvius, Schule—scola, Rose—rosa, Lang—longus, Acker—ager, Nase—nasus, Herr—herus, Flamme—flamma, Falsch—falsus*, etc. However, in spite of this, I am far from believing that these languages are sisters born of the same mother. Whether the Germans had these words in their language when they still inhabited the shores of the Caspian Sea where they knew no Romans, or whether, on the other hand, the founders of Rome had already brought the words into the confines of Etruria without knowing any Germans, it seems evident that the two people did not learn them from each other. However, they could have drawn from a third language, and perhaps that language could have owed its origin to a previous

---

3. Here are some of his primitive words.

Ten or Tan	Fire
Qui	Force
Eid	Hand
Pot	Heroic, people
Cap	Anything concave that contains something
Ran	Imitating the sound of a frog, hence *rana*
Bar	Probably origin of the German words *Wort* and *Mahre*
Nel	River
Pol	Labor
Mut	Silence; being mute
Coel	Sky
Mun	To supply
Tum	Perfection
Kol	Service
Mer or mar	Shining or vivid
Tan	Fish
Ner	Force
Rom	Elevation

language, and so on, to a primitive language. However, there is a lack of sufficient proof to assert this opinion.

§ 20

If we compare two completely different languages, choosing words that two peoples likely had at a time when their languages were all simple, limited, and in their infancy, so to speak, we will not find the slightest similarity between them. Even if we assume the existence of a primitive mother language, we would also have to agree that one of these languages separated completely from the mother language and adopted entirely new words. To do this, let us embark on a brief analysis of two languages that are completely different and with which I am very familiar, German and Hungarian.[4]

Here are the most common words in these two languages [with English and French equivalents][5]:

---

4. Having noted the assumption that the Hungarian language is a branch of Illyrian or Slavic in the work of some scholars, I take this opportunity to declare that it is as far removed from the first and the second as German is from Greek, and that it does not have the least connection with any other European language.

5. Kempelen renders a number of Hungarian forms in a way that does not correspond with actual Hungarian spelling, and the following footnotes represent a combined effort by the editors, working with Csilla Varga, to correct these spellings and forms.—The eds.

Nouns

English	French	German	Hungarian
God	Dieu	Gott	Isten
Man	Homme	Mensch	Ember
Woman	Femme	Weib	Aszszony[6]
Child	Enfant	Kind	Gyermek
Life	Vie	Leben	Élet
Blood	Sang	Blut	Vél[7]
Hand	Main	Hand	Kéz
People	Peuple	Volk	Nemzet
Beast	Bête	Vieh	Marha[8]
Dead	Mort	Tod	Halál
Cow	Vache	Kuh	Tehén
Horse	Cheval	Pferd, Ross	Lò
Sheep	Brebis	Schaaf	Júh
Dog	Chien	Hund	Kutya
Milk	Lait	Milch	Téi[9]
Tree	Arbre	Baum	Fa
Stone	Pierre	Stein	Keö[10]

6. Modern *asszony*.
7. Modern *vér*.
8. This form means 'beef'; the Hungarian word for 'beast' is *vadállat*.
9. Modern *tej*.
10. Modern *kő*.

Adjectives

English	French	German	Hungarian
Large	Grand	Gross	Nagy
Small	Petit	Klein	Kiss[11]
Full	Plein	Voll	Teli
Empty	Vide	Leer	Üres
Strong	Fort	Stark	Erös[12]
Hot	Chaud	Warm	Meleg
Cold	Froid	Kalt	Hideg
Beautiful	Beau	Schön	Szép
Old	Vieux	Alt	Eöreg[13]

Adverbs and Prepositions

English	French	German	Hungarian
Far	Loin	Weit	Meszsze[15]
Near	Proche	Nahe	Közel
Again	Encore	Noch	Még[16]
Fast	Vite	Geschwind	Hamar
After	Après	Nach	Után
Only	Seulement	Nur	Tsak[17]
Now	À présent	Itzt[14]	Most
Where	Où	Wo	Holl[18]
Already	Déjà	Schon	Mâr

11. Modern *kis*.
12. Modern *erős*.
13. Modern *öreg*.
14. Modern *jetzt*.
15. Modern *messze* (*meszsze* means 'lime').
16. This means 'more'; again is *újra*.
17. Modern *csak*.
18. Modern *hol*.

Verbs

English	French	German	Hungarian
I am	Je suis	Ich bin	Vagyok
I live	Je vis	Ich lebe	Élek
I die	Je meurs	Ich sterbe	Halok[19]
I sleep	Je dors	Ich schlafe	Aluszom[20]
I hear	J'entends	Ich höre	Hallok
I see	Je vois	Ich sehe	Látok
I love	J'aime	Ich liebe	Szeretek
I speak	Je parle	Ich spreche	Szolok[21]
I say	Je dis	Ich sage	Mondok
I laugh	Je ris	Ich lache	Nevetek
I cry	Je pleurs	Ich weine	Sirok[22]
I run	Je cours	Ich laufe	Futok
I know	Je sais	Ich weiss	Tudok

Let us now decide if a single one of all these words could have been derived from the primitive word from which the Hungarian word originated. From the word *Qui* in Court de Gébelin's primitive words cited above, we could, for example, derive the German word *stark* and the Hungarian word *Erös*. We may also derive the German word *Hand* and the Hungarian word *Kéz* from Court de Gebelin's *Eid*, the words *Volk* and *Nemzet* from *Pot*, the words *Frosch* and *Béka* from *Ran*, the words *Arbeit* and *Munka* from *Pol*, the words *Wort* and *Szò* from *Bar*, the words *Fisch* and *Hal* from *Tan*, and the words *Himmel* and *Meny* from *Coel*. We could more strongly assert that in the beginning there were only a few species of quadrupeds and that they later degenerated, a tiger giving birth to a cat, a donkey to a horse, a dog to a wolf, and a crocodile to a lizard. They, at least, would have retained some similarity to their parents, whereas the words we have just listed have no similarity at all, since they retain not a single syllable or tone that could disclose their etymology.

Admittedly the Hungarian language, like every other language, has adopted several words from its neighbors, but these are strictly the names for things that the Hungarians did not have at the time when they wandered

---

19. Modern *meghalok*.
20. Modern *alszom*.
21. Modern *beszélek*.
22. Modern *sírok*.

in hordes without culture and without many needs. They found names for things that suited them among the peoples they met and adopted them, although these were often distorted and pronounced in their own idiom. Here are some examples:

English	French	German	Hungarian
House	Maison	Haus	Ház
Tile, brick	Tuile, brique	Ziegel	Tégla
Rope	Cordon	Schnur	Sinor[24]
Clock	Horloge	Uhr	Ora[25]
Wheelwright	Charon[23]	Wagner	Bognár
Coachman	Cocher	Kutscher	Kocsis
Tower	Tour	Thurn	Torony
Sack	Sac	Sack	Zsák
Turnip	Rave	Rübe	Répa[26]
Priest	Prêtre	Pfaff	Pap
Master	Maître	Meister	Mester

Some very basic words in Hungarian have a correspondence with German words, but this may be attributed to chance, since they are very few in number. For example: *Wasser—Viz* (water); *Ich esse—eszezem*[27] (I eat); *Herr—Ur*[28] (mister), and perhaps a few others.

Can we assume that the following eight words were derived from the same primitive word, and that they could have been changed by the transposition of letters or by a corruption in their pronunciation to such a point that not a vestige of their original structure remains? These words all have the same meaning: *petit* in French, μίκρος (mikros) in Greek, *parvus* in Latin, *kiss*[29] in Hungarian, *little* in English, *klein* in German, *piccolo* in Italian, and *mali* in Slavic.

---

23. This is not a word in French. Kempelen may mean *cartier* but this is unclear, and the translations across this row seem to be more on the side of approximations—the eds.
24. Modern *zsinór*.
25. Modern *óra*.
26. Modern *fehér répa*, literally 'white carrot'.
27. Modern *eszem*.
28. Modern *úr*.
29. Modern *kis*.

§ 21

It has been observed that the words for numbers are very similar in many languages that are different in all other respects. If we compare the words for numbers in all the European languages except Hungarian and countries under Russian domination, we will find a great many similarities among them. However, if we go further and compare words for numbers in three other parts of the world where the populations, because of the great distances that separate them, have never interacted, we find enormous differences. Our readers might perhaps like to find some examples here:

Hungarian	Turkish	Lamut	Korean
Egy	Pir	Omun	Jagner
Kettö[30]	Iki	Dzur	Tourgy
Harom[31]	Ursch	Jean	Socsom
Négy	Tord	Dagan	Docso
Öt	Pesch	Dongan	Caseto
Hat	Alti	Niugun	Joseljone
Hét	Jedi	Nadan	Jeroptehil
Nyolcz[32]	Sokis	Dziebkan	Jaderpal
Kilentz[33]	Tokus	Jigin	Ahopcon
Tiz[34]	Un	Dzian	Jorchip

---

30. Modern *kettő*.
31. Modern *három*.
32. Modern *nyolc*.
33. Modern *kilenc*.
34. Modern *tíz*.

Formosan	Fetu	Guinean	Hottentot
Taush	Wanni	Dèa	Q'kui
Bogio	Abièn	Aoüe	K'kan
Charhe	Abiéssan	Otton	K'ouna
Kiorh	Anan	Cné	Kaka
Nokin	Anum	Atton	Koro
Dekie	Essia	Troupo	Nanni
Memi	Essam	Keoüe	Honko
Thenio	Aoqui	Quiaton	K'hyssi
Senio	Acoa	Kené	K'hessi
Kon	Edu	Ao	Gysso

Ostyak-Samoyed	Kalmyk	Tangut	Avar
Oker	Nege	Dschyk	Szu
Schida	Choyor	Ny	Giggu
Nakor	Gurba	Ssuum	Hanku
Thett	Dörbö	Dscysz	Onku
Nomblach	Tabu	Dnga	Tziloku
Mocktin	Surga	Uruch	Ankalga
Hälsch	Dolo	Dhun	Giuhtku
Stagwet	Naima	Dsguat	Mokbeggu
Okrasiawet	Gessu	Dsg-tomba	Utsgu
Pagowet	Arba	Dsgyn	Entzelgu[35]

§ 22

It is as difficult for me to convince myself that these 120 words originated from the same ten primitive words as it is to imagine that all apple trees originated from an oak and all lindens from a pine.

If, among all of these words, there is a single word that was not derived from a fundamental primitive language but was invented by a given society, it follows that a hundred could have been invented, then a thousand, or even an entire language.

When one wishes to study the difference between languages in depth, one should not stop at single words, but should principally examine syntax

---

[35]. All of the above forms are taken from Schulze 1769—the editors.

and structure. Words may change over long intervals of time to become almost unrecognizable. Continuous interaction among nations has resulted in different dialects, and the art of writing, refined over the years, has also produced a considerable number of changes. We can see this in the German language, where many words look quite different than they did six hundred years ago, and a present-day German almost never hears them. The words in this language may undergo many more changes in the next six hundred years, however, changes in sentence construction will never be significant. If one thousand years ago they said "with the hand," they will not say "the hand with" a thousand years from now. They will not say "happyun" instead of "unhappy," neither will they say "have I six horses stable in my" instead of "I have six horses in my stable."

The difference in gender-defining pronouns will probably never be lost; they will not say, in French, le femme, or le vache, etc. Yet all the peculiarities of speech that we have just cited are present in Hungarian, which is proof that its structure is different from all other European languages and that consequently it cannot share a common origin. This unique language merits a further detailed study of some of its characteristics.

To begin with, instead of prepositions, Hungarian only has postpositions, that is to say particles attached to the end of nouns. *Erdö*, for example, means *forest*; *Erdöben* mean *in the forest*. *Vass*[36] means *iron*, and *Vassböl*[37] means *made of iron*. Simply changing the last syllable of verbs expresses the subject as well as the object of the action. For example, *szertem*[38] means *I love*, whereas *szeretlek* means *I love you*. A syllable added to a noun expresses the possessive adjective: *sziv* means *heart*, *szivem* means *my heart*, *szived* means *your heart*, and *szivé* means *his heart*.

The French verbs *I can* and *I do/make* (in French this is simply *faire*) are not considered to be auxiliaries in Hungarian: to compensate for this, a syllable is inserted in the middle of the verb. *Látok* means *I see*, and *láthalok* means *I can see*; *csinálok* means *I do*, and *csináltátok* means *I make it do* (*j'écris*). When I say *I write* indefinitely and without also indicating what I am writing, in Hungarian the verb always has to end with a *k*, such as in *irok*. However, if I want to say *I am writing this letter*, the verb must end in an *m*, as in *ezt az levelt irom*[39].

The affirmative particle *yes*, which exists in almost all languages, is completely missing in Hungarian. When Hungarians reply to a question,

---

36. Modern *vas*.
37. Modern *vasból*.
38. Modern *szeretem*.
39. Modern *ezt a levelet írom*.

they either have to repeat the verb in the question, for example, to "Have you eaten?" they reply "I have eaten," or *ugy*[40] which means *of course*, or *igenés*, which means *even too much*.[41] The particles that form prefixes in some languages are suffixes in Hungarian: *szerencsés* means *happy*[42], and *szerencsétlen* means *unhappy*.[43]

When there is a question of quantity, the noun is always in the singular. They do not say, "In this stable there are six horses," but rather *six horse*.

Some words in Hungarian can, on their own, express something for which other languages require three words. For example:

My older brother	Bátyám
My younger brother	Eótsém[44]
My older sister	Néném[45]
My younger sister	Hugom[46]

This language has many other unique characteristics, but since they are not directly relevant to our study, we will spare the reader the details. All that has already been said is enough to convince him that this language, in addition to its unique words, also has a completely different sentence structure. Those who have heard Hungarians speak will agree that there is something moving and even heroic in their language which is not evident to such a degree in any other European language.

§ 23

The proponents of an innate primitive language should at least indicate which of our living languages is most in accord with this primitive language.[47] If it is innate to man, how could he have lost it or changed it? How

---

40. Modern *úgy* means 'so'; 'of course' is *természetesen*.

41. Modern *igen* means 'yes', and *és* means "and", but the two words do not combine to make a word meaning 'even too much'.

42. This actually means 'lucky'; the word for 'happy' is *boldog*.

43. This actually means 'unlucky'.

44. Modern *öcsém*.

45. This should be *nővérem*; *néne* means 'aunt'.

46. Modern *húgom*.

47. Some people say it is Phoenician, others say it is Hebrew that has retained most of the primitive language. J. Webbe gives his support to Chinese, Reating to Abyssinian, Boxhorn and Cluverus to Scythian, Mylius to Cimbrian, Jac. Hugo to Latin, P. Ericus to Greek. Stiernholm and Rudbeck go so far as to say that Swedish is the mother of all languages.

could man change the circulation of his blood? Can the innate language be a lesser work of our Creator than our pulse? If man, destined to live in a community, came forth from the hand of the Creator with a complete language, he would naturally have conserved this gift just as he has all his other physical characteristics and would have propagated it with his species as the animals have done with their cries. Someone abandoned in infancy wandering alone in the forest would know this innate language to such a degree that, should he meet another human being, he would be able to communicate in the common language of all human beings without having to learn the latter's language, similarly innate and common to all men. A rooster crows today as he has crowed for a thousand years, and the white parrot still cries *cacatou* as he did on the first day of his creation.

§ 24

Let us consider the first human beings of both sexes, having been endowed with the universal language by the Creator. When they met, what would they have to say to each other in this newly created world where fruits were their nourishment, branches their shelter, and grass their bed, and where they knew no needs other than the primal needs for food and procreation. Under such conditions, their language would naturally have been very limited.

What words would they have used to describe things still unknown such as gold, silver, iron, lead, copper, and all of the semi-metals still buried deep in the bowels of the earth? What would they have called wood, still hidden from their view by its bark, or the intestines and bones of animals hidden beneath fur and feathers, or all the primary materials from which so many thousands of instruments, tools, and clothes were to be shaped? What were their words for the thousands of actions, works, and crafts not yet attempted? If we assume that the first man had a complete language, then we must also attribute to him all ideas and thoughts, without which he would know only how to speak like a parrot.

§ 25

What Mr. Adelung [1793] has said on this subject seems very true to me:

> "Having God Himself invent language and communicate it to mortals is very convenient, but not very satisfactory. The entire structure of language only points to the fact that it is the work of man. Its structure also suggests that man did not invent it

by chance, nor for pleasure and amusement, but by the force of man's great need, his very nature, to speak and be a part of a community, without which he could not be man. Furthermore, the structure of language indicates that it was not invented by geniuses or people with great knowledge, but by simple man formed by the hand of his Creator. Although he was endowed with all manner of faculties and talents, he still lacked development. We have to believe that man used his own capabilities if we do not want to amass wonder upon wonder. Like an animal, he could move about as he wished, and seek his nourishment by instinct alone. However, being at the same time very much above animals, he had the talent and the faculty to invent a language that could animate and stretch his reason. Without understanding, no language can be invented: the corollary, however, is that without language no clear understanding can take place. Both advance at an even pace and complement each other. What makes research into the origin of language so difficult is that man, brought up in a community and already civilized, can no longer place himself entirely in the natural state in order to recall how he perceived objects and by what means his still dormant soul made his perceptions intelligible to others. Just as each person can no longer recall ideas developed during childhood, similarly tradition cannot instruct us on the human spirit's initial development. Allegory and fables always precede history! Thus, a nation has nothing but the words of its language to show the development of its culture and knowledge if it has been lucky enough to preserve that language, pure and uncorrupted, since its beginning."

It was Mr. Herder [1789] who, in large measure, clarified this long obscure topic, and who demonstrated by principles that man himself had invented his language out of necessity. If we wished to cite some of his principles here separately, we would risk distorting the whole, since the parts are linked together. One must read this excellent treatise in its entirety. It certainly merits attention.

Lord Monboddo's excellent work [1773/1785] can also be recommended to those who wish to go into this matter in greater detail. This profound philosopher has written on the formation of ideas, on the nature of man, on the beginning and progress of social life, and on language. A truly philosophical spirit permeates this book, showing a deep and all-encompassing erudition in Greek and Roman antiquity. Superintendent General Herder has written a preface to the German translation in which, while paying homage to the author, he also mentions some topics on which they disagree. The work and the preface [by Herder] are very interesting, instructive, and amusing.

3: The organs of speech and their functions

§ 26

An anatomical description of all the organs that Nature uses to form speech—an examination of each bone, muscle, membrane, and ligament—would lead us too far afield. One could have easily extended this work by another volume if, in elaborating on this subject, one wished to cite all the relevant physiological and anatomical treatises. The immortal Haller has left us an entire volume on the subject of respiration alone [1757-1782].[1]

If teaching someone how to play the violin were being discussed here, we would be straying too far afield if we began by giving a description of each part of that instrument and their interconnections, the various types of wood used in its construction, the sound post, the strings, the bridge, the pegs, etc. We would be straying even further if, wishing to instruct the student more thoroughly, we went on to tell him about the muscles and tendons that move the fingers and explained their names and functions. Instead, with a well-made violin and bow in hand, it becomes a matter of teaching the student how to use his fingers and draw the bow in order to create a beautiful sound. We know that we have a resonating throat, a concave mouth and a mobile tongue. How are they used to produce speech?

Briefly, in order to give readers who have not yet had the opportunity to acquire knowledge of the internal parts of the human body that contribute to speech I shall explain each individual organ—its structure, its use, and its performance.

The principal organs of speech are the following six:

1. The voice
2. The nose
3. The mouth
4. The tongue
5. The teeth
6. The lips

---

1. Volume III discusses respiration and voice.

On the Voice

§ 27

Voice alone is far from being speech. It is only one component, one organ. One can loudly and clearly run through the entire musical scale with only one vowel, without forming a single syllable, let alone a word.[2]

More accurately, the voice is not absolutely indispensable to speech. It is only useful in allowing speech to be heard over a greater distance. If people always remained near each other and if they all had sensitive ears, they could communicate in a very soft voice using air alone. One could then take air, by itself, without sound, for the principal organ of speech.[3] However, since we are discussing only loud and sonorous speech here, we should consider the sonorous voice—air made to vibrate by certain organs—to be necessary. The following, therefore, is a subdivision of organs: the lungs, the trachea, the larynx, and the glottis, which together produce the voice.

The Lungs

§ 28

The lungs are composed of two bodies, the right body always being larger than the left. Both are shaped like a sugar loaf, or an irregular cone that is somewhat truncated at the top. They are composed of cellular tissue and consequently are capable of taking in air. When they are compressed by the diaphragm and the ribs, the air they contain is forced out. If, later, pressure from the ribs is diminished and the diaphragm is lowered, outside air enters of its own weight. This is the mechanism of respiration.

§ 29

When someone is in a tranquil state and respiration is following its normal course, the lungs draw air in and, once full, they immediately force it out again. However, once they have expelled the air, the lungs do not refill immediately, but pause for a moment. Therefore, the lungs remain empty[4]

---

2. An entire air can be sung with a few consonants accompanied by the voice alone, as for example with l, m, and n.

3. With my speaking machine I can speak distinctly with air alone by placing a small piece of wood in the reed to prevent vibration.

4. When we use the term *empty* here we do not mean that the last atom of air is

for a longer span of time than when they are full. Inhalation is always accomplished more slowly than exhalation.

§ 30

The reverse of what we have just discussed occurs during speech. One inhales more rapidly during intervals of discourse. Once the lungs are filled, the air, which has to be converted into voice and overcome various obstacles in its way, exits slowly. The lungs therefore are filled with air longer than when they are empty.

§ 31

The subject we are discussing does not require that we examine the destination of the air, so indispensable to the human body, or how it contributes to the body's preservation as a whole. Whether it serves to cool the blood or to nourish it, what quality of air is useful or detrimental to health—these are not our concern. We will consider air only insofar as it contributes to the formation of speech. We shall only note that our bodies require that the lungs be filled with air for a certain amount of time. During speech the lungs are in an agitated and unnatural state, because air is retained in them. We may observe that people who have been talking excitedly for some time must breathe rapidly in order to regain their equilibrium and restore the peaceful uniformity of ordinary respiration. Preachers, professors, singers, comedians, reciters, and others can render a better account of how much the lungs are affected by this effort.[5]

§ 32

Breathing is not as periodic as the pulse, nor is it as dependent on man's will as other movements of the body. It is not periodic, since man can accelerate or slow down its rate, exhale or inhale, or hold his breath for a while. However, it is not entirely subject to man's will because he cannot

---

expelled from the lungs. A small quantity always remains, since a few words can always be very distinctly articulated after ordinary exhalation. The word *empty* here serves to indicated the opposite of *full*.

5. *Multa loquens quoniam amittit de corpore partem.* Lucretius, Lib. IV. v.545. ["Since by much speaking a man loses a part of his body." Lucretius, Book IV, p. 287, line 54 (Rouse 1924).]

dispense with it completely and is, sooner or later, forced to resume breathing in spite of himself.

We know that all violent movements and exertions of the human body cause variations in breathing, slowing it down or accelerating it and, at times, completely interrupting it for short intervals. Even the slightest movements can cause variations of this nature. For example, it is enough only to turn one's eyes elsewhere or to change the position of one's hand in order to disturb periodic and regular breathing. We may observe that once we have finished a certain task, even a light one to which we have devoted our undivided attention for a given length of time, we take a deep breath to get us prepared for the energy demands of the next task, or simply to restore the spirit we might have lost during our efforts. While we are sleeping peacefully, our breathing is usually regular and marked by even intervals. But once we are awake, our first movement is to take a deep breath in order to prepare ourselves for matters that require activity. At a social gathering when someone deeply absorbed in his own thoughts is unexpectedly addressed, his first reaction will be to take a deep breath. He will be prompted by two needs: first, to give new energy to his vital spirits, now called upon to respond to something else, and second, to fill his lungs deeply with air so that he is prepared to give the necessary response.

§ 33

Changes in spirit also influence our breathing. Shock, fear, anger, pity, joy, love—all of these have an effect on our lungs, just as they do on the heart. These two parts are generally very closely linked, not only in proximity, but in their intimate functional connections. It is not only movement and violent passions of the spirit that have an effect on the lungs. Even the least trifles cause the same changes proportionally. When the mind focuses its attention on the smallest object, such as a grain of sand, respiration sometimes stops entirely so that the body will not make the slightest movement that could distract from the application of our senses. When we subsequently go on to examine another object, for example a fly, the lungs will most certainly take a deep breath, and then stop their action for a short time.

It is very interesting to observe the variation in the actions of the lungs. One can guess someone else's mood simply by observing his breathing, without his having uttered a word about the condition of his spirit. Whether he is calm, worried, content, or irritated, we can often observe a sudden change come over people who are in the calmest of spirits, and can easily determine the moment one thought ended and another began. This may be observed not only when the new idea is a sad or disagreeable one, but even when a thought is completely neutral. The spirit, following its normal course, stops momentarily as it takes a new direction. To do this it needs new energy, which it finds in fresh air deeply inhaled.[6]

§ 34

Often there are defects and flaws in respiration. Just as a bad violin player will never learn how to draw his bow properly, an awkward speaker will never know how to gauge the amount of air he needs and how much he should save in his lungs for any period of time. Thus, he often runs out of air in the middle of a sentence, and pauses to inhale at an inappropriate moment, or compresses his lungs with great effort in order to borrow from the last pockets of air in his lungs, which should always be held in reserve. All of these actions have a bad effect on speech patterns. We can see that children, just starting to speak, only slowly learn how much air is necessary for speech, for in the beginning they inhale before each word. Adults who are not too adept at reading breathe in the middle of a word they cannot immediately pronounce in order to hide their embarrassment by pretending to run out of air. By this device they hope to gain time to spell out the difficult word.

Diseased or weak lungs or illness in other parts of the body can cause many irregularities in breathing, but we shall leave this area to medicine. Here we are only concerned with the organs of speech in their normal state.

The Trachea

§ 35

This is the channel through which air enters and leaves the lungs. It is a somewhat flattened cylindrical tube, composed of cartilaginous rings and fibers that can shorten it by contracting and lengthen it by relaxing. Its upper portion is connected to the larynx, while its lower portion is divided into two branches, or short tubes, one of which leads into the right lung and the other into the left lung, so that the two parts are united in a single trunk.

---

6. We could say more on respiration, but since it would not be directly relevant to speech, we will not bother our readers, who are interested only in what is germane to the principal topic of this book. Maybe we have already gone beyond our stated limit of saying no more than what is absolutely necessary.

§ 36

Galen, and after him all the Ancients, and even some more modern men, was of the opinion that the trachea contributed much and was indispensable for the formation of the voice. This belief continued until Dodart [1700], who clearly proved that its sole function was to serve as a conduit for air between the lungs and the glottis, that it had no role in causing air vibrations, and had no other function than that of the wind trunk of a pipe organ.

I myself harbored the same mistaken idea for some time while I was building a speaking machine. When I pressed a finger against the trachea, over the sternum at first, I felt distinct vibrations. This always made me hold on to the idea that one somehow had to duplicate a channel capable of similar vibrations in order to make a machine speak. I was, however, confronted with a thousand insurmountable difficulties. The numerous fruitless trials would have almost made me lose my enthusiasm for my enterprise, had not Dodart's work absolutely assured me that the vibrations of air were not a result of the trachea's vibrations, but that on the contrary, the trachea vibrated because of the vibrations of the air within. We shall see this more clearly in what follows.

The Larynx

§ 37

Above the trachea there is a short stub of a tube, wider than the trachea itself, but much shorter. It is composed of cartilage, muscles, membranes, and ligaments. It has the shape of a box, or an urn, whose anterior portion is somewhat more elongated and more serrated than its posterior portion, which is shorter and more open at the top. This portion is mobile, rising at times and falling at others, when one is speaking or swallowing, a fact that can easily be observed by pressing a finger against it.

§ 38

This part includes the seat of the voice, that is to say the "glottis," which we shall discuss first. To protect this most precious and useful gift to man, the Creator used all the precautions He could to protect it from external attacks, by providing it with a mobile cover[7] that prevents foreign bodies from falling into its narrow opening and obstructing it. This small cover resembles a

---

7. The epiglottis.

miniature tongue, pointed at its end, which can be lowered by its posterior portion to cover the entire opening of the larynx. It is an elastic cartilage, normally curved upward at its point, closing only when something threatens to enter the larynx. Since the opening of the esophagus is directly behind the larynx and food has to go over it to reach the esophagus, this cover is indispensable. It acts as a drawbridge over which anything destined for the stomach has to pass. If by chance this drawbridge is not lowered in time, or does not seal completely, or, while swallowing, the esophagus receives too much food or liquid, these foreign substances may enter the larynx and epiglottis. The immediate result is an unbearable irritation and tickling in the larynx. With convulsive effort, nature tries to rid itself of the foreign body by violently compressing the lungs so that air is forced out with such impetuosity that it carries along everything in its path. This, too, is the mechanism of the cough.

§ 39

It is also the epiglottis that creates a sound when one hiccups. However, it is not the primary cause as many people think. One should not look for its cause in the throat either, since this sound results from action of the diaphragm. When the diaphragm is suddenly lowered by a convulsive movement, outside air violently enters the lungs. This current of air closes the epiglottis, which is normally open, sealing it like a valve and producing the sound of a hiccup. If one could foresee the moment of the diaphragm's convulsive movement, he could, with effort, hold his epiglottis open. Air could then enter without creating too much noise, such as during rapid breathing. However, one is usually unprepared. The spasm of the diaphragm occurs when it is least expected and the epiglottis is relaxed. Fortunately, the air in the lungs can expand. Otherwise, the diaphragm could be easily damaged since the epiglottis closes suddenly at the moment of the diaphragm's greatest tension. We know how tiring and debilitating hiccuping can be when it lasts for any length of time.

§ 40

Table I, Fig. 2, represents the trachea (*D*), the larynx (*G*), and the sealed epiglottis (*H*). Chewed food, moving over the tongue, passes over the closed epiglottis and falls into the esophagus (*K*).

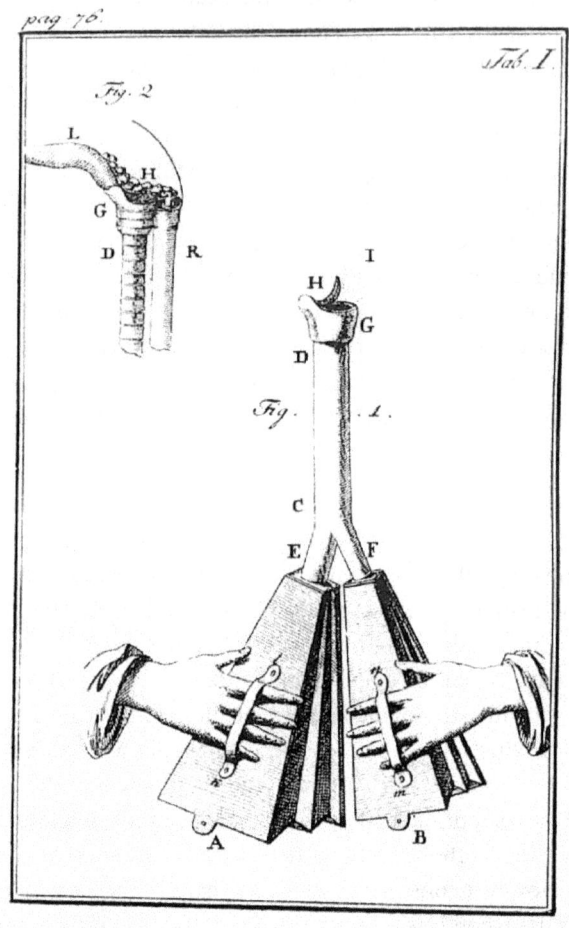

§ 41

With a diagram—not an anatomical but a mechanical imitation of nature—I will try to illustrate what we have already said about the organs of speech.[8]

---

8. I am of the opinion that people who have not frequently witnessed the anatomical dissection of a cadaver, and who consequently have not acquired the ability to readily recognize internal organs, will have difficulty in forming a correct idea about these things from drawings and engravings only. Since most of my readers are in this category, I thought I would be rendering them a service by helping their imagination with the method I adopted. It will also serve to prepare the reader for the explanation of the speaking machine.

In Table I, Fig. 1, with the two bellows, *A* represents the right portion of the lung, which is somewhat larger than the left portion *B*. Above this, *C* and *D* represent the trachea, *E* and *F* the two branches or tubes, *G* the larynx, and *H* the epiglottis. One can imagine the fingers of both hands acting as the ribs. The bellows do not have valves like ordinary bellows, but they draw in and discharge air through the same opening, which is exactly the mechanism of the lungs. We can therefore represent inhalation and exhalation clearly in the following manner.

The two posterior planks of the bellows must be imagined as attached to an object. When the ribs, represented by the fingers, compress the two bellows, air exits through the glottis at *I*. If, subsequently, the two hands return to their original position, the fingers lift the bellows by means of the straps *k-l* and *m-n*, and then space is created for air to enter and refill them. One must also note that in nature it is not only the ribs that control respiration; the diaphragm also makes a contribution, primarily in the manner already described. Although our diagram does not include the pressure caused by the diaphragm, it gives a reasonable idea of how respiration works.[9]

The Glottis

§ 42

Below the epiglottis and inside the larynx are two horizontally stretched membranes or skins[10], each forming the surface of a semicircle, and together forming a complete circle. They are attached to the inner wall of the larynx by their rounded outer edges. Their right sides are turned inward toward each other such that they form a straight line when they come together (i.e. the diameter of the circle). When they touch each other along their entire length, they seal so exactly that they do not allow the least atom of air to pass through. When they separate, they form a lenticular opening, resembling the reed of an oboe or a bassoon.

§ 43

If this opening is not wide enough for the air pressed out of the lungs to find a clear outlet, but is forced to break through with some effort, it will

---

9. Moreover, one can dispense with the idea that the diaphragm is absolutely necessary for respiration. Haller [1700, vol. 3, section 1, §36] says that the diaphragm sometimes falls during exhalation and conversely rises during inhalation.

10. Linguists today refer to the two membranes as the "vocal folds". –the eds.

rub against the two edges of the membranes and make them vibrate. These vibrations are so extraordinarily rapid that the blows the air receives from the repeated beating of the membranes blend with each other and cannot be distinguished by the ear, much like the spokes of a wheel which, turning at high speed, seem to combine into a solid disc before our eyes. In this manner, the repeated vibrations of the air are perceived by our ear as a single sound, which we call *the voice*.

§ 44

The opening we have just described will always be referred to as the "glottis" in this work. It has its limits. When it is open in the center along its short diameter about a tenth or twelfth of an inch, the voice ceases because the air can pass through freely without creating any friction. The more this membrane contracts and the closer its edges are to being a straight line, the higher the tone. In other words, the tone becomes shrill. One can think of them as two strings. The more a string is stretched, the higher its tone, and in the same manner, the more the membranes of the glottis approach a straight line, the more they are stretched and consequently the more rapid their vibrations, which produces the shriller sound. Air passing over the glottis has the same effect as a bow over the strings of a violin. It rubs against the edges of the glottis and sets them in motion more or less immediately, depending on their tautness. From this point of view our voice should be placed among string instruments.[11]

Dodart does not find the explanation for the difference in tones in the tension of the glottis, but instead in the expansion and contraction of its opening. He therefore places the voice among the wind instruments. However, it is very easy to combine these two points of view, though each opinion carries its own considerable weight. The glottis cannot undergo a single change; that is, it can neither expand nor contract without having its edges relaxed or taut. Conversely, the edges cannot be taut or relaxed without an expansion or contraction of the glottal opening. Therefore, Ferrein's tension and Dodart's opening are inseparable. One is as necessary to the voice as the other. The nature of the mechanism seems to demand that the opening of the glottis and the tension of its edges always maintain an exact proportion. If the edges are very taut, they require a greater quantity of air, pushed with more force, in order to vibrate. Once the air forces a passage through the contracted opening, the friction against the edges becomes so great that it makes them vibrate.

---

11. This was the opinion of Mr. Ferrein [1741].

§ 45

Perhaps the best illustration for the high and low tones of the human voice is the trumpet or the hunting horn. The mouth represents the glottis, the mouthpiece of the trumpet represents the larynx, and the lips are the two membranes of the glottis. The rest of the instrument serves to make the sound more shrill, or to increase or aggrandize it, or to articulate it by serving the same purpose as the mouth does for the voice. The more we wish to raise the tone, the more we press the lips and the more force we will have to use to expel the air out of the contracted opening. Through this example we can clearly see how much effort people who sing or play wind instruments have to make in order to produce higher tones.

Here, the funnel-shaped mouthpiece of the trumpet and hunting horn serves as the larynx, and the lips, which serve the function of the glottis, are tightly compressed. In instruments that are played with a reed, like the bassoon and the clarinet, it is the other way around: the mouth becomes the larynx and the glottis is the instrument's reed. When these instruments are held to the mouth, the lips become the ligaments and the muscles, which more or less contract the glottis, represented by the reed, to determine the degree of the tone. We will also show that in order to invent instruments that produce sounds similar to the human voice, it is necessary to follow the plan that Nature enjoined as our guide.

§ 46

Coming back to the human glottis, we shall again make use of a mechanical instrument in order to have a clearer idea of its structure and movements.

Let us look at Table II, Fig. 1—a wooden hoop over which a skin has been stretched like a drum and split from a to b along its diameter. As long as this box is left undisturbed, the two edges of the slit meet each other. However, if the circle is compressed a little in the direction a to b, as in Fig. 2, the diameter ab is shortened while the circle's other diameter, cd, is lengthened by the same amount, as the skin is pulled toward the sides. The result is a wider or narrower opening, depending on the degree of pressure applied to the sides.

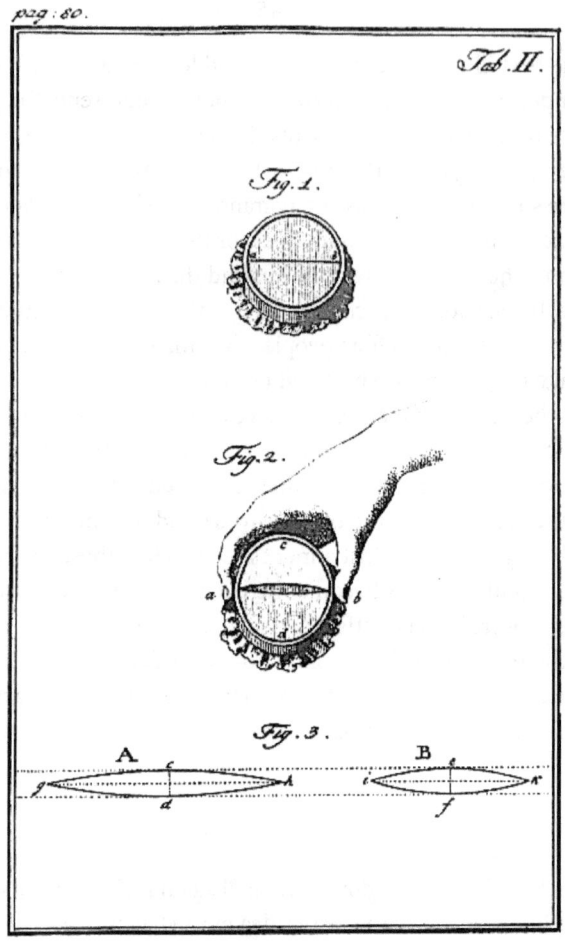

§ 47

This small opening, barely a tenth of an inch in length, is capable of an incredible number of variations. If two strings of equal thickness are under equal tension, consequently producing the same tone, but one is stretched proportionally about 2/1000 parts more than the other, a trained ear can notice the dissonance. There are some who claim that a good voice can divide the interval between two tones into 100 degrees. If that is so, the diameter of the glottis, which is just 1/10 of an inch, can, in an ordinary voice of twelve tones, produce 1,200 variations. If we consider that each membrane of the glottis has its own particular variations, we would have to double that figure, bringing it up to 2,400. It would then follow that an inch can be divided into 24,000 parts.[12] There is no instrument with which we can mark such a small division on a body. Dodart went farther by dividing the inch into the astonishing number of 963,200 parts. He determined that one could imagine a line, however short, as being infinitely divisible. It would then become a question of knowing how far any executed division depended on one's intention and ability, and how many degrees a well-trained human voice could produce distinctly and at will between one tone and another. It seems that this matter has not yet been decided.

§ 48

If the voices of women and children are normally[13] clear and high, while on the other hand the voices of men are lower, it is because the former have a smaller larynx, the membranes of their glottises are shorter, and in general all the parts are more delicate. Since at one point we compared the edges of the glottis to strings, we shall maintain that analogy when explaining this natural phenomenon.

If two strings, one being shorter than the other, are stretched with an equal force, the shorter string will always produce a higher note because its vibrations are shorter and consequently more rapid. To make the longer string vibrate in unison with the shorter one, it would have to be stretched farther. Using this premise, we shall assume that in Table II Fig. 3, of the two glottises, A is that of a man, and B that of a woman. They are both equally open at the center as shown by the dotted parallel lines, $cd = ef$, the only difference being in the opposing diameters gh and ik, where the first is a third longer than the second. It follows, then, that the sections of the circle gch and hdg are longer than those of iek and kfi. If we also assume that the two objects are under equal tension, then case B will produce a higher tone than case A.

If we wish to have A produce the same tone as B, the two angles g and h have to separate from one another, so that the two halves of the circle will be under greater tension, just as the longer string in the case we discussed

---

12. Encyclopedia. Voice. Formation of the Human Voice. [Kempelen does not indicate which encyclopedia is being referred to here. –the eds.]

13. I say *normally*, because there are women, even children, who have low voices and conversely men who have voices that are clear and high, just as a man may sometimes have a small nose and a woman a large one. There are always exceptions to the general rule.

earlier would have to stretch farther in order to vibrate in unison with the shorter one. If greater tension is applied, the two halves of the circle at *c* and *d* must come closer to each other. Thus, the glottis *A* will contract quite a bit, let us say by about a third, while *B* will remain in its original state, and its diameter *ef* will be a third longer than at *A*.

If, on the other hand, *B* contracted and went up by a tone, then *A* would have to contract by a greater amount in order to produce the same tone, and the two halves of the circle in *A* would flatten out almost to a straight line, and consequently would soon reach their limit and cease to produce an effect. On the other hand, portions of circle *B* would still have several degrees of higher tones to produce before they attained their limit and reached a straight line.

§49

This clearly demonstrates why a man's voice cannot attain the high tones of a woman's soprano.[14] On the other hand, high female voices cannot produce the low tones of a male bass. We can, similarly, find the explanation in what has already been discussed. If the edges of the small glottis *B*, had to stretch, they would create a disproportionately large opening *ef*, because in the process of stretching, the edges would be pulled so far apart that air could pass freely over them with no further opportunity to cause any friction or vibration. From this, it follows that if someone wishes to surpass the limits of the natural voice he will either have to separate the edges of the glottis as far as possible, or draw them together entirely. In both cases the voice stops naturally.

§ 50

We will note yet another condition that might contribute to lowering the voice. On either side of the "lips" of the glottis, and between its ligaments, there is a cavity known as *Ventriculi Galeni*, or *Sinus Laryngis*. These are barely noticeable in a fetus, wider in children, better developed in adults, and very large in aged people. In his *Anatomie*, Lieutaud augments this observation by adding that he has examined these cavities in animal dissections and has found that they are generally deeper in animals that have a lower voice, such as oxen.

---

14. The falsetto does not enter into this discussion because it is not a natural tone but a forced one. By using this method, a natural voice may be raised three tones higher than the singer can obtain by straining his lungs, just as higher tones may be drawn from a flute by blowing air in with greater force.

3: THE ORGANS OF SPEECH AND THEIR FUNCTIONS

§ 51

I know of no animals, except fish and some insects, that are not equipped with a voice. Vicq-d'Azyr [1779:106] has described the trachea, the larynx, and the glottis of different quadrupeds, birds and reptiles, and has depicted them in very beautiful engravings.

§ 52

Some scholars claim that monkeys have no voice. Camper [1779] maintains that nature deprived the monkey of a voice by giving it two sacs which hang next to his trachea. Herder [1784:223] says, "The monkey is mute: more mute than all other animals, each of which, including the frog and lizard, have their characteristic sound." These authors probably did not have the opportunity to study monkeys extensively. I can, in this case, assert that monkeys do have a voice, and a strong and piercing one at that. I had, for many years, a female monkey of medium size in my home. She produced different high-pitched sounds. For example, when she was petted or scratched, she always growled. From her youth she was used to being with people. Therefore, when she was left alone in a room, she called so loudly for company that she could be heard through closed doors. When she was irritated, she emitted a special cry, but joy also made her let out even higher cries, for example when a person to whom she was especially attached came in, or when she was offered a favorite food. She preferred my sister to everyone else. When my sister was out, she crept around very sadly and voiced her discontent over this absence with distinct sounds, resembling the syllables *um, um, ma, ma*. She would finally calm down once she heard my sister's carriage arrive, and would immediately leave her retreat and hurry across the room to greet her on the stairs. I cannot exactly describe her sounds, but it seemed to me that they bore some resemblance to those of a partridge, except that they were connected with a very distinct <a > or <i>.

Many people may think that what makes monkeys mute is that they remain silent unless they are tame. In order to succeed in hearing the voice of this species of animal, they must be tamed to such a degree that they may be allowed to go about without a chain. At least my female monkey was at that stage. She had the run of the house, though she was not initially given this liberty. The first year she was with us, she suffered a severe illness and became so weak that she could barely turn from one side to the other as she lay on her bed. In order to ease her pitiful condition a little, and having no reason to fear the natural mischief of these animals, we removed her chain.

Her illness lasted several weeks, and when she finally recovered her strength returned very slowly, by almost imperceptible degrees. Thus, we delayed replacing her chain from one day to the next. Gradually we could see that she was not abusing her freedom and we left the chain off entirely. She would go about in the courtyard and at times would climb over the roofs like a cat, but the moment her name was called she would return immediately. Because she was a female and would periodically damage furniture and clothing, we were obliged to chain her at times. When, after a few days, she was given her liberty again, it was a joy to see her run about the house announcing to everyone with lively cries her joy at being free. She would redouble her cries when one sympathized with her over her difficult captivity.

§ 53

Convinced by my personal experience that monkeys do indeed have a voice, I cannot see why their sacs would prevent them from producing a voice since they do have all of the necessary organs. On the contrary, I think that monkeys might speak much better than parrots if they were as inclined to imitate our sounds. I have often observed that when a frog wants to croak, it inflates a bladder about the size of a nut on each side of its throat near the end of the jaw. With these sacs or bladders, it has an impressively strong voice in proportion to its body size. It is even probable that these sacs are of great use in producing the frog's croaks, since with its rapid breathing the frog could not sustain its croaking efforts for long and would only produce short, interrupted sounds. It is possible that the frog's lungs are very small and that nature gave it these bladders so that it could pump air, and thus maintain its croaking sounds over longer periods. These bladders may be to the frog what the eolipile (boiler) is to a steam engine.[15] If we dare avail ourselves of yet another mechanical proof, I could allude to my speaking machine here. Two of the very largest ox bladders can be attached to the duct serving as the trachea, and when filled they do not hinder the voice in any way. I even had to, by design, fit my speaking machine with a sac in the shape of a small bellows, as will be seen later in its description.

---

15. According to Bomare's entry for *grenouille* 'frog' [1764a:548], it is only the male frogs that emit cries. One can find the same [in his article for *singe* 'monkey']. These animals have very loud cries and therefore a voice [1768b:264-278]. Buffon and Daubenton [1749-1804, vol. XV, p. 5] describe a certain type of monkey they designate "Howlers" because of the cries these animals emit.

§ 54

Various other observed flaws and defects in the voice should also be mentioned. There are the falsetto voices that can almost never produce a single clear sound. The reason given seems to be well founded. It is claimed that in some people one membrane of the glottis is naturally shorter than the other. This always creates unequal tension in them, so that the tone is ambiguous, vacillating, and false. This produces an unpleasant enunciation.

§ 55

There are also people who, while speaking in a deep voice, suddenly shift to a tone so sharp that it causes a disagreeable shock to the ear. This sometimes happens in the middle of a phrase. One could almost conclude that they have two glottises and that they alternate between them at inopportune times. I would not know how to determine the real reason, but I imagine that these people want to imitate the inflections of the voice, being one of the biggest embellishments to rhetoric and giving them [tremendous] energy of expression. However, not having the right 'ear', they do it awkwardly, imagining that it suffices just to change tone, without concern for what they are doing. Although voice inflections are among the greatest embellishments of speech, giving it zest and expression, this particularly drastic shift has an awkward result.

There are also people who are unable to use their organs of speech properly. They never learn how to give their glottis the correct opening so they cannot produce a firm tone, or sing the simplest ballad. An incorrect "ear" might be another possible reason for this flaw.

§56

All voice ceases when the membranes of the glottis are eroded by illness, or have become paralyzed and have consequently lost some of their elasticity. Such people can only speak in a very soft voice, with breath alone. Nevertheless, they can still be understood at a short distance.

Goiters, sore throats, tumors, swellings, mucus, and coughs all pose different obstacles to speech. The position of the larynx is changed by swellings and contusions, preventing it from rising and falling. The membranes of the glottis are weighted down by foreign bodies attached to mucus, preventing them from producing vibrations with the necessary vivacity. The voice then becomes hoarse and disagreeable, very much like the way violin strings, when touched by a light object, give a repugnant sound.

§ 57

When the glottis is not opened wide enough during respiration—as when it is open wide enough only for singing and speaking—it will also produce a sound during inhalation. This is because the edges of the glottis are subject to the same friction and vibrations when air enters as when it leaves, just as a violin string produces the same tone whether the bow is going up or down. I have often observed talkative women gossiping with their neighbors at such a spirited pace that in order not to lose an instant, they pronounced entire phrases on the inside while inhaling. One can often observe this phenomenon in Catholic churches, where everyone prays to himself. If one finds himself next to someone praying in a low voice and with great fervor, one can hear him pronounce as many words inside the mouth as outside, with no discontinuity at all. I can, if I want to, loudly and distinctly pronounce words on the inside. However, the sound has an annoying, hoarse, and disagreeable quality.

§ 58

Until now, we have we have examined what produces voice, and we shall finish by citing what makes it cease. We shall have occasion to make use of the latter in what follows.

The voice ceases:

1. When the glottis is open too far.
2. When the glottis is too tight.
3. When lung pressure is interrupted.
4. When the lungs are completely devoid of air.
5. When the mouth and nose are closed.
6. When the epiglottis falls and covers the glottis.

The Nose

§ 59

All quadrupeds ordinarily breathe through the nose. Some, such as the dog, fox, wolf and several others, also use their mouth during very hot weather.[16]

At rest, man normally breathes only through his nose, but if he is in motion, or if his nose is partially blocked, he will also keep his mouth open in order to allow air to enter more freely. Small children rarely breathe through their mouths. Since the nose is the principal channel for breathing, and since its opening is directly over the larynx, natural order seems to demand that we discuss it before we mention the mouth, although the latter organ is more important for speech.

The interior structure of the nose can be compared to an arched canal, or a mine entrance, whose base is narrower than its rising inner walls, and which terminates in a gothic arch at the top. The channel of the nose is separated along its length by a partition that divides it into two parts, or further channels. In addition to the principal opening that leads to the throat, the sides have several other openings which we shall not describe here, as they are not relevant to speech. The entire structure of the nose is bony and covered by a membrane. At their anterior extremity, all three partitions terminate in cartilage and are covered with flesh and skin. When these are removed, the bony structure revealed is somewhat like the etching in Table III, Fig. 1. This channel passes horizontally over the arch of the mouth, called the palate, up to the throat, following the former's inclined slope.

---

16. Since horses never breathe through their mouth, many Tartars slit the nostrils of their horses in order to help them breathe more easily when they gallop at great speed.

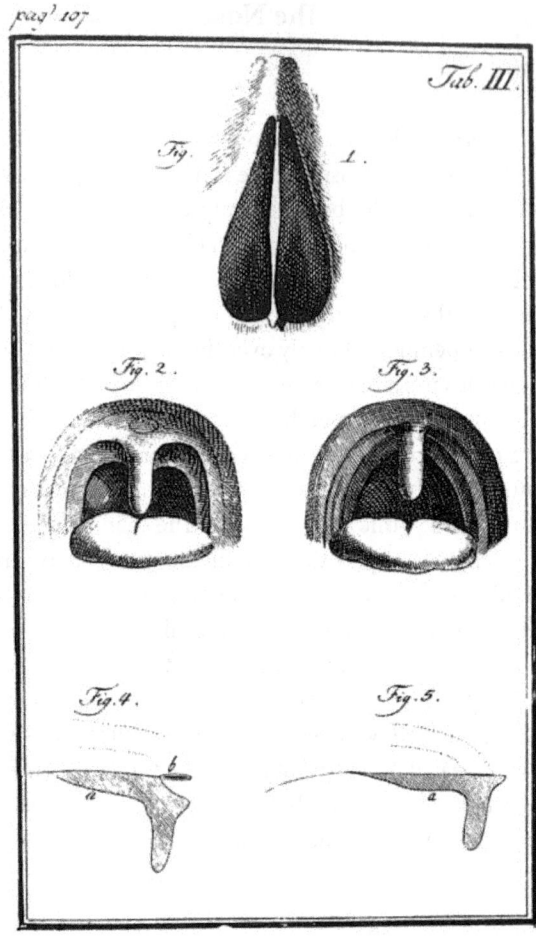

§ 60

People who have lost the intermediate cartilage of their nose, either through illness or through accident, or whose nasal cavity has been plugged by a growth or by dirt, always have something defective in their speech that is repugnant to the ear. The only two sounds or letters pronounced through the nose are M and N. To form the sounds that our ears are accustomed to hearing, the resonating air has to be divided into two by the cartilage inside the nose. Otherwise, M and N will not sound the way they should.[17]

17. Just as in pronouncing L, the tongue, pressing against a point opposite the

§ 61

The opening through which air passes from the throat into the channel of the nose is a sort of valve that is open at times and closed at others. This valve is called the soft palate, or *Velum pendulum palati*. The soft palate is formed by two rounded bodies of skin which hang at the end of the palate over the epiglottis (Fig. 2). A small, fleshy tongue, commonly called the uvula, originates and is suspended from the center of these bodies of skin. In its entirety, the structure can be represented as two double arcades, resting on the same column at the center. Over the arch formed by these arcades is the opening leading to the nose, as indicated by the dotted circle in the diagram.

The entire arch is composed of flesh, is supple and mobile, and can be raised or lowered. When it is raised, its surface covers the nasal passage and is in the form shown in Fig. 3. Fig. 4 and 5 show the side views. In the first of these figures, the uvula is pendent, thus the entry of the nasal passage *b* is left open. In the second, the soft palate is pulled upward, exactly covering the orifice.

When the soft palate is entirely absent, or when it is defective to the point that it does not completely cover the entry of the nasal passage, no vowel or consonant can be pronounced distinctly except M and N, and the voice will always be nasal.

We shall return to this topic later when we discuss each letter separately. We shall currently consider the purpose and the function of the soft palate.[18]

---

palate, leaves an opening for air on either side, dividing the air into two streams, thus forming the L sound.

18. In order to avoid any error, I have marked the soft palate as only a small tongue, or valve, in all of the profile views. Lieutaud [1782:337] also calls it a valve.

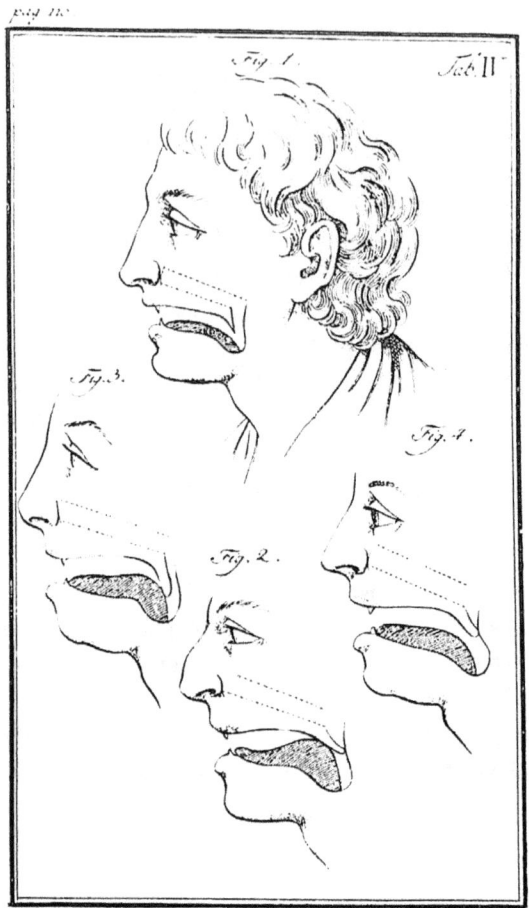

§ 62

1: When the soft palate hangs absolutely straight, and the posterior part of the tongue is lowered so far that it does not touch the uvula, the two channels are open, and the air can enter and exit freely through both the mouth and the nose (Table IV, Fig. 1).

2: The soft palate can block both channels simultaneously when its edge leans against the part opposite the throat and the posterior part of the tongue curves up to the soft part of the palate (Fig. 2). Although the mouth is open, air cannot escape, because of the obstacles formed by the soft palate. This is true even when air pressure is as high as possible.

3: The soft palate opens and closes each channel alternately, leaving one or the other open. In other words, the channel of the mouth is open at times and that of the nose is open at others. The first case occurs when the soft palate presses its lower edge against the slightly raised posterior portion of the tongue (Fig. 3). The second condition occurs when the soft palate abandons the tongue and pushes against the posterior part of the throat (Fig 4).

Later, when we discuss each letter separately, we will often say that the nose is blocked. In these cases, we are speaking of the soft palate we have just discussed, since the nose cannot be blocked in any other manner than externally, with the fingers, or by plugging the nostrils, alternatives which are not under consideration here.

Since we are discussing this singular organ, we should mention some of its other functions that are not directly related to speech, but which occasionally create a sonorous sound. These merit our attention inasmuch as we have neglected discussing them until now. Among these are the snore, the cough, the sneeze, and the noise made when blowing the nose. We shall consider each of these topics separately.

The Snore

§ 63

When someone is sleeping and his uvula is in one of the positions described above, he does not snore. However, there are three other situations that differ very slightly from the preceding ones and result in snoring. The first of these is when the sleeper is breathing through his nose with his mouth closed and the uvula is not completely open, but allows only a very narrow passage for air. In that case, the soft palate acquires some of the properties of the glottis. That is, it is shaken by the force of air flow and immediately starts to beat repeatedly against the inner walls of the throat, thus producing a sound somewhat different from that produced by the glottis, because it is always hoarse and loud.

The second of these situations occurs when the sleeper breathes in air through his mouth while his nose is blocked by the soft palate. If, at the same time, the back portion of the tongue is raised too high and almost touches the soft part of the palate[19], the result, as in the preceding case, is too small an opening; the soft part of palate shakes and acts in the same manner as the soft palate in the preceding case.

Finally, the third situation occurs when the sleeper breathes through both channels simultaneously; the soft palate is not completely pressed against the posterior inner wall, nor is the tongue lifted against the soft part of the palate, causing the soft palate to tremble. Sometimes snoring is heard only during inhalation, sometimes during exhalation only, and often in both situations. These three situations are, then, what snoring consists of.

There exists another kind of snore, but I would not name it as such. It includes sighs, moans, and cries that escape from the glottis of a sleeping person, when the glottis is not sufficiently open. This is therefore not, properly speaking, a snore, but a sound of the voice occasioned by the action of the ligaments of the glottis.

There is yet another type of noise, heard at times, that cannot be labeled a snore. It occurs when air passes over one of the channels whose orifice has been somewhat constricted, but not enough to cause a vibration. The passage, being too narrow to allow copious quantities of air to pass easily, does not allow the air to escape without creating a certain sound that cannot, properly speaking, be called a snore.

The Cough

§ 64

The cough has much in common with the snore, the only difference being that one coughs while one is awake for a deliberate purpose, and in a more violent manner than a snore. The following is how the noise made during a cough is produced. When the nose is blocked, the posterior part of the tongue is so elevated that it slightly touches the soft part of the palate. If air is then pushed violently, this part will vibrate and produce the noise of a cough. Nature uses this method to rid itself of mucus and other matters that attach themselves to the throat, the soft palate, or the larynx that affect the clarity of the voice considerably.

The violence with which air is forced out sweeps along all of the foreign bodies. For this reason, when someone who has been silent for some time wishes to speak, he often coughs or spits before he begins, to rid himself of mucus collected during the interval of silence and to make

---

19. Later, in describing the mouth, we shall state what we mean by the soft part of the palate. In the meantime it can be seen in the diagram, Table III, Figs. 1 and 5, letter *a*.

his throat more supple. Many people have adopted the habit of coughing lightly before they start to speak. Others do so intentionally, to gain time in order to mentally review what they are about to say, or to find the appropriate words with which to begin. The cough is almost always followed by an ejection from the mouth.[20]

We also sniffle through the nose. The action of sniffling is produced by holding the mouth closed and forcefully inhaling air through the nose, thus setting the partially closed soft palate in motion, as during a snore. This results in a more muted sound than a cough.

By sniffling, the mucus ordinarily in the nose is pulled into the throat where it is collected by repeated sniffles and is finally ejected through the mouth. Many people, especially children, have the habit of swallowing it.

The third movement of this nature takes place in the epiglottis. When the opening of the trachea or its cover (the epiglottis) is covered with phlegm and tries to expel it, the epiglottis falls. Then the opening for the voice, which lies underneath, expands as far as possible, and a torrent of air, rushing impetuously out of the lungs, finds no obstacle in its path to the opening of the glottis except the epiglottis. Meanwhile, air, having gained the advantage, makes the epiglottis vibrate, producing a sound similar to that made by horses at the end of their neighing. When only a small amount of phlegm is detached from the trachea by this movement, the rest remains attached to the less sensitive inner walls of the throat. However, if the phlegm is more abundant, it is ejected by a special movement of the mouth, or is swallowed, which is more often the case.

Through this, we can see that these movements are different, since they are performed by different organs. However, we lack the proper terms for their definition since, until now, they have received too little attention.

§ 65

There are no other differences between these last movements and a proper cough, except that in the former the epiglottis offers less resistance to the internal air, while resistance is at its highest during a cough. Finally, when forced, the epiglottis opens abruptly and lets the air escape, which produces a blast of air and the familiar sound of the cough, repeated three or four times.

---

20. Later, when we discuss the functions of the tongue, we shall also describe the mechanism of this operation.

The Sneeze

§ 66

The sneeze is another way for the nose to rid itself of dust and other causes of intolerable tickling. It is not only things attached to the nose that cause this tickling. The nose, seat of the sense of smell, is very easily irritated, and is sensitive to all sorts of external stimuli. It responds to infinitely nuanced stimuli, from the gentle fragrance of a rose, to the harsh smoke of pitch, to the effect of tobacco and hellebore. Even a ray of sunshine can cause a sneeze.

It is not our intention here to elaborate on the causes of sneezing but only to show which organs are used in its execution. When one wants to sneeze, a large amount of air is inhaled, then, one or both channels are blocked (Table IV, Fig. 2). Air within the lungs is compressed with great effort, and finally, one or both canals open suddenly and allow the air to issue with great impetuosity. If the objective is not attained the first time, that is to say, if the causes of irritation are not removed, the sneeze is repeated more often. It is thus possible for one to sneeze a hundred times or more. Excessive pressure and violent sneezes affect almost all of the limbs and the intestines, and weaken the entire body.[21] Since this is the greatest effort made by the diaphragm it can have many dangerous consequences, including ruptured veins, hernias, blindness, hemorrhage, and even death. Therefore it is not without reason that we say "To your health" or "God bless you" to someone who sneezes. We mean to say "may God preserve you from a fatal accident at this moment."

Blowing the Nose

§ 67

Blowing is another function of the nose. When one wishes to rid the nose of excess moisture, the two nostrils are pressed together with the fingers, a large quantity of air is inhaled through the mouth, the tongue is pushed hard against the soft part of the palate[22] and air is violently forced into the nose. When the air in the nose is compressed, the fingers are relaxed, but only enough to allow the nostrils to flare somewhat, creating a passage

---

21. The celebrated Haller says that a continuous fit of sneezing lasting several months has been observed. *Phisiologie, Liv. VIII. Sect. III,* § 36.

22. If the mouth is closed by the lips alone, the cheeks will puff up while the nose is being blown.

for the moisture in the path of the compressed air. Thus, air under pressure entrains the moisture as it rushes out. This process often results in a sonorous sound that can be heard at a distance. If the nose is very full of moisture, it is not necessary to press on the nostrils; one need only blow hard through the nose while the mouth is held shut to expel moisture without too much noise. If there is very little moisture, or if it is very fluid, a simple clearing will have little effect, since the air may escape with little opposition and will consequently entrain little or none of the moisture on the inner walls of the nose. The sound heard when the nose is cleared while it is held closed is due to the nostrils taking on the characteristics of the glottis and producing a sonorous noise by their rapid vibration. These vibrations can be felt even by the fingertips.[23]

§ 68

If I may, I would like to mention here an observation that has nothing to do with speech and is consequently not germane to my principal topic, but which seems interesting enough to be offered to physiologists for future experiments. It seems to me that the uvula, or rather what I call the valve of the nose, is absolutely indispensable for swallowing food. I think of this natural function as it is depicted in Table V, Fig. 1a with the throat area sealed on all sides. When food arrives at this space, having just passed over the tongue, it is met by the jointly rising larynx and pharynx. At the same time, the interior walls of the throat contract somewhat, helping to shrink this space and consequently compress the food from all sides. Since the larynx is covered by the epiglottis, which allows nothing to enter, and the other side of the throat—the funnel-shaped pharynx—is always open, the compressed food, moistened with saliva and therefore somewhat fluid, finds no other exit than the opening of the esophagus which then receives it and pushes it into the stomach with a vermicular movement. The positions of all the organs that cooperate in this function are shown in Fig. 2. By pressing the fingers against the throat one can easily convince oneself that the two channels, the larynx and the pharynx, rise during the act of swallowing. During speech, however,

---

23. It has been generally observed that when air is forced through small openings with membranous edges, a vibration results and consequently a sound is produced, as when air rushes out through the contracted opening of the anus. This noise can also be imitated by the lips. Similarly, if a cupped hand is placed in the cavity of the armpit such that it is well supported all around by the lowered arm, the compressed air issues from one side and then the other, producing a sound very similar to the first sound mentioned. Some people can accomplish the same thing by applying one cupped hand against the other, etc.

the larynx rises, especially when the letter I is being pronounced. However, it rises to twice that height during swallowing.

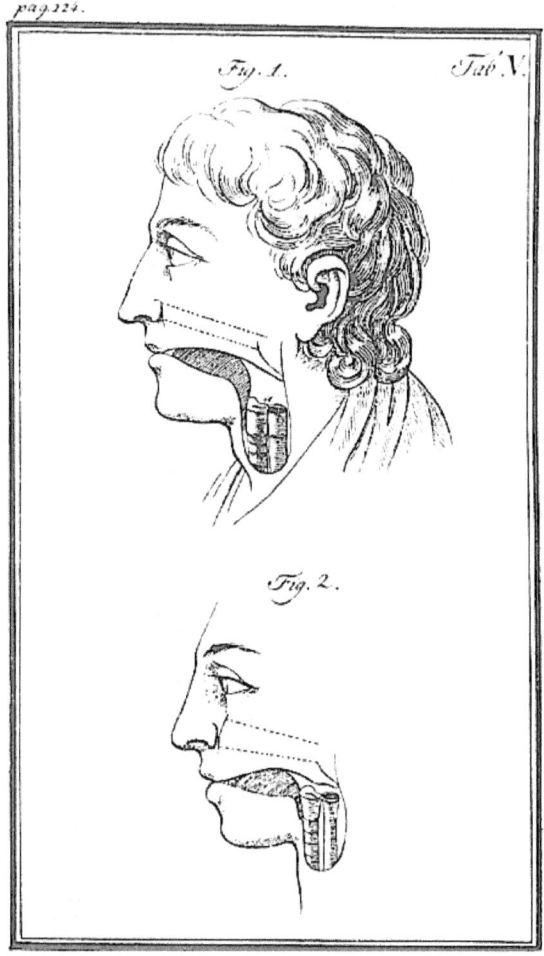

We have stated all of the above in order to prove that the valve of the nose, that is to say the soft palate, is necessary for swallowing. Let us imagine that it is missing and that the nasal passage is open. Would not some particles of food always be present in the nose? And would that not lead to an irritation which would be immediately followed by a sneeze, disturbing the entire process of swallowing? As such, we are on a firm basis if we assume that when people have difficulty swallowing coarse food, or if it is impossible for them to even swallow at all, the fault lies in the soft palate, which has either been mutilated or is naturally too small to completely seal the inner opening of the nose. Therefore, these people are only able to eat very soft food that can flow into the esophagus on its own without the need for any strong pressure.[24]

The Mouth

§ 69

The mouth is too well known to everyone to require an extensive description. By the mouth we mean the space that stretches between the two cheeks, from the lips to the soft palate. Its skeleton is made of the bones of the upper and lower jaws. The first is composed of several parts, while the second is of one piece in adults. Both are furnished with teeth, and the tongue lies between them as if surrounded by a balustrade. We shall consider the teeth and tongue in separate paragraphs. To the extent that the mouth cooperates in the formation of speech, we have only two things to observe: the soft palate, and the mobility of the lower jaw.

§ 70

The palate, the vault or cover of the interior of the mouth, is hard for three-quarters of its length, from the incisors toward the throat. Soft skin, horizontally stretched, bordering on the soft palate, begins in the fourth quarter of its length. We call this skin the soft palate. In some instances, the posterior part of the tongue presses against the vault to close the channel of the tongue,[25] as we shall observe on every occasion the situation arises when we describe each letter separately.

§ 71

Nature's principal purpose in providing the two jaws with teeth was to grind food, necessary for our nourishment, with tools, in the manner of a mill, in order to make it softer and more easily swallowed and digested. She could not have achieved that end had she not made at least one jaw mobile and

24. I knew a woman and a young girl who for years lived only on bouillon, milk, coffee, and chocolate, and who thought they were committing a dangerous excess when they allowed themselves a soft-boiled egg. I did not have the opportunity to verify if this was due to the state of their soft palates. Nonetheless, I believe I noticed something in the speech of these people which confirmed my suspicion.

25. Later, I shall explain what I mean by *the channel of the tongue*. At this time, note only that by this expression I mean the interior space of the mouth, between the tongue and the palate, over which the voice must travel.

capable of being separated from the other so that food could be introduced between two millstones, so to speak. The upper jaw always remains firm and immobile, but the lower jaw can be lowered. The mouth opening, especially between the incisor teeth, cannot be too small, so that large pieces of food can be seized and cut up. The incisor teeth can ordinarily be separated by an inch, but in adults this distance increases up to 1¾ inches. The lower jaw is shaped as illustrated in Fig. 1 of Table VI. At its two posterior ends, which are curved at the top, there are two fork-shaped elongations a and b. The first, a, is often somewhat rounded and fits into a small box near the opening of the ear, thus forming a true hinge. The other end, b, ends in a sharp edge with a somewhat thick and fleshy muscle m along its length, which can, like a lever of the third class, lift the lower jaw and its teeth as far as the upper jaw and push against it with force.

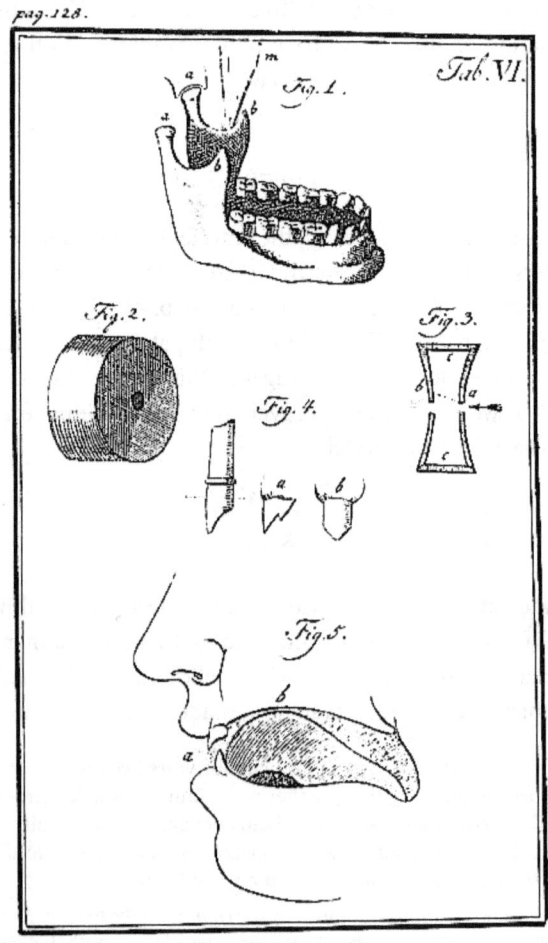

§ 72

This mobility of the jaw fortuitously becomes useful for speech, because the tongue, which completely fills the inner space of the mouth, could not easily make the movements necessary to form letters if the jaw could not be lowered. This would prevent the enlarging of the interior of the mouth and giving the tongue room for play. While it is true that one can, with some effort, speak intelligibly through clenched teeth, this type of speech is so far removed from the charm of natural sound that it is repugnant to the ear. Thus, it becomes the characteristic manner of expressing a desire for vengeance, fury, and the gnashing of teeth. The tongue pulls back into the throat so that its tip is in the middle of the mouth, where it has free space for its movements. It forms the majority of letters there, but almost all are very indistinct. In addition, the teeth do not meet too exactly, so that the sounds of speech, passing through their openings, have a muted quality. Thus, it is obvious that for the perfection of speech it is not only necessary that the lips part, but also that the two rows of teeth separate in a definite ratio. We shall determine this ratio in the discussion of vowels.

§ 73

Finally, we shall note that all the organs in the mouth, as well as its walls, have to be constantly moist in order to perform their functions exactly. A large number of glands, distributed throughout, provide the necessary moisture. Without moisture, the tongue becomes too rigid and inflexible to perform its rapid movements. In addition, the contact made whenever the tongue presses against other parts of the mouth is not as effective as when moisture is present. We may observe sick people, whose organs have been dried up by fever, speaking with difficulty and babbling unintelligibly.[26]

---

26. One of the greatest difficulties in constructing a speech-imitating machine is moisture, since it is difficult to spread evenly and causes the interlocking parts of the machine to expand, making them seize up. Anyone who can succeed in modifying his machine so that it can distribute moisture evenly will soon achieve remarkable improvements.

The Tongue

§ 74

Haller gives exactly the description of the tongue that I need for my topic. I can do no better than to translate it, omitting what he says about its muscles, which the limits of the task at hand do not allow me to cite. He says:[27]

> "The tongue is a piece of flesh that is short, broad, blunt at its end, free along its entire upper length, proportional to the bony cavity of the palate, shorter on its underside, equipped with glands, and free at the end near its tip. Its back rises from the epiglottis and is slightly inclined along the rest of its length. On its upper surface its width is divided along the middle by an almost imperceptible channel which divides it into two halves, so to speak. The entire tongue is very mobile and adept at assuming all sorts of forms and shapes. It can push against the upper and lower teeth, the anterior, mid and posterior parts of the palate, and the gums. It can pull its tip backward or push it beyond the space between the teeth. It can extend into the cavities of the cheek and probe into all their spaces. It can, finally, extend beyond the lips, curl about itself, flatten, or form a hollow with its back, or pull its sides together to create a cylinder, all of which demonstrate its extraordinary agility. It is attached to the hyoid bone, the throat, the glands, and the epiglottis by its muscles and outer covering. The frenulum of the tongue is a fold of this double covering which connects the mid portion of its lower surface to the skin of the mouth. It is said that when this connection is too short, it prevents the free movement of the tongue and articulation, so that the letters R and L cannot be pronounced distinctly. Nevertheless, it would be harmful if this connection were severed in all those who mumble because it is too short and they cannot extend their tongue outside their mouth. Celsius knew a man who could not speak even though his frenulum had been cut."

§ 75

The principal purpose of the tongue appears to be to distribute and spread saliva evenly in the mouth, to push food under the teeth, to collect and move it about inside the mouth and to push it under the teeth again, and

---

27. In his *Physiologie*, Book IX, Sec. II § 8, Of the Tongue.

finally, when it has been sufficiently chewed, to gather the smallest pieces and push them backward into the throat.

§ 76

Just as air, or voice, is one of the principal components of speech, the tongue is the principal organ to fashion and shape it. It remains idle only for a very few sounds or letters. The vowels need it as much as the consonants. Later, we shall try to determine the position it has to take for each letter, but it is enough to say here that sometimes it contracts, sometimes it half-blocks, and at other times it completely blocks the channel of the tongue, which we shall always name as such because of the primary organ that this cavity contains. The tongue remains still or vibrates against the palate or the teeth, and thus is almost always in motion. The first inventors of speech must have found this continuous movement of the tongue so striking that the majority used the name of this organ to express the idea of speech.[28]

§ 77

Sounds other than speech produced by the tongue are clicking, spitting and whistling.

Clicking is produced when the tongue, pushing hard against the entire length of the palate, suddenly pulls away at the same time as air is being forcefully inhaled. Air, entering the mouth all at once, produces a sound similar to that made when a tightly sealed case is opened quickly. The clicking used to spur horses is produced in the same manner, except that the tongue is partially pulled away in the area near the molars while its tip remains pressed against the palate, behind the incisors. This produces a sharper click than the first method.

§ 78

Spitting is accomplished by the tongue in the following manner. When there is a surplus of saliva, or anything else in the mouth which has to be ejected,

---

28. *Language* can be translated as γλωσσα (glossa) in Greek, *lingua* in Latin, *nyelv* in Hungarian, *jezik* in Illyrian. In addition, πολυγλωσσος (polyglossos) means 'multilingual' in Greek; *multarum linguarum peritus* means [in Latin] 'he who speaks in several *tongues*'. *Nyelveket beszèlni* and *jezike govoriti* both mean 'to speak languages (or *tongues*)'.

the tongue collects the material about its tip, presses its mid-section against the palate immediately behind the incisors, while its tip curves downward to touch the lower teeth. The lower lip is slightly raised to prevent saliva from flowing out, but not high enough to meet the upper lip completely. When the saliva is not too thin or too fluid, it remains suspended between the tip of the tongue and the two, often parted, lips. The compressed air inside the mouth rushes out with force the instant the tongue pulls away from the palate, entraining the saliva that was impeding its passage. This eruption is accompanied by a sonorous blast somewhat similar to the sound of a pop gun. Sometimes it is also accompanied by the voice, or an exclamation like <pfuy> or <tfuy>, but these are incidental and have nothing to do with spitting directly. Rather, they are additions made by the glottis. When the saliva is thick and sticks to the tongue, the latter sometimes pushes against the upper incisors with its mid-section and pulls away as it rubs against their sharp edge, so that the teeth, acting as scrapers, push the thick saliva as far as the very tip of the tongue. The thicker the saliva, the noisier the act of spitting and the longer the trajectory of the spit. I have seen people who, as they lay on their beds, could hit the ceiling with their spit as often as they pleased; standing, they could launch it three or four toises (a toise measuring 6.4 ft.).

§ 79

To explain whistling, let us take for example a small round brass box with two concave sides and a small hole in the center (as shown in Table VI, Fig. 2). When this box is held against the lips while air is blown into the hole or sucked out of the same opening, a sound similar to a whistle produced by the mouth will result. The smaller the box, the sharper the sound. This can be explained in the following manner: the box contains air, and when more air is blown in, it does not travel in a straight line directly to the opposite hole, but expands (as air always does when it is blown through a hole) in eccentric rays. This is illustrated in Fig. 3, where a side view of the preceding figure illustrates air flowing through point a. Although part of the air issues through the opposite hole b, the rest, that is to say, that portion which has separated from the current of air in the center, pushes against the air already contained in the space c. Since air is naturally compressible it contracts, but, because of its elasticity, it also tries to re-expand against the pressure of the incoming air. This alternating transfer of pressure, which goes on at great speed and results in an exceedingly rapid vibration of the air between the holes, is the actual and sole reason for the sound.

It is very simple to apply this mechanical explanation of whistling to the mouth. The lips are closed except for the small opening near the middle, analogous to one of the holes in the side of the box described above. The tongue pushing against the palate with its mid-section, leaving only a narrow channel along the middle for air, can be compared to the other side of the box with a hole. The space between the lips and the tongue corresponds to the interior of the brass box. If air is drawn in or blown out when the mouth holds the shape just described, a sound similar to that made by blackbirds, or other chirping birds, will be produced.

The reason why I classify whistling as more a function of the tongue than of the lips, where it might seem to belong by preference, is the following. If one wishes to whistle a tune, the tones have to be high at times and low at others. Since this result cannot be achieved without the tongue, it must play the primary role in this process. The opening of the mouth changes very little, or not at all, during the variation of tones. However, the more the tongue pulls away from the posterior region of the palate, the lower the tone produced, since the space between the tongue and the lips is thus increased. The larger this space, the deeper the sound, and in the opposite case, the smaller this space, the sharper the tone, as has already been observed during the discussion of the small brass box.[29]

§ 80

Before moving on from the tongue, we must acquaint our readers with a book, both because it is a rare volume and because it deals mainly with this organ. The reader will be astonished by the level of blindness attained by an exalted imagination. In 1667, F. M. B. ab Helmont wrote a small book of 12° (folios) entitled *Alphabeti veri naturalis hebraïci brevissima delineatio, quæ simul methodum suppeditat, juxta quam, qui surdi nati sunt, sic informari possunt, ut non alios saltem loquentes intelligant, sed et ipsi ad sermonis usum perveniant*.[30] He boldly purports that all the letters of the Hebrew

---

29. This can be confirmed in all instruments. The longer and thicker the string, the bigger the flute or violin, the larger the horn, the deeper the sound.

Those who do not know how to whistle will not learn how to do it from this description, because whistling depends a great deal on the ratio between the opening of the lips and that of the tongue, which cannot be defined in words, but which is easy to find by repeated trials.

30. "A brief sketch of the true, natural Hebrew alphabet that at the same time supplies a method in accordance with which those who have been born deaf can be educated in such a fashion that they not only understand others who are speaking but also themselves arrive at the use of speech."

language, which must be of direct divine origin and in which God always preferred to speak, could be perfectly written according to the position the tongue takes in pronouncing them. Therefore, the letters are shaped in accordance with a plan in nature ordained by God. He goes even further and verifies that the letters of the alphabet must be formed in this manner and not otherwise, because as the tongue completes the pronunciation of one letter, it begins to get into the position it has to take in order to form the next one. His imagination attributes curvatures and contortions to the tongue which it never takes for the letters he discusses, and for which it does not have the ability under any circumstance. It is inconceivable how he could not clearly feel his own tongue as he pronounced certain letters, to know whether it was still, toward which side of his mouth it curved, or how he could believe that his tongue could take the positions he describes when a Hebrew letter was being pronounced.

He had a profile view of a head engraved for each letter, with a depiction of the tongue's position. The letter, in its ancient and modern form, was engraved on the edge of the cap adorning each head, so that its shape could be compared with the position of the tongue. We shall give our readers, who will not have the opportunity to see this already very rare book, a copy of four of these heads (see Tables VII and VIII). I selected letters for which normally the tongue is not at all involved, or remains completely still during their pronunciation. Helmont depicts the tongue in remarkable contortions (Fig. 1, *Aleph*, Fig. 2, *Beth*, Fig. 3, *Mem*, and Fig. 4, *Pe*).

3: THE ORGANS OF SPEECH AND THEIR FUNCTIONS 61

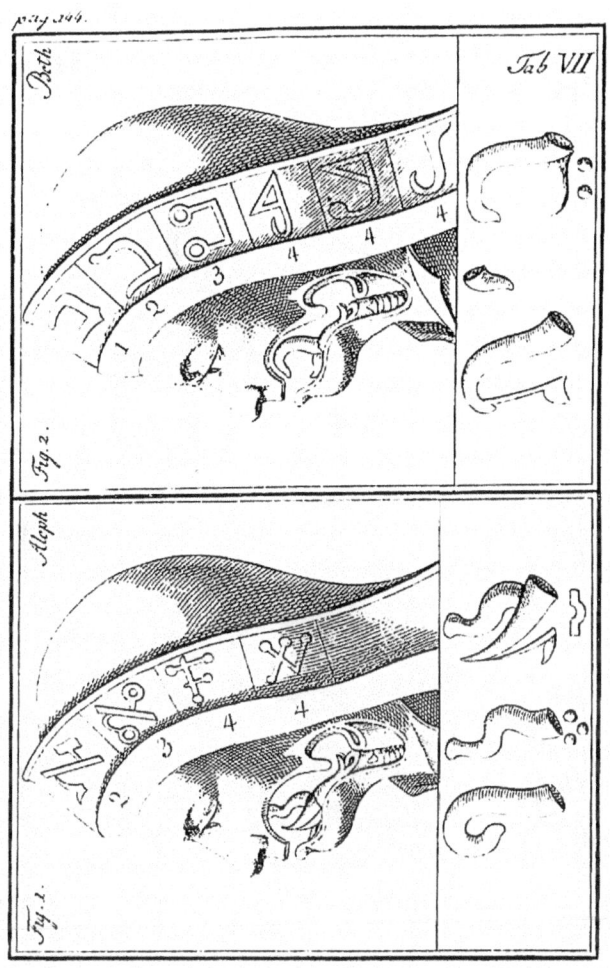

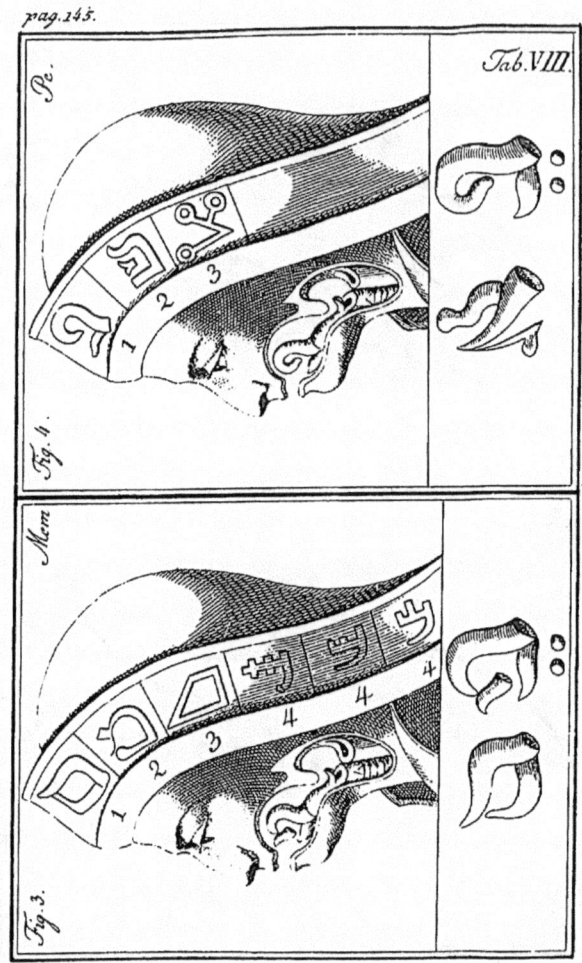

In this depiction, the letters, in truth, do have a passable resemblance to the position of the tongue. However, if we may be allowed the same liberties as Helmont, we can easily find letter shapes for all languages in any tongue position we might care to imagine.

There are other glaring errors in these engravings in addition to the position of the tongue. For example, for *Beth*, *Mem*, and *Pe*, the mouth has to be closed, while the nose has to be blocked for *Aleph*, *Beth*, and *Pe*. Actually, he did show the nose opening with its valve, that is to say, the soft palate or uvula, but he probably did not imagine that it took part in the formation of speech, since he depicts it in the same position for all the letters.

3: THE ORGANS OF SPEECH AND THEIR FUNCTIONS 63

The linking or transition from one letter to another is part incomprehensible and part ridiculous,[31] and several other of these observations are simply absurd.[32] Let us judge whether such nonsense can be useful to the deaf and mute, as the title proclaims. Such representations and descriptions are more likely to mislead these people, already burdened with too many problems, and make them despair of ever imitating one letter with their own tongue.[33]

31. Page 62 of Helmont's book indicates what follows after the transition from *Aleph* to *Beth*.

Question: *Quomodo connexio hujus litera cum subsequenti ex ipsa litera natura deduci potest?*

Answer: *Finis actionis ejus consistit in adscensu linguæ, in quo opus habet, ut pergat, ad initia litteræ Gimmel, prout quilibet facile jiducare poterit.*

[Question: How can the connection of this letter with the following (letter) be deduced from the very nature of the letter?

Answer: The end of its delivery consists in the ascent of the tongue, in which it (the tongue) has the action of proceeding to the beginnings of the letter 'Gimel', as anyone will easily be able to judge.]

There are a hundred similar cases which might have seemed very logical to the author, but which no one after him will be able to understand since no trace of them can be found in nature.

32. We shall cite two more examples:

Page 67 where the subject is the letter He. *Videtur autem in illa mystica quædam significate generationis occultari: omnia enim animantia, fervore libidinis agitata hujus quasi literæ sonum anhelando producere videntur, & proptera factum esse probabile est, quod HAEC imposita sit nominibus ABRAHAMI ET SARAH, & non alia, quia ex illis generari debedant multi populi.*

[Moreover a certain mystic signification of generation appears to be hidden in it (the letter He): for all animate things, when shaken by the ardor of desire, are seen to produce, panting, a sound like that of this letter, and it is probable that on this account it came about that this (letter) and no other, was imposed on the names of ABRAHAM and SARAH, since from them many peoples had to be born.]

Page 75: On the letter *Mem*. *Si quis aliquanto exactius ad mysticam ejus significationem respicere velit, præsertim quatenus finalis est, ubi os nostrum spiritu, & quasi semine vivo repletur, facile animadverti posse videtur aliqua harum rerum analogia: per ipsam enim, omnis MULTIPLICATO ET PLURALITAS indigitatur, & tum figura ejus caluditur, tanquam pragnans aliqua mater quæ virtutem sui MULTIPLICATIVAM utero suo firmiter inclusit.*

[If anyone should wish to refer somewhat more precisely to its mystic signification, especially where it is final, when our mouth is filled with breath and with a kind of living seed, it seems that some analogy of these things can easily be considered: for truly, through it (the letter Mem) all multiplication and plurality is uttered, and then too its shape is closed, just like some pregnant mother who has firmly enclosed in her womb a power multiplicative of herself.]

33. The author asks the reader to forgive him for having spent too much time on this short little volume. He only did it to demonstrate of what little use it could have

§ 81

In general, many extraordinary and extravagant things have always been said and written on the topic of the tongue. Diodorus Siculus [see [2011]], for example, wrote a pretty story about a people, assumed to be the Taprobanes, based on a report of the honest Jambulus and accepted in good faith.[34] The latter related that, among other characteristics, these people had a unique tongue formation, produced in part by nature and in part by artifice. Their tongue was almost double, being split in such a manner that it became a double tongue almost to its roots, making them very adept not only at imitating all articulated human languages, but also in producing bird songs with all their variations. Even more astonishing was their ability to converse with two different people simultaneously, responding to each and maintaining a continuous dialogue with each by using half their tongue with one and the other half with the other.

The Teeth

§ 82

Ordinarily we have 16 teeth on each jaw and therefore 32 on both. They are divided into three classes: first, the incisors, second, the canines, and third, the molars. The first are always four in number, and are set in the rounded front part of the jaw. They are all sharp, but the upper more so than the lower. Their shape resembles the mouthpiece of a recorder (see Table VI, Fig. 4). They serve to cut the pieces of food to be carried into the mouth. Often incisors have two cutting edges, one being slightly higher than the other (see point *a*).

Next to them, on either side, is a tooth of the second class, more pointed and somewhat longer than the incisors themselves (see point *b*). In carnivorous animals, these are much sharper and have slightly curved points so that they may be driven, like hooks, into the flesh of prey and hold on to it.[35]

---

been in deciphering the organization of speech. For when it became publicly known that he was working on a speaking machine, the possibility of his building such a machine was repudiated in a certain publication by citing the work of different authors, familiar to him for some time, among whom was the aforementioned Helmont whose book he had read many years earlier and rejected because of its inutility.

34. Diodorus Siculus, Book II. (see Delphi Classics 2011 edition)

35. These teeth are called the *canines*, leading some to use the name as evidence that man always belonged to the carnivorous class of animals, because nature gave him the

Next to them, on either side, are five grinding teeth. They are wide, square at the top, and notched crosswise. In Latin, they are very appropriately named *dentes molares* ["grinding teeth"], because grinding food is their unique purpose. The last grinding teeth are included among them. At times these appear at a later age, and are therefore called "wisdom teeth". Some people place these teeth in a fourth class, but they are nevertheless grinding teeth like the others, and although they do not appear until later, they have the same shape and position.³⁶

§ 83

From the description just given, and from what has already been said about the mobility of the lower jaw in the section on the tongue, one might conclude that there is nothing more to be said about the function of teeth in grinding food. However, two observations remain to be made in order to exhaust the topic completely.

First, the lower jaw not only has the ability to be lowered like a hinge, but can also move from side to side, allowing the grinding teeth to rub against each other. If this were not the case, the teeth would only compress food, breaking up hard and dry substances by pressure alone. Being large, having no sharp edges, and using pressure alone, how could they cut meat, cartilage, or other elastic materials and tear their fibers? Nature took care of this problem by giving the jaw horizontal motion. True, grinding takes place only because the teeth have ridges and can rub against each other. If grain is placed between two flat and immobile stones, and if enormous weights are heaped on the upper stone, the grain will never become flour. It is absolutely essential that one of the stones turn and create friction. Millstone faces are evenly notched in order to augment friction; so, the notched grinding teeth rub against each other and represent a true mill.³⁷

---

teeth that belong to this class only and are characteristic of it.

36. They have different names in Latin: *Dentes sapientiæ, cranteres, sophronisteres, genuini, intimi, postremi, serotini.* See [the article in von Haller 1756 on *Dens* 'tooth'— the eds.].

37. This horizontal movement of the jaw can be better observed in horses, cattle and other ruminating animals because their jaws are proportionately longer than ours and consequently the obviation of the lower lip from the center of the upper lip is quite considerable. Man's jaws are too short and his cheeks are too fleshy to make their small horizontal motion remarkable.

§ 84

The second observation concerns the front teeth, that is to say, the incisors. Here we may observe yet another movement of the lower jaw which is also horizontal, but is hardly more than the distance of half an inch. The lower jaw can be pushed forward so that the cutting edges of the two rows of incisors are on top of each other. At times, the lower incisors extend even beyond the uppers. Their objective, however, is not to meet at their cutting edge. The lower incisors must remain slightly to the rear and slip behind the upper incisors. Normally, when one is at rest and the mouth is closed, the molars rest on each other, but the upper incisors, which are somewhat longer then the molars, project beyond the lower incisors, and in some cases cover them completely.[38]

§ 85

We shall try to explain Nature's purpose for this arrangement with a mechanical experiment. If we wished to use an instrument with two-well fitted parallel cutting edges, somewhat like a pair of large tongs, instead of ordinary scissors, we could not cut wool, hair, cloth, tree branches, tin, or a hundred other things, or could only do so with difficulty. In order to cut with greater ease, scissors whose cutting edges slide over each other had to be invented so that those parts not immediately severed by the cutting edge are torn by pressure. Tinner's snips, for instance, are nothing if not cutting edges, but they tear, or rather separate one part from the other by pressure. The same result is achieved by the incisors. Since they do not have a very good cutting edge, they separate food by pressure rather than by cutting. If they were to accomplish this task by pressing their cutting edges against each other, they would have had to have a different configuration, and their cutting edges would have been of one piece. However, since they are aligned one next to the other, there is always something of a small gap between them. They are unable to cut anything completely, and would always leave some uncut portions linking the part inside the mouth with the remainder still outside, which would then have to be torn off by hand. This experiment can be easily verified by trying to bite off some soft wax from a larger piece, about the thickness of half an inch, while the incisors are held perpendicular to each other.

---

38. In some people, the opposite case can be observed; their upper teeth slide behind their lower teeth because their lower jaw is too long. However, this only happens rarely and is disfiguring to the physiognomy.

Finally, we should note that if teeth had the cutting edge of a knife, continuous use would soon blunt them and nature would not always have enough time to replace what is worn out with a bony material as hard as the teeth themselves.

§ 86

We shall presently see the part teeth play in the formation of speech. If we take into consideration that people who have lost all their teeth still speak very intelligibly, we must rank this organ behind all the others. We can do without teeth entirely when necessary, and this cannot be said about any of the other organs of speech. However, we must admit that because they are hard and somewhat sharp, teeth contribute to making the sounds of speech more pleasant, since all the sounds passing over them are clearer, more sonorous, and more distinct than those that slide over blunt and moist edges. They are directly involved only in S, and letters derived from it, like SH, J, and Z, as well as in F, V, and the English <th>. Later, when each letter is discussed separately, we shall demonstrate precisely how the teeth are used. Here we shall only add that the manner in which speech takes advantage of the situation just described is by sliding the lower teeth behind the upper.

When the lower teeth drop somewhat below their natural position (see Table VI, Fig. 5), so that their cutting edges are still slightly covered by the upper teeth (see point *a*) and the tip of the tongue pushes against the roots of the lower teeth while its back pushes against the palate (see point *b*), leaving a small channel open in the middle, then air flowing through the space between the roof of the palate and the tip of the tongue and over the cutting edge of the lower teeth is divided in half, so to speak, and produces the hissing sound of the letter S. This sound, and all the others related to it, are better formed when the mouth is completely devoid of teeth rather than when some incisors are missing. This is because in the former case the function of the teeth is performed by the continuous line of the gums, while in the latter case the empty spaces between the teeth cause an astonishing number of distortions in all the sibilant tones. This can be observed in children, who already speak well, but whose pronunciation is disturbed when they lose their baby teeth.[39]

---

39. This condition could have led Amman [see Ammann and Foot 1972] to infer that the S is produced by the air that is forced out through the spaces between the teeth: *Si linguæ pars media leuiter attollitur, & anterior ita dentibus adaptatur, ut Spiritus nonnisi per dentium interstitia tenui radio prodire queat, S. inde formatur. Dissert. de Loquela.*

[If the middle part of the tongue is raised slightly and its foremost part is fitted to the teeth in such a way that the breath can be produced only through the interstices of the

§ 87

Finally, a few inconsequential sounds produced by the teeth, such as chattering and gnashing, remain to be discussed. The first is made by quick, consecutive up-and-down movements of the lower jaw so that the lower teeth hit the upper teeth. The second, gnashing, is produced when the teeth rub against each other in the manner just described. Chattering occurs naturally when one is shivering or in a fever, and gnashing occurs most frequently during sleep.

The Lips

§ 88

All animals have something which serves to close their mouth. In some, as with birds, this part is rigid and is composed of two horn pipes sharpened to a point which interlock on their concave sides to form the beak. In some animals this part constitutes thin flaps of skin and in others it is fleshy. In man it is the lips. At their edge these are covered with skin so fine that the blood vessels beneath the surface are visible, giving them a pleasing red color in healthy people. The lips are capable of many movements. The upper lips can be drawn upward and the lower lip can be pulled down so that the teeth are uncovered. They can separate much farther than the teeth, for example, during a yawn. Their corners can be drawn together toward the middle of the mouth. The lips then contract, in vermicular wrinkles, to form a round hole, large at times and small at others. They can also be extended beyond their natural position, stretching the red skin very far as, for example, while smiling. They can extend forward as they move away from the teeth and form a funnel, or they may pull inward between the two rows of teeth, so that they cannot be seen at all.

§ 89

The utility and necessity of this organ can be seen the moment man enters the world. A child born without lips could not suck his mother's milk. If the nipple were placed between his bare gums, large openings would remain on both sides and the infant would suck air in instead of milk. According to the general laws of suction, when a liquid is to be sucked, all inlets have to be

---

teeth in a slender shaft, "s" is formed from it. *Dissertation on Speech*.] If this were the case, then someone with no teeth could not pronounce an S.

airtight. Nature could have done nothing wiser than to surround the mouth with a soft material which can take on many different shapes, and can surround the nipple of the maternal breast and squeeze it in such a manner that even the least atom of air cannot enter the mouth.

§ 90

Lips are equally indispensable to man when he wishes to drink. He always drinks by sucking and drawing liquids in. Whether he drinks from a vessel or directly from a source, the lips always have to be somewhat immersed in the liquid in order to prevent air from entering the mouth. A man with no lips would have to tilt his head backward and pour liquid into his mouth.

§ 91

Like man, horses and other ruminating animals drink by suction. But because their mouth has a wider slit, they must immerse it more deeply into the water in order to avoid sucking air in from all sides. However, since their noses are also immersed, water would enter through both the mouth and the nostrils when they inhale, save for the following technique. The horse, for example, (see Table IX, Fig. 1), folds his lower lip b in a special way so that only its anterior portion b is pulled backward, slightly opening its mouth, while the rest of the opening (from point b to point c) remains closed. If he then submerges his lips as far as the dotted line from points d to e, representing the surface of the water, he may then draw the liquid in. Having the slit of his nostrils above the jointing of the lips also helps because in this configuration, water cannot penetrate the nostrils. Nevertheless, many animals, wary of water in their nostrils, do not immerse their mouths deeply into the liquid. Thus, some air is always drawn in with the water. This can be heard as a hiss with each repetition.

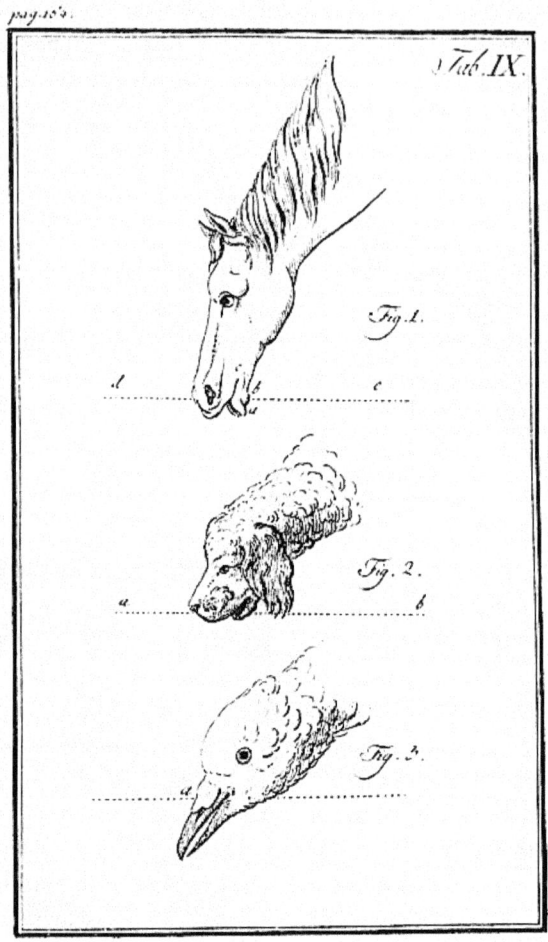

§ 92

Carnivorous animals have a different structure and do not drink by sucking. Their mouths have a proportionally wider slit than those of herbivores. Their lower lips can neither close nor partially open like those of the horse, and their nostrils are situated in such a manner that they would be completely submerged if the lips were immersed. For example, if the dog in Table IX, Fig. 2, immersed his mouth up to the line from *a* to *b*, his nose would be underwater. Nature therefore provided him with another means for quenching his thirst. She gave him a thinner, wider, longer, and more mobile tongue which he extends and curves like a spoon, plunges into the water, and pulls back into his mouth, without having to touch the surface of the water with his lips.

§ 93

Birds, who have absolutely no lips, accomplish this task in yet another manner. There are those that suck and others that do not. Those with a beak that has a thick and somewhat mobile membrane at the back, covering the nostrils, plunge the beak completely into the water, up to the feathers, and suck, for example the pigeon (see Fig. 3). Air does not enter their nose during inhalation since water, under atmospheric pressure, shuts off the valve a, and seals the nostrils. Other birds with no similar membrane, for example the chicken, have nostrils which are either entirely open or partially closed. These birds plunge their beak up to the nostrils, fill it with water and immediately lift their head so that the tip of the beak is in the air. They then open their beak and let the liquid fall into their throat of its own weight, where it drops into the esophagus and is pushed all the way down. This awkward procedure must be repeated until their thirst is quenched.

§ 94

In addition to their principal function of sucking, which has already been discussed, the lips have other uses and purposes. Their inner surface is, in a manner of speaking, studded with small lenticular glands which continuously moisten the mouth and keep it in a slippery state. They also collect the excess saliva and expel it. If they did not exist, the mouth could never be completely closed and consequently could neither collect saliva nor prevent it from constantly dripping. The continuous flow of air might also dehydrate the mouth. Finally, by contracting and closing, except for a small opening, the lips serve another purpose, namely that of blowing.

§ 95

The lips render speech a very important service. Without them, we would forfeit many beautiful letters in all languages as well as many forceful and energetic syllables and frequently used expressions. The [sounds of the] letters B, P, F, M, V, and W are owed to them entirely, excluding their contribution to the clarity of vowels, as we shall indicate later.

§ 96

The sounds produced by the lips, other than those of speech, are as follows. When the lips are tightly pressed and their corners pulled back as for a smile, the cheeks are pressed against the jaws and air is blown violently against the lips so that they are pushed away from the incisors. Then, the skin between the upper lips and the nose as well as the skin between the lower lip and the chin will puff out like a bladder. The air will then shape an oblong and very narrow opening in the middle of the lips and produce a sound similar to the whistling of mice or the crying of puppies.

If the lips are closed flat and pushed forward slightly, air forced across them violently will make them vibrate and produce a sound similar to that made by horses getting rid of the dust in their nostrils. If sound accompanies the air, a rumbling similar to that of a drum is produced.

There is also a clacking sound that imitates a trotting horse. This sound is produced when the lips are pushed between the teeth, covering their cutting edges, and if, while they are held in this state of tension, they are repeatedly and rapidly separated, a clacking sound will be produced.[40]

The Kiss

§ 97

The kiss, not an entirely negligible function of the lips, is also associated with a definite sound we dare not ignore. The entire universe knows how to kiss; however, the majority may never have reflected on the origin of this most pleasurable sound. If one wishes to give a friendly resonant kiss that speaks from the heart, the lips are pursed to form a circle, as if a cherry pit is about to be expelled from the mouth, and are firmly pressed onto the object to be kissed. Thus, the edges of the round opening are so compressed that they are completely sealed, leaving no opening. This position is held for some time while a means of separating the lips is sought. But since the pressure they exert via the anterior portion of the lower jaw against the object being kissed is too strong, they are not easy to detach at the same time as air is being inhaled. If, while in this position, the head is suddenly drawn back and the mouth is

---

40. When I draw my lips between my teeth and press hard, and then separate them with a strong burst of air, and if, at the moment the air erupts, I fling the middle portion of my tongue up against the palate, I can imitate applause perfectly and can repeat the sound rapidly. In my youth, when I wished to applaud at the theater and my hands were otherwise occupied, I could applaud as loudly with my lips as I could with my hands. I learned this from an Italian, but have never heard it from anyone else since then.

pulled away from the object to which it is attached, then the lips, under strain from the first effort and suddenly free from pressure, separate, allowing air to enter the mouth with a snapping sound. It must also be noted that the object being kissed also contributes toward producing a louder sound, because it remains sufficiently close to provide an obstacle to the inhaled air, forcing it to find a path between the kisser and the object being kissed, and giving the sound greater éclat. One can verify this by blowing a kiss into the air; a sound will be heard, but it will not be as strong or as lively as in the first scenario.

A soft kiss is no different, except that the lips are not pressed as hard against the object being kissed and are therefore pulled away with less force. Sometimes the head is not drawn away quickly, or the lips remain pressed together but pull apart slowly, allowing air to enter from both corners. In these cases, the sound produced is not as loud.

Yet another manner of kissing is with the open mouth pressed against the object to be kissed, the lips closed but not completely so. During inhalation, the skin being kissed is lifted, as if by a suction cup, and when the lips are suddenly pulled away, a moist spot remains. However, this is somewhat disgusting and is not a proper kiss.

§ 98

All of the observations I have made on the organs of speech and have cited until now have convinced me that the plan of nature's creator had, as its principal objective, the living creature's primary need for nourishment, essential for its survival. Consequently, all the organs we ascribe to speech were not made for this purpose specifically, but once extant, were slowly and haphazardly used by man. Man, naturally inclined to inventiveness, used them to produce speech. All quadrupeds have organs similar to ours, with slight differences in size and configuration, yet none of them have an articulated language. Only the glottis, it seems to me, was expressly created for sound, and has no other purpose than to give animals the means of producing a noise: a call, a cry, or a song. However, we can imagine animals and man in perfect wellbeing, relative to their natural needs, even when they are deprived of this organ.

Man's first language might have only been a cry, like that of an animal. Could man, who far surpasses other animals in wisdom, inventive spirit, and imitation, have sensed that a louder or softer cry, a sharper or duller tone, a sustained or interrupted sound, moist at times and dry at others, but basically always the same, was not enough to express his daily increasing needs? It is possible that these needs were compounded once he was in a community of his fellow men and he thus searched for other sounds on purpose. He may have learned by accident or by necessity. Perhaps, for no other premeditated reason, he produced an ordinary sound with his mouth closed and observed that this resulted in another, more muffled, sound from his nose. Thus, he would have already invented the letter M, and a medium for noisemaking, the nose. If by chance he had placed his tongue against his palate, or closed his mouth with his lips, he could have produced a T or a P, and would have discovered the usefulness of his tongue and lips. In time, he could learn to produce speech with his organs of nourishment.

Not all of the capabilities of these organs have been discovered by all nations, nor are all used in their languages. For example, New England's neighbors in America do not know two very interesting letters formed by the tongue: L and R: they replace [them] with an N and say "Nobstan" instead of "Lobstar."[41] On the other hand, if we were to hear the speech of all the people of the universe, especially that of savages, we would most certainly hear entirely unknown sounds that would be, in part, impossible for us to imitate.[42]

Even Europeans, in their own languages, do not have the sounds of all the other languages of Europe. German does not have the French J, French does not have the German CH, and neither of these languages has the English <th>. The Bohemian RSCH and the Hungarian <gy> are foreign to other nations. Suffice it to say that all the evidence combines to support the arguments that other than the glottis, no organ was expressly created for speech and that the nose, mouth, tongue, teeth, and lips were no more originally created for speech than fingers were created for playing the flute or eyes for reading, even though they later became necessary for speech by the invention of language.

---

41. [See Wallis 1674, p. 29. Wallis appears to be referring to the Wampanoag language. –the eds.]

42. It is not without purpose that in discussing each organ I list and describe, as clearly as possible and to the extent of my knowledge, all the sounds other than those familiar to us that that organ can produce. From which one can draw the conclusion that in addition to the far from negligible ones known to us, a large number of other letters can exist. Perhaps some of the sounds that I have cited and many others that have escaped my attention, could be an integral part of the language of people unknown.

4: On the sounds and letters of European languages

On the alphabet

§ 99

If one were to assemble a general alphabet for all the European languages and assign a special character to each sound encountered therein, that alphabet would most certainly exceed forty letters. Most of the letters would either consist of deviations from the common alphabet adopted long ago, which, in their written form, would be distinguished by special marks or the addition of other letters. Alternatively, they would be pronounced differently by various nations according to special usage and not according to their accepted written form. This deviation is at times very remarkable and almost imperceptible at others. I shall try, to the extent that my knowledge of languages will allow, to point out these nuances and to classify them in such a manner that each nuance is linked to its principal letter and is accompanied by one or more words in the language where it is most frequently used. The manner in which each sound is produced, the composition of its mechanical structure, and how it deviates from the principal letter will be revealed when each principal letter is discussed individually and described in detail.

§ 100

This is my general alphabet: A, B, D, E, F, G, H, CH, I, K, L, M, N, O, P, R, S, SCH, J, T, U, W, V, and Z.

Before going any further, I must give an account of why I have omitted some letters of the common alphabet and why I have added others. Those I have omitted are C, Q, X, and Y.

§ 101

I have omitted the letter C because it does not have a unique sound in any language. It is a K in German, and only serves to double that letter (as in *Brücke* and *Decke*). In French, before an E or an I, it is a simple S (as in *celui* and *civile*); before an A, O, or U, it is a K (as in *car, colle,* and *cuve*). Before an E, or an I in Italian, it becomes <tsch> (as in *cita*, which is pronounced *tschita*). In Germany, the Latin C is pronounced as a <ts>. They say <tsivitas> and <tsedo> rather than *civitas* or *cedo*.

The letter Q is nothing but a K in all languages. In German, *bequem* is pronounced <bekuem>, *quahl* as <kuahl>. In French, *qui* is pronounced <ki>, *quand* as <kand>. In Latin and in Italian *quando* is pronounced <kuando>. The Greeks, Hungarians and Illyrians have no Q at all.

X is a letter composed of K and S. *Dixi* in Latin is pronounced <diksi>. In French, *fixer* is pronounced as <fikser>. In German, *axt* is <akst>. Similarly in Greek, <ksi> is not a special sound but a combination of K and S that becomes K, <gs>, or <chs> according to the dialect spoken.

Y is only an ordinary I in pronunciation.[1] Its inutility has long been recognized and it has begun to be banished from the German language. *Bei* is as good as *bey*. In French *Il-i-a* will become the same as *il-y-a*. The ancients did not have a Y in their writing; they only kept it in words borrowed from the Greek, such as *Hymen, Physica, hydrops,* etc.

§ 102

I have added CH, SCH, and J to the common alphabet. In German, the CH is a single and not compound sound. However, it is represented by two letters in its written form. Having a single sound, it consequently merits its own place and character in the alphabet of the German language just as the χ does in Greek. Later, in a separate paragraph, we shall demonstrate that the mouth has a special position for the production of this letter.

In the Hebrew and Arabic languages, SCH has a special letter. In Hebrew it is ש, and in Arabic it is ش. The other European languages usually use a combination of common letters to designate this sound.

In French, J is also a distinct letter, as in *jamais*. It is in fact close to the aforementioned German SCH, but it does, nevertheless, have a different sound. For, if one wished to change a J into an SCH in French and say <schamais> instead of *jamais,* the substitution would be revolting to an ear

---

1. The υ of ancient Greek does not belong here. It is a completely different sound in pronunciation, probably similar to the French *u*.

accustomed to the French language. There are people who never learn how to pronounce this letter well, which suggests that it must have a unique sound. Its structure, which we shall discuss later, will better convince us of this fact.

§ 103

The following is an enumeration of all the speech sounds that are encountered in Europe, together with their derivatives.

A	The Latin A in *arma*.
	The German A of many German provinces as in *Gabe*.
	The High German A in *aber*.
B	This letter is the same in all languages except when it is changed into a V in the Greek and Spanish languages.
D	Is the same everywhere.
E	The common E in e*xemplum*.
	The French in *trouvé*, the Hungarian in *és*.
	The French open E in *bête, fête*, similarly the open <ai> in *mais, vrais*, and probably the H of ancient Greeks.
	In some German provinces the first E in *leben, gene* and *Esel* is pronounced *læben, gæben*, and *Aesel*.
F	Is the same in all languages.
G	The Latin G in *gallus*.
H	The German H in *Haut*.
CH	The German CH, deeper in *Sache*.
	and the other, sharper German CH in *ich, dich*.
I	The common I in *ille, ville*, and *wind*.
	As a consonant in German in *Jahr* and *Jammer*.
K	The Greek κ in κεφαλή, the German in *knall*, the Hungarian in *kár*.
	The simple German K before a vowel, which is pronounced as <kh> in most parts of Germany, where *Kind* and *Kunst* sound like *Khind, Khunst*.
L	The common L.
	The deepest L of the Poles and Turks.
	The palatal L of the French and Italians in *fille* and *figlia*.

M	Is the same in all languages.
N	The common N in *nos, nuit, ein*. The French N in *an*, the German in *Anker* and *Dank*. The Spanish and Bohemian Ñ and the French <gn> in *campagne*. The Italian in *segno*. The French in *enchanter*, and *ainsi*.
O	The German O in *tonne*, the French in *homme*. The German O in *Wohl*, or the French in *eau*. The German Ö in *örter* and the French <eu> in *heureux*.
P	Is the same in all languages.
R	The common R. The Bohemian <rsch> in *Prigjti*.
S	The common S in *sauer* and *sister*.
SCH	The Hebrew שׁ, or the German SCH in *Schande*. The French <ch> in *chapelle* and *vache*.
J	The French J in *jamais* and *jurer*.
T	The common T. The Greek Θ and the English <th> in *with*. The English T[h] in *the*.
U	The German U in *Uhr*, the compound Greek [ου], or the French in *ou*. The Greek υ, or the German Ü in *würde*, the French U in *vertu*. The Hungarian Ü in *szüz*.
V	The French V in *vrai* and *vivacité*.[2]
W	The German W in *wassen* and *entwickeln*.
Z	The ζ of modern Greeks, similar to the French Z in *douzaine* and *donnez-en* and the Latin *Zeus*.[3]

---

2. Actually, the Germans also have this V in writing, but they pronounce it as an *F*, saying <Fiel fom Fater> instead *of Viel vom vater.*

3. The German Z does not belong here, as it is nothing more than a compound of T and S. *Zeit* or <Tseit>, *Herz* or <Herts>, are identical.

Here, then, are all the letters and sounds that one encounters in European languages. We shall discuss them in greater length in the two following sections.

On Vowels

§ 104

There are ordinarily five principal vowels in speech: A, E, I, O, and U. These have their subdivisions (Ä, Ö, Ü, etc.) that correspond roughly to semitones in music. They can only be produced in the following manner.

§ 105

1. The glottis resonates in the same manner for each, the nose being blocked.
2. The voice, as it emerges from the throat, is led by the tongue as if by a channel to the lips. This channel expands and contracts in proportion to the amount by which the tongue is raised or lowered, especially in its posterior portion. The wider or narrower the channel, the more the sound differs.
3. The appropriate size of the mouth opening finally completes the formation of the sound and gives it its clarity.[4]

§ 106

A vowel is therefore a sound made by the voice as it is led by the tongue to the lips, which in turn allow it to issue through their opening. The difference between one vowel and the other is produced only by the wider or narrower passage that the tongue or the lips, or the two together, allow for the voice.[5] The nose and the teeth do not take any part in the formation of a vowel.

    4. It must be noted that this lesser or greater mouth opening is not absolutely necessary for the production of various vowels. All the vowels can be produced distinctly by changing the position of the tongue alone and leaving the mouth opening identical to that necessary to produce an A, but the sound produced will be repulsive. However, these letters will regain their clarity when, following nature's course, the lips participate in the production of the vowel. Since we are only discussing pure and simple speech here, we shall always consider the appropriate mouth opening without digressing into what can be obtained by artifice.

    5. Dionysius of Halicarnassus was quite mistaken when, in speaking of vowels,

§ 107

Let any consonant be selected and examined for the three aforementioned conditions of vowels. A small deviation or augmentation will be discovered in each instance. We shall consider the four letters L, R, S and M. For L, the anterior portion of the tongue is pushed hard against the palate, and consequently it does not lead the voice directly to the lips. This is contrary to the second point. For R, the passage of the voice is interrupted by the vibrations of the tongue against the palate, which is also contrary to the second point. For S, the voice does not resonate at all, which is contrary to the first point. For M, the voice issues through the nose, which is contrary to the second and third points. Therefore, one could find, if one wished to pursue the point, something contrary to these three points for each consonant.

Here, then, is the basis for the natural difference between vowels and consonants: for the former the voice resonates alone, while for the latter it is linked with another sound or noise, such as a hiss, a growl, a puff of air, etc., which one might say destroys the purity of the voice.[6]

§ 108

Elaborating further, for vowels there are two sluice gates, openings, or doors through which the sound of the voice must pass. One of these openings is formed by the tongue, and the other is formed by the lips. The expansion or contraction of these two paths does not take place at the same time. In other words, when the channel of the tongue expands, the mouth's opening does not simultaneously expand. In fact, quite the opposite occurs with some vowels. For U, the mouth is closed except for a small, tight opening, while the channel of the tongue is open as far as possible. For I, the mouth is passably open, while the channel of the tongue is closed except for a small opening.

---

he said that the tongue served no purpose and that the vowels were produced by the mouth alone:

Omnes autem arteria spiritum cohibente, & simplici oris conformatione proferunctur, lingua interim nihil adlaborante, ipsa quieta. Vol. V. de compositione verborum.

[All are produced by the windpipe confining the breath and by the simple shaping of the mouth, meanwhile the tongue does not labor at all, but is entirely at rest. Vol. V. *On the composition of words.*] Since we are only discussing pure and simple speech here, we shall always consider the appropriate mouth opening without digressing into what might be obtained by artifice. [See Singer's 1976 edition of Dionysius of Halicarnassus. –the eds.]

6. Why is Italian the best language for singing? Surely there can be no other reason than the fact that all of its words end in vowels, that is to say clear and pure sounds.

4: ON THE SOUNDS AND LETTERS OF EUROPEAN LANGUAGES

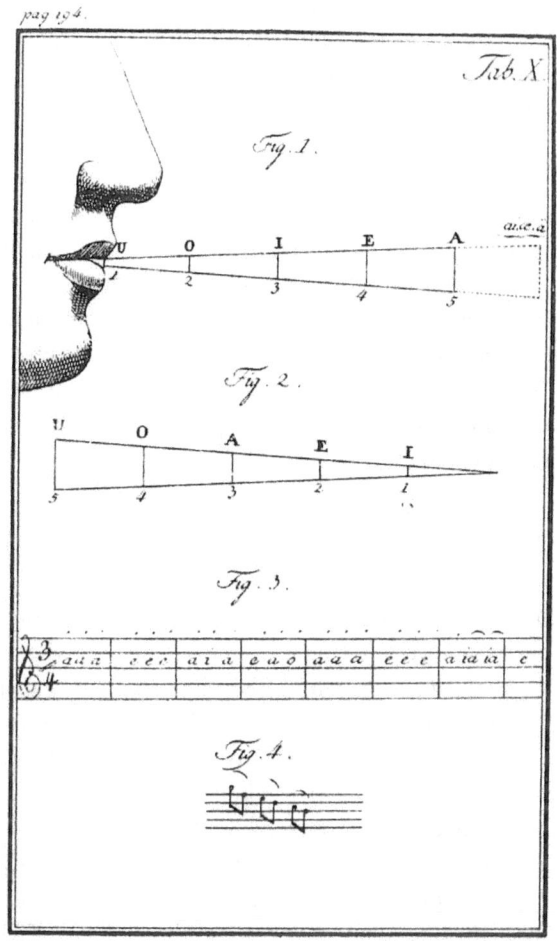

§ 109

Table X has two scales that give a better idea of this relationship for each vowel. One scale, Fig. 1, represents the mouth opening, the other, Fig. 2, represents the opening of the channel of the tongue for each vowel. These openings are divided into five parts. The mouth is least open for U, which is to say it is open to the first degree. It is open to its widest for A, or to the fifth degree.[7] The channel of the tongue, on the other hand, is open widest for U,

---

7. Beyond these five degrees on the scale of the mouth, there should be a sixth which would be required for the French <ae> or <ai>. However, since this vowel does not belong with the five common vowels, I have only marked it with a dotted line on the

or to the fifth degree, and least for an I, or to the first degree. The other vowels fall between these two extremes and, relative to the size of the opening of the mouth, are in the following order: U, O, I, E, and A. Relative to the tongue channel opening they are in the following order: I, E, A, O, and U.

This can be easily checked. One has only to stand in front of a mirror and pronounce A and U alternately, and the difference will be remarkable. If the five vowels are pronounced in the aforementioned order, the gradually increasing mouth opening will be clearly seen. The opening of the tongue channel cannot be seen, except for the vowels where the mouth is adequately open. For the others, one has to rely on touch. If one places a finger against one's throat, on the larynx, and pronounces U and I, the two vowels farthest apart, one can feel how this cartilage, so closely linked to the base of the tongue, rises and falls with the tongue in proportion to the expansion and contraction of its channel.

§ 110

In discussing vowels, I should add another small observation that could provide material for further thought. It seems to me that when I pronounce the different vowels in the same tone, they have a quality perceptible to my ear that makes me think of a certain melody. Yet, as I know very well, a melody can be produced only by the variation of tones into highs and lows. If, as shown in Tab. X, Fig. 3, I write a line of vowels in a certain order derived from the tongue channel opening scale on the same music stave line, and if I pronounce them all at the same height or depth, it always seems to me that they form a sort of song. At least, I find that in spite of myself I tend to sound those letters that have a wider mouth opening higher than those with a smaller opening. However, since this observation really belongs more to music than to speech, we shall not explore its accuracy any further and will leave its definition to those who have a more musically trained ear. I should only add here, for those who wish to duplicate the experiment, that each vowel should be distinct, pronounced after a slight pause, and that a musical measure must be observed for its duration.

Professor Kratzenstein, in an ingenious dissertation that was awarded a prize by the Imperial Academy of Sciences in St. Petersburg, not only solved the problem of the origin of vowels and how they could be reproduced, but also invented and built a sort of organ that imitates the human voice and produces the sound of each vowel.[8] When this dissertation

---

figure and thus defined its special place.

8. This dissertation was printed under the title *Christiani Theophili Kranzensteinii*

appeared in 1780, I could already produce all the vowels except I with my speaking machine. I hoped to acquire a duplicate of the St. Petersburg organ for the sole purpose of succeeding in finding that vowel. However, upon reflecting on its description, I observed that in this apparatus each vowel had to have its own conic pipe. Having learned from experience that to produce compound words in their entirety the voice should not issue from many pipes, but through a single one, I presumed that such an I, issuing from its own pipe, would hardly be useful to me, and that pursuing this notion would involve unnecessary cost. Moreover, the following year a scientist from St. Petersburg who had heard Mr. Kratzenstein's organ came here and listened to my speaking machine. He assured me that Mr. Kratzenstein's vowels were no better and no more distinct that mine. I therefore abandoned the idea. Soon after that, I discovered how to produce an I with my machine. Nevertheless, I must admit that I would be very happy to see and hear Mr. Kratzenstein's machine.[9]

A

§ 111

This first letter is fundamental to all languages. All children pronounce it first, since it is the easiest. The position of all of the speech organs for its pronunciation is the most natural and the most comfortable.[10] In its pronunciation:

---

tentamen resolvendi di Problema ab Acad. Scient. Imp, Petropolitana ad annum 1780 publice propositum ub publico Academmiae conventu die 19 Septembris Praemio coronatum [Christian Theophilus Kratzenstein. An essay on resolving the problem publicly proposed by the Imperial Academy of Science at St. Petersburg in the year 1780 and awarded the prize in a public meeting of the academy on the 19th day of September]. An abstract can be found in the Act. Acad. Petropolitana pro Anno 1780.

9. Since we are discussing the vowel I here, I should relate an amusing personal anecdote. In *** [editors' note: Kempelen employed asterisks to denote a withheld location], a wealthy and beribboned nobleman in a handsome carriage came to see me, and asked to hear my speaking machine, which, at the time, was still fairly defective. He asked me, among other things, to reproduce the vowels in their normal order. I declined, telling him that I lacked the letter I and had not discovered how to produce it in spite of all my efforts, "Eh," he replied "how can you suffer the lack of that in a town like **** where all manner of artisans abound; can't you find someone who could quickly make an I for you?"

10. *Prima notissimaque infantis vox, cum qua vitæ hujus spiritun hausimus, neque re ulla eget alia, quam hiatus oris solo sine ullo cæterorum motu instrumentorum* ['First and best known is the infant's cry with which we first drew the breath of this life; nor does it require any other thing than the mere gaping of the mouth without any movement of

1. The glottis resonates.
2. The nose is blocked.
3. The tongue is recumbent and its channel is open to the third degree.
4. The teeth take no part at all.
5. The lips are open to the fifth degree.

This sound can be produced by someone lacking a tongue, teeth and lips. It is for this reason that it can be easily imitated by instruments.

§ 112

We shall observe three different As. The first is the true A, that is to say, an A as it is pronounced in Latin in *arma*. The French, Italians and Illyrians have an identical A in their languages. The Germans, the English, the Danes, and the Hungarians often form deviations of it. Sometimes they give it a more open sound, and at others a more closed, deep sound, as we shall presently indicate.

The second A is somewhat deeper, as in the German word *Gabe*, and is not as open as in *arma*, at least not in all the German provinces. In some provinces, the E before I is pronounced exactly like the Latin A. They say <main>, <dain>, and <sain> instead of *mein, dein,* and *sein*. However, in words written with an A it is usually a deeper, more closed sound than *mein*, for example the A in *Stadt, schlact,* and *Wahl*.[11]

The third, an even deeper A, is the English A in *talk* and *tall*. The Hungarians also have two As. The sharp A that they mark with an accent as Á and pronounce like the Latin A in the words *Szás* and *Ház*. The other A is written without an accent, as in *Hamar* and *az*. The Hungarian and English A's differ only in that the first is sustained for a short time, while the second is held longer.[12]

Although the difference between all of these A's is due, in part, to a larger or smaller mouth opening, it is primarily a consequence of the

---

other instruments'. Scaligero (1540) I, 38].

11. Here, as in all similar passages in this work, it is never a question of how something is pronounced in a certain province, and even less whether it is pronounced badly or well. When one is discussing speech in general, it is sufficient that a sound is used in a given nation's language, and that it is occasionally encountered in one's own language for that sound to belong to human speech.

12. The common Austrian and Bavarian dialects have a still deeper A, for example in *aber, wahr* and *gar*. However, since this is nothing but a Latin or French O, and consequently the substitution of one letter for another, it does not belong to the class of A's.

changes in the channel of the tongue, where all of these As are formed, between the third and fourth degrees, that is to say between an A and an O, in so many subdivisions.

§ 113

We could have justly ranked the Latin <æ>, the common English A, the accented German Ä, and the French <ai> in the class of A's, because we shall later find that they are much closer to the Latin A than they are to the E. The mouth, as well as the channel of the tongue, are more open than they are for the first A, and consequently <æ> is not only far from approaching an E, which is more closed than the A, but on the contrary, it deviates very far from an E, as we shall prove later. However, since <æ> is usually interchanged with an E and is placed in the category of the latter, I did not wish to wander too far from this customary usage and placed it with the derivatives of E, where it will be discussed further in the section on E.

E

§ 114

The position of the speech organs for the pronunciation of E is the same as it is for an A, the sole difference being that the lips are open to the fourth degree and the channel of the tongue is open to the second degree.

One finds three natural variations of the letter E. There is the Latin E as in *ecce* and two others, one of which is sharper and the other deeper. The first, which is the French accented É in *vérité*, or the Hungarian in *és*, is close to an I, and lies in the middle of an E and an I. In its pronunciation, the tongue channel is somewhat more contracted than it is for the ordinary E but not as much as it is for an I. The second, or deeper, E is the Latin <æ> or the French <ai> that was mentioned when discussing A. This letter differs from the common E because for its pronunciation, the throat and the lips are more open than they are for all other letters. Therefore it is very odd that the French add an I to the A to designate <æ>, since I is actually the very vowel that is farthest from A.

The mute E in French does not belong to the E class at all, since in its pronunciation it completely ceases to be an E and sounds like a brief Ö, for example the final E in *mechante*. The same is true for the E in *le*, for example, *le chien* is pronounced <lö chien>, with a brief Ö.

I

§ 115

For the pronunciation of I, the middle portion of the tongue presses against the palate and spreads out in such a manner that its two edges touch the upper molars, while its point is lowered in front and pushed against the lower incisors. The middle part of the tongue, thus pushed against the palate, leaves only a small opening with a lenticular diameter. The lips are open to the third degree and the rest is identical to the preceding vowels.

§ 116

I is the same in all languages and does not have a single derivation or deviation in its vowel quality. On the other hand, it is the only vowel that at times performs the function of a consonant. By the addition of an almost imperceptible change in the tongue, it is immediately transformed into a consonant. This only confirms what we asserted earlier, that a vowel can consist solely of the pure human voice, and that once it is tainted by the addition of another sound, or noise, it ceases to be a vowel.

In the German words *Jahr* and *Jammer*, the I is a consonant produced in the following manner. As we said earlier, to form an I the tongue only allows a very small lenticular opening as an outlet for the voice. If the I has to be changed into a consonant, no changes occur other than a slight additional contraction of that small opening, which causes the quantity of air accompanying the sound of the I to emerge forcefully. This produces a slight noise, or breath, that deprives the I sound of its clarity, and thereby turns it into a consonant. It is easy to observe that in pronunciation one must always use more energy to produce a J than an I.

One can also consider the J as a simple CH accompanied by voicing. A CH, as it is pronounced in the German word *ich*, has absolutely the same position as a J, the only difference being that the CH is produced by air alone, without voicing, while for the J the voice also resonates. There are people who never find the correct opening required for a J. They make it either too big or too small. In the first case, they always allow a coincident CH to be heard, saying <chia> instead of *ja*. In the second case, the I remains an ordinary I and then they say <ia>. To confirm this experimentally, pronounce a word, elongate the CH, and subsequently let the voice be made to resonate. A perfect J will be heard.[13]

---

13. Here we are concerned only with the letter J as it is pronounced in German. It

O

§ 117

There are two types of O. One is the Latin or French open O as in *hoc* and *homme*. It is very close to the third A that has already been discussed, but is slightly more closed. There is no reason, then, to describe it further. The other O is even more closed, and is a sound used often by Germans, as in *Wohl, soll, Krone,* and *schon*. The French express it by <au>, as in *aux* and *aucun*. In some words, they even use three vowels for this sound, as in *beaucoup* and *vaisseau*. This O has the channel of the tongue open to the fourth degree and the lips to the second. When, in what follows, we speak of the five principal vowels, the O we mention will always be this second, or German, O. It is probable that the Greeks also had these two types of O, and made a distinction between them in their pronunciation.

§ 118

The intermediate sound of an O (or its semitones, if I dare use the expression) is the Latin <œ>, the French <eu>, or the German and Hungarian Ö. It is most aptly named <œ> since it actually combines something of these two letters. The tongue is in the position for an E, while the lips are open to the degree for an O. If the E is protracted, and if at the same time the mouth is closed to the second degree as if for an O without changing the tongue's position in any way, a perfect Ö will be produced.

U

§ 119

For U, as it is pronounced by the Germans, the channel of the tongue is always open the widest, or to the fifth degree, whereas the mouth is open the least, or to the first degree.

All nations use this U in their language, but designate it differently in their writing. The Greeks and the French do not have a special letter for this sound in their alphabet. The former join o to υ, from which the ου finally evolved. The French imitated them and adopted O and U. The English, who pronounce U as <ju>, denote it <oo> when it sounds like the German U, as in *root* and *foot*.

---

should not be confused with the French J which is another letter altogether.

§ 120

The υ of the ancient Greeks, which is the origin of the German Ü and the French U, is formed solely by the tongue. The tongue, which is recumbent for the U, moves forward for the Ü and takes the position for an I, while the lips remain closed to the first degree as for a U. Thus, it seems that those who write this vowel as <ui> are quite right, since the two letters do actually take part in its formation. Whether I is pronounced with the mouth closed to the degree necessary for U, or whether U is pronounced and the mouth opening remains unchanged while the tongue is placed in the position necessary for I, a perfect Ü will be produced.

§ 121

The vowels and their derivatives are twelve in number:

1. The Latin A.
2. The deepest German A.
3. The even deeper Hungarian and English A.
4. The universal E.
5. The French E in *verité* and the accented Hungarian É.
6. æ, the German Ä, and the open French E.
7. The universal I.
8. The German O, or the French <au>.
9. The Latin and the French O.
10. œ, the German Ö, or the French <eu>.
11. The German U, the French <ou> and the English <oo>.
12. The German Ü, the υ of the ancient Greeks, and the French U.

If another sound between these existed, or if there was a variation, it would almost certainly be imperceptible to European ears, or of such little consequence that it would not merit a distinct and special designation.

§ 122

These twelve vowels, denoted by their numbers, are ranked in order according to the relative size of the mouth and tongue channel openings. The list begins with the smallest opening, the others follow by degrees, up to the largest opening.

	Opening of the tongue channel		Opening of the mouth		
Smallest opening	1.	I	11.	U	}
	12.	ü	12.	ü	}
	5.	é	8.	O	} These pairs all have
	4.	E	10.	œ	} equal openings
	10.	œ	7.	I	}
	3.	a	5.	é	}
	2.	a	4.	E	
	1.	A	9.	o	
	6.	æ	3.	a	
	8.	O	2.	a	
	9.	o	1.	A	
Widest opening	11.	U	9.	æ	

On Diphthongs

§ 123

If, in accord with the etymology of the word "diphthong," one thought that he should hear two different sounds at the same time as is possible with a violin when two strings are played simultaneously, he would be deeply mistaken. The human voice can be compared to a flute, especially since the first has only one glottis and the second has only one hole to blow into. It is as difficult to sound two notes simultaneously on a flute as it is to pronounce two sounds distinctly at the same time with the human voice. To be precise, there are no diphthongs in speech, and even fewer triphthongs. They can exist only in writing, and, in accord with Mr. Adelung's opinion, they should really be called double letters.

To better determine what diphthongs, once adopted, do in speech, we must first single them out and then divide them into two classes. In the first we shall rank those that are, in fact, represented by two letters in writing, but are pronounced as a single sound. The second will consist of those that are not only written with two letters, but are also expressed as two vowels in pronunciation. The diphthongs of the first class are simple sounds that differ from the five principal vowels and, in a manner of speaking, form their semitones. To express these in writing, definite characters were required, but since the early writers did not find such characters in the alphabets borrowed from other nations who perhaps did not have these semitones, they combined two known characters or letters to express a third, just as in painting two colors are mixed to produce a third. They might not have had the courage to invent new letters, or did not wish to do so out of modesty, or they might have been afraid of being misunderstood. They erroneously confused this written construction with pronunciation and very inappropriately named such a sound, which was always a single sound, a diphthong. To represent them in writing, the Romans, and later the French, placed letters next to each other such as <ae>, <eu>, <au>, and <ai>. The Germans placed one on top of the other, Ä, Ö, and Ü. Finally, some more modern Romans connected them completely and thus <ae> became æ, and <oe> became œ.

§ 124

As to the second class of diphthongs, they are more appropriately named, since they are actually expressed as two vowels in pronunciation. However, these are never blended into a single sound, but each is heard separately. Two vowels, written next to each other, are joined into one syllable in pronunciation and slide together. In other words, the voice slides from one vowel to the other without a special stress on the second, just as one passes from one tone to the other in music without stopping. In music this is indicated by a curved line placed above the notes, as shown in Fig. 4 of Table X. The French often make use of this type of diphthong, for example in *veille, miel, oeil, pointe, taille*, etc. Often they allow other, unwritten letters to be heard, as in *roi* and *loi*, where the I is pronounced as an A. The Germans do the same thing. In *mein*, they turn the E into an A, in *euch*, the E is changed into an A, and the U into an I, and the resulting pronunciation is <aich>. In general, the German language has the distinction that when two vowels follow each other they always become a diphthong, as in *Weise, Hui, Freund, Weib, Strauss*, and *Eiche*.[14] It is only in compound words joined by two vowels that this does not occur, as in *bearbeiten, geirrt*, and *beurtheilen*. Double vowels, as for example *Aal* and *See*, are only stretched simple vowels.

§ 125

In the Italian and Latin languages two vowels are rarely found in one syllable. When two vowels follow each other immediately, they are always

---

14. The article *die*, when it is pronounced *di*, does not constitute an exception since the *e* is omitted, and it could just as easily be omitted in writing. However, if one had to pronounce it, it would only form a single syllable with I.

separated into two syllables, that is to say they are pronounced separately with a stress on each syllable, just as two notes not connected with a slur are played in music. For example, in Italian *mai, assai, sei, mia, io, voi*, and *suo*, and in the Latin *aer, chaos, mea, ei, leo, Deus, via, quies, scio, diu, herois, boum, sua, lues, frui*, and *duo*. *Diei* has three consecutive vowels, each of which forms a separate syllable. <au>, however, is an exception. In *aurum, fraus*, and *aula*, the two vowels form only a single syllable. It has not, as of yet, been determined whether the Romans pronounced *Aula* as the Germans pronounce *faul*, or as the <au> of the French, or as the German O in *Ohr*, or even if they said <ohla> instead of *Aula*. A passage in Terence allows us this last conjecture, in which case <au> ceases to be two separate vowels. There are a few additional cases in the Latin language where two vowels are blended into one syllable as in *heu, seu* and a few others, but their number is very limited.

To conclude what we have to say about vowels, I will add that each vowel can form a syllable with each consonant, whether it is preceded or followed by that consonant, for example, <am>, <ma>, <es>, <se>, <if>, <fi>, <ol>, <lo>, <ur>, <ru>, etc. This detail is of great importance for a speaking machine.

On Consonants

§ 126

A consonant is a sound or letter that cannot be expressed by itself in a clear manner. Moreover, to render its pronunciation distinct, it must be combined with another letter, be it a vowel or a consonant, that might precede or follow it.

The word "consonant" ([Latin] consonans ['sounding together, agreeing']) itself, is very aptly chosen, because it expresses perfectly that which it must describe. The qualities that characterize and distinguish vowels from consonants were cited in the chapter on vowels. Consequently, any letter that does not have those characteristics is a consonant.

§ 127

It is now a matter of establishing the principles according to which consonants may be suitably ordered into types or classes.

In his "Primitive World" [ch. 4, p. 131, 1775], M. Court de Gébelin classified all of the consonants in the French language according to the organs that contribute the most to their pronunciation, characterizing them as weak or strong. Here is his table:

Mode of Production	Consonants	
	Strong	**Weak**
1. Labial	P	B
2. Dental	T	D
3. Nasal	N	M
4. Lingual	R	L
5. Guttural	Ca	Ga
6. Sibilant (sifflante)[15]	S, Ce	Z, T (between two vowels)
7. Shibilant (chuintante)[16]	Ch	J, Ge
8. Labio-dental	F	V
9. Palatalized	Ill	Gn
10. Guttural-sibilant	X	
11. Gutturo-labial	Que	Gue

It is to this author's deep knowledge and vast erudition[17] that we owe a number of important discoveries on the origin of languages. He is the author of the most recent work on this subject and has far surpassed those who treated the topic before him, all of whom are cited in his work. But if, in general, science only ever makes slow progress, this truism is an especially apt one for the topic at hand. It has not been pursued with enough diligence until now, which is why we are confronted with so many areas that are still obscure, or whose discoveries have not been completely developed, or are even presented in a false light. The proof lies in the very table presented above. The author gives such an inexact idea of the subject that, unable to use it as a basis for my work, I had to search for another that was more analogous to the nature of the matter. Nevertheless, before I expound upon it, I believe that I should give an account of why I decided not to adopt M. Court de Gébelin's table.

15. Linguists today would refer to this class as "anterior sibilants". –the eds.

16. Linguists today would refer to this class as "non-anterior sibilants". They are sometimes also called "shibilants". –the eds.

17. While in Paris in 1783, I had the pleasure of meeting this learned man shortly before his death. I showed him my speaking machine, which at that time was still quite imperfect. We frequently discussed the mechanism of human speech and he appreciated some of my discoveries so much that he assured me that if there was to be a second edition of his work in his lifetime, he would have to make several changes.

§ 128

First, I would not concur with his division of consonants into weak and strong because I do not find a P to be any stronger than a B. Is the sound heard when a B is pronounced any weaker than the sound of a P? What I shall expound upon below, in my discussion of consonants, will better explain my ideas, and at the same time will justify my reasons for not adopting M. de Gébelin's system.

It should also be noted that the letters T and D are not dental at all because the teeth have no role in their production. I checked this experimentally with people whose upper teeth were completely missing, but who, nevertheless, pronounced these two letters perfectly. Rather, these are lingual consonants because they are pronounced principally by means of the tongue.

I do not find any basis for asserting that the letter M is less strong than the letter N.

The letters L and R are consonants that depend on the movement of the tongue. One can be pronounced as loudly as the other, and if one used equal pressure from the lungs in the pronunciation of both consonants, one would find that the sound of one is no weaker than the sound of the other. When pronouncing *Cyrillus*, is the letter L heard any less than the letter R?

The sounds <ca> and <ga> are formed by the posterior portion of the tongue and are consequently not gutturals.

The letter T between two vowels has no analogy with the letter Z in the French language. Whether it conserves its pronunciation as in *été* or changes into an S as in *nation*, it never changes into a Z. One does not say <nazion>.

The word "palatalized" [mouillée, literally 'moist'] does not have the same meaning as the word "watery," since neither the tongue nor the mouth put any more moisture into the pronunciation of *ill* than into pronouncing the simple consonant L. The epithet is probably used to indicate that this letter is pronounced as it is in the French word *mouillé*. One could just as easily say an L as in *grille* because it is pronounced the same way in both words, but since this designation is generally accepted, I see nothing amiss in its usage. It remains only for me to note that the letter L is lingual, while the sound <gn> is nasal, as I shall prove below.

X is not a unique letter, but is composed of the letters K and S, or C and S. The letters KS and CS are pronounced as <iks> or <ics>.

In the French language, the lips do not contribute to the pronunciation of <que> and <gue>. If the author names them gutturo-labials, he does so in error. Moreover, the letter Q does not differ at all from K or <ca> in pronunciation.

§ 129

According to my system, consonants may only be classified into the following four categories:

1st Class	Mute consonants.[18]
2nd Class	Spirant consonants.[19]
3rd Class	Voiced consonants.
4th Class	Spirant and voiced at the same time.

First Class

§ 130

Mute consonants are those which, on their own, produce no sound and cannot be pronounced or heard without the help of another letter. The letters K, P, and T form this class. To produce a sound, they must be followed either by a vowel or by another consonant. Moreover, they can be heard only after the second letter has been pronounced. When a syllable begins with one of these letters it is not heard until the ensuing letter has been pronounced, as for example, the French word *cas*, which is pronounced <kas>, as well as *peste*, *prince*, *tort*, and *trois*. Conversely, if a word ends in one of these letters, it must be followed by an aspiration or mute sound, which renders its pronunciation distinct.

When in the French language one of these letters occurs at the end of a word, as *estomac*, *trop*, and *tant*, it is not pronounced unless it is followed

---

18. Linguists today would call these "voiceless stops".

19. *1792 German into French translator's note:*
We could not find a word to exactly convey the meaning of the German term *Windmitlauter*. It denotes those consonants that are produced solely by air, without the involvement of the sonorous voice. We thought that the term *soufflantes* that we adopted most closely approached the meaning of the original.

Present editors' note: linguists today would refer to the set of *Windmitlauter/soufflantes* as "voiceless fricatives".

by a silent E, as in *pipe* and *tante*. The Italians do not have a single word in their language that ends in one of these three letters. They are always followed by a vowel which is pronounced distinctly, as in *sacco*, *troppo*, and *bastante*. The Italian, unaccustomed to the weak aspiration that the German language requires in the pronunciation of these letters, dwells either too long or too little on the tone of the aspiration. It is only through painstaking attention that he attains the correct degree.

In the German language there are numerous words that end in the letters K and T, but very few that end in P. The greatest number of these words are of the feminine gender, thus a final E is added to make their pronunciation less harsh, as in *Lampe*, *Treppe*, *Suppe*, and *Kappe*.

Second Class

§ 131

Spirant consonants are those that are formed with aspiration, or by air forced out of the mouth in various ways without simultaneous voicing. They may be heard weakly without the help of another consonant or vowel, but always in a manner distinct enough to mark the difference between one letter and the other. These consonants are F, H, S and SCH.

Let us experiment with the letter F, or <ef>. Once the sound of the é is over, let the F be held for a while. The letter is recognizable. This is also true at the beginning of words. If the sibilant tone of the letter S, or CH, is maintained before it is followed by a vowel or a consonant, for example in *s-uite* or *ch-asse*, it will be accurately discerned that these words begin with an S or a CH, even before the <uite> and <asse> are heard.

Third Class

§ 132

I describe voiced consonants as those that must always be accompanied by voicing, and whose sound cannot be produced by the action of air alone. It must be well noted that here we are discussing only normal, audible speech, for when one whispers or speaks in a low voice, all of the letters are produced by air without concurrent voicing. The letters that belong to this class are B, D, G, L, M, and N. To convince oneself of this, one need only place a finger against his throat as one of these letters is pronounced. The easily felt vibration will prove the existence of voicing. To avoid being erroneously led into believing that this motion of the throat is caused by vowels added to the consonants, one need only sustain the sound of one of these letters without immediately proceeding to the following vowel, and it will become evident that the movement of the larynx is caused by the consonant, for example, *L-ivre*, *R-ome*, and *M-ere*.

§ 133

This third class of consonants is subject to yet another subdivision known as simple and compound. Simple consonants are produced with concurrent voicing, the speech organs remaining in the same position: for example, the letters L, M, N, and R.[20] On the other hand, compound consonants are those consonants for which the organs do not keep the same position but must change in order to be heard. In other words, in pronouncing them, the channel of the mouth or the tongue must first be closed and should not open except to finish the sound of the letter: B, D, and G are such letters.

Fourth Class

§ 134

I include consonants that are simultaneously voiced and spirant in this class. That is to say, these are consonants whose pronunciation is not brought about by the voice alone, but which require aspiration as well.

There are some letters for which a hissing produced by the tone of the voice is first retained within the mouth and then forced out through a very small opening, creating a noise that is heard along with the voice. This noise is somehow comingled with the voice. These letters are R, J as in the French word *jamais*, the French G when it falls before an E as in *génie*, the German letter W, the French and Latin V as in *vrai* and *volo*, the Z in *zéphir*, *mazette*, and *Zona*. All of this will be clarified when we discuss the nature of each letter separately.

---

20. It must be noted that in the pronunciation of the letter R, the tongue does not actually remain immobile, but moves with a very rapid vibration. However, since the movement is uniform, this letter can always be classified as a simple vocal consonant.

On Consonants in Particular

§ 135

I shall now attempt to detail the origin of each consonant, insofar as I believe I have discovered it to be in nature. I shall do so with as much clarity and precision as I am capable of. To this end, as I discuss each one of these letters, I shall indicate to which of the aforementioned classes it belongs and for what reasons. I shall also demonstrate the position of the five most essential organs of speech. Lastly, I shall reveal the difference that exists in the pronunciation of the same consonants among diverse nations, as well as anything else that remains to be said on the subject.

Where necessary, I will add figures to clarify the subject under discussion. Finally, I will mention commonly observed mistakes in pronunciation and the best means of correcting them.

B

§ 136

The letter B is a consonant of the third class, or a compound voiced consonant.

It is a consonant because it cannot be heard distinctly unless it is linked to a vowel. It is compound because it cannot be pronounced with a single and constant position of the organs, but must change to another in order to be heard. I place it among the voiced consonants because it produces a sound before the accompanying vowel is heard, although that sound is not that of a vowel but more of a muffled whisper.

The position of the organs for the pronunciation of this letter is the following:

1. The voice resonates.
2. The nose is blocked.
3. The tongue is recumbent.
4. The teeth take no part at all.
5. The lips are closed.

This letter has many similarities to a P. The evidence that this opinion has always been held lies in the fact that so far all those who have written on speech find no difference between a B and a P other than that the first is gentler or softer, and that the second is pronounced with greater force or more harshly. Hence, in German one pronounces a soft B and a hard P.

This explanation, however, is far from satisfactory. If we were to teach the pronunciation of a B to someone who did not know how to pronounce it, and if we taught that it should be pronounced more softly or gently than a P, he would pronounce a slightly higher P or even with aspiration like a <phe>, as experience has often proved to me. Conversely, we might say to always pronounce the B always like a P, only somewhat more softly, or even like a W, with the idea that in this manner they would differentiate between the two letters. Thus in Austria, I have often heard <ponus>, <wonus>, <wellum>, and <warwarus> instead of *bonus*, *bellum* and *barbarus*.

Some have thought that the addition of an M to the P would result in a certain softening that would change this letter into a B. For a long time I held that a B was pronounced as if it were preceded by a brief M, that is to say like the sound <mbe>. However, after a long series of observations, I realized my error. During my experiments, I somehow stretched the B for three or four seconds, and as a result I tended to let the sound issue through the open nose in order to make it resonate longer, which inevitably produced the sound of an M. This confirmed my preconception that this letter was in competition with M. It is an axiom that with the mouth closed and the nose open, no letter except an M can be pronounced. Moreover, during my observations of the letter B, whether isolated or at the beginning of a word, I thought my idea was correct. However, considering a B between two vowels, as for example in the Latin words *ibi* and *ubi*, I soon realized that not even the least trace of the M remained. Otherwise, one would have heard <imbi> and <umbi>. I therefore concluded that another cause for the difference between a B and a P must be sought.

There are, in speech, some almost imperceptible details that produce the greatest consequences, and without which it is impossible to produce the desired sounds. This is especially true in the case of the letter B. Here we have a few general observations to make that can also be applied to other letters such as D, T, <ga>, and K. The principal one is that with B, the voice always resonates. This is not true of a P.

§ 137

To determine the exact difference between a B and a P, which is our principal concern here, we must define exactly what constitutes a P. In pronouncing a P, the mouth and the nose are closed as they are for a B, but the voice takes no part at all. Air within the mouth, forcefully compressed by the air pushed out of the lungs, seeks an exit. The closed lips obstruct that exit for a time. If they finally yield, and their resistance is no longer at equilibrium with the pressure of the enclosed air, the latter pries the lips open and emerges forcefully. The vowel which accompanies the P, be it an A, an E, or any other vowel, emerges at the same instant as the voice as in <pa>, <pe>, <pi>, etc.

§ 138

B, on the other hand, begins with the voice and is accompanied by it throughout its duration. This alone would already denote a great difference from a P, which remains completely silent. However, there are some small nuances that will render the difference even more obvious. If I might be allowed to introduce some observations here that could serve as fundamental rules:

The voice is nothing but a current of air. To maintain that current, the air issuing from the trachea advances in order to make room for the air that follows it. Once this current is interrupted the voice must stop, just as a current of water stops when the floodgates are closed.

The following consequence might be drawn from this principle: the voice should abruptly and completely cease the moment the mouth and nose are closed and all exits are obstructed. If we think of the voice as a current of water, this conclusion would be valid. But since it is composed of air, which has a completely different characteristic than that of water, namely that it is compressible, the result in this case is entirely different.

On the contrary, the voice can be made audible while the mouth and nose are closed, but only for a short time, and feebly at that. This takes place in the following manner: the interior space of the mouth is filled with air that is not compressed, but is in its natural state. The glottis, like a valve, cuts off the air contained in the lungs. When the voice has to be made audible, the air within the lungs is compressed and the glottis opens slightly, allowing the air a very narrow exit. It finds enough space in the air already contained in the mouth to enter as it produces a sound. Once the air within the mouth is as compressed as the air in the lungs, equilibrium is reestablished and the flow of air ceases and the voice with it. This is why the voice can only last for a short time (about a second). It may also be observed that the voice cannot be too loud, as we have already stated, because it is confined and consequently muffled, just like the sound of a violin coming through the walls of an adjoining room is heard less distinctly than if that obstacle did not exist.

In addition to the compression of air, nature makes use of another expedient to procure space for the air leaving the lungs. The walls of the space above the glottis, that is to say, the soft parts of the throat, expand, or rather are inflated by the air. If one looks into a mirror while slowly pronouncing a B, he will be convinced that even before his mouth is opened, his throat and the lower part of his chin both inflate slightly. However, this expedient is limited by space as well: when these parts are inflated to the last degree, the voice must cease, but if in addition to this the two cheeks are inflated, the voice can be sustained a little longer.

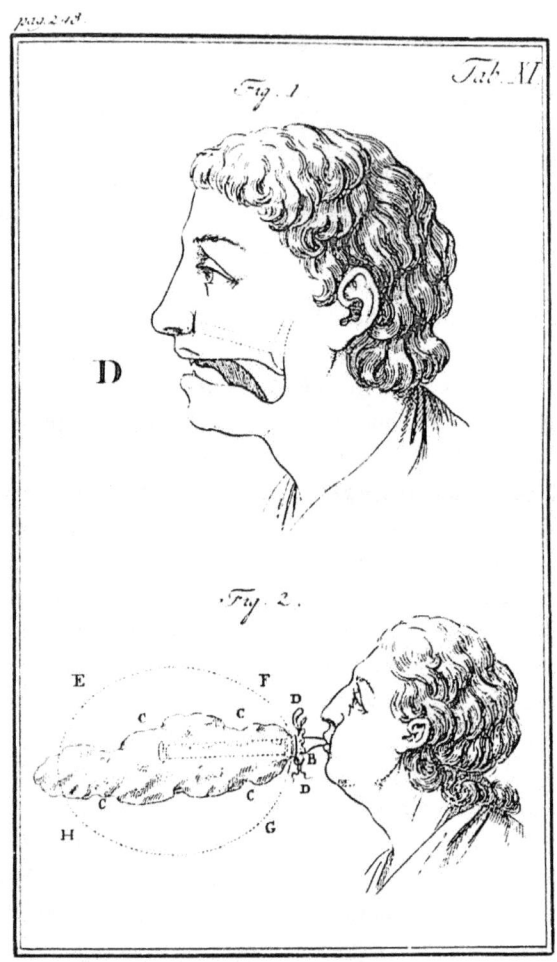

§ 139

An experiment will demonstrate this description more clearly. As in Table XI, Fig. 2 *d*, place an ordinary flute into an ox or pig bladder (see C-C-C), and let the flute be firmly affixed above the hole near the mouthpiece (see D-D). When air is blown into the flute, a tone will be heard for as long as the bladder yields. However, once it is completely filled and distended like a drum and occupies the expanded space E-F-G-H, it becomes impossible to produce any sound from the flute.

Before proceeding to another letter, I feel that I should forewarn those among my readers who wish to carry out these experiments of potential pitfalls. To avoid these, they must remember that to pronounce a B, the nose must be blocked. However, the nose blocks itself so imperceptibly that someone not used to carrying out such experiments often thinks the nose is blocked, when in fact it is open. I therefore advise compressing the nose firmly with the hand during the experiment with the pronunciation of B in order to be convinced that no air is escaping.

Flaws in the pronunciation of the letter B

§ 140.

In general, this letter is pronounced well. I have never observed errors in its pronunciation, save its substitution for a P. This happens rarely, if at all, to the English, French, Italians, Hungarians, Illyrians, and most other European nations that I know. It is only the Germans who often use a P instead of a B. In Germany, one may find entire provinces in which inhabitants have never pronounced a B and would, furthermore, be incapable of pronouncing one. They say <prun> and <pierre> for *brun* and *bierre*, etc. They also change the B into a W, saying <awer> and <hawer> instead of *aber* and *haber*. This error is so habitual that they retain the habit even when learning foreign languages. This alone makes their pronunciation striking, lifeless, and absurd to the ears of foreigners.

The pronunciation of the letter B is not easy for those who are not accustomed to it. It is, however, possible to learn. I would in this case advise beginning with words where B is preceded by an M (for example, *umbra, ambulo, tumba, sombre,* and *humble*). This is because the M, pronounced with the mouth closed, performs the functions of the previously-discussed muffled sound which must always precede a B.

D

§ 141

The letter D is also a consonant of the third class (a compound voiced consonant). What I have said about the letter B from the introduction to the detailed position of the organs is, word for word, applicable to this letter. There is a very small difference between the pronunciation of a B and a D, and it is limited to a single variation. For the pronunciation of a B, it is the lips that block the egress of air, whereas for the pronunciation of a D, it is the tongue that performs this function. All the rest is identical. The affinity between D and T is analogous to that which exists between B and P, and what has already been said about a hard P and a soft B is also applicable to a hard T and a soft D.

The position of the organs is as follows:

1. The voice resonates.
2. The nose is blocked.
3. The flattened tip of the tongue presses against the palate, behind the upper teeth first.
4. The teeth take no part.
5. The lips are open.

Table XI, Fig. 1 illustrates the position of the organs of speech in profile. This will help in examining how the difference of air retention by the tongue rather than the lips can cause such a marked difference and produce a completely different letter. We know that in wind instruments such as the flute and the oboe, the tone changes in a fixed ratio in proportion to how much air is allowed to escape through the instruments' several openings. In the hunting horn and the trumpet more space can be filled by air blown into them, and thus they produce lower tones. The same variation may be observed in speech, although it does not consist of higher or lower tones, but of something that I can only explain by comparison. Just as the ear can accurately differentiate the tone generated by a gut string from one produced by a steel or brass string, even when they are in unison and consequently have the same vibrations, similarly it can find the essential difference between a B and a D, even when they are pronounced in the same tone, and even though they both consist only of what is heard as a muffled sound that suddenly bursts in a vowel.

This difference can be found in the following two points:

1. As we already know, the voice resonating in an enclosed space has a larger space to fill for the pronunciation of a B than for the pronunciation of a D.
2. When the voice finally bursts in a vowel, it has a completely different configuration of passage and exit for these two letters. These two factors are perceptible enough to the ear to allow for immediate differentiation.[21]

---

21. The extraordinary range and sensitivity of the human ear manifests itself principally in people who are born blind. I can cite a memorable example in the person of Miss de Paradis of Vienna, so celebrated for her musical talents. She lost her sight

4: ON THE SOUNDS AND LETTERS OF EUROPEAN LANGUAGES 103

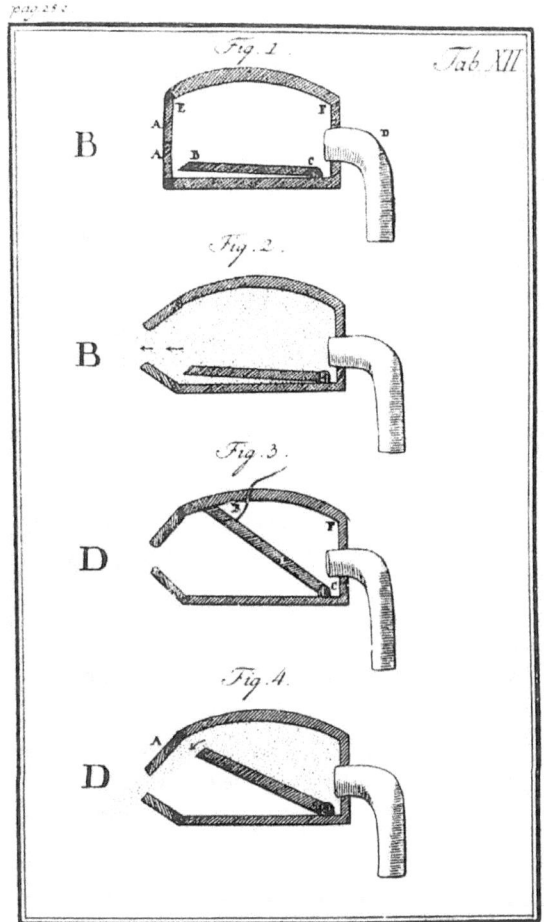

§ 142

Table XII, Fig. 1 will serve to further clarify this matter. It is a side view of an oblong box, the top of which is slightly vaulted along its length. This will serve as a representation of the interior of the mouth as it is shaped

---

completely at the age of two, her ear, on the contrary, acquired such sensitivity that at the age of 16 she could, when led to a wall, determine the exact length of the building by the sound of her footsteps. When she had taken only a few steps into a room, she would first observe whether it was large or small, and would even announce its approximate size. At a distance of ten steps, she could tell if the person talking to her was seated or standing. I was an eyewitness to all these accomplishments.

during the pronunciation of a B. The two side walls have been removed. At point *A*, there are two little doors that represent the lips. Points *B* and *C* are a small board, hinged at *C*, which fits exactly between the two side walls. This board can be raised or lowered at its end, *B*, and performs the functions of the tongue. Point *D* represents the trachea.

It must be noted that:

1. When the doors *A* are closed, the space to be filled by the voice runs from points *E*, *F*, *C*, *B*, and back to *E*.
2. When the two doors open (see Fig. 2), the voice issues straight through the center of these doors, following the illustrated dotted lines.

For D, on the other hand, see Fig. 3. In this illustration, the tip of the small board *B*, representing the tongue, rests against the cover, representing the palate.

1. The space to be filled by the voice ranges from points *B*, *F*, *C*, and back to *B*. It consequently takes less than half the space of that for the letter B (Fig. 1).
2. When the tongue leaves the palate and drops, the sound can no longer issue in a straight line, as indicated by the dotted lines in Fig. 2, but strikes against the upper lip (Fig. 4) and falls in the direction indicated by the dotted lines. Thus, these two different circumstances constitute the difference between the pronunciation of a B and a D.

Flaws in the pronunciation of B and D

§ 143

The majority of what was said earlier relative to flaws in the pronunciation of B are similar to those in the pronunciation of D. One slight difference is that a D is easier to pronounce when it is preceded by an N, for example in the words *bands*, *lande*, and *onde*. Since the position of the tongue and the other organs of speech are the same for an N as they are for a D, and since the voice, which must seem to be confined for a D, resonates through the nose for an N, the transition from an N to a D is quite easy and mistakes are rarely made.

When a D occurs at the beginning of a word, or when it is not followed by an N, it is often changed to a T, for example <toigt> and <tocteur>

instead of the French *doigt* and *docteur*. However, this is not a case of incorrect pronunciation, but of substituting one letter for another.[22]

F

§ 144

F is a consonant of the second class (a spirant consonant).

1. The glottis is silent.
2. The nose is blocked.
3. The tongue is at rest.
4. The upper incisors push against the edges of the lower lip.
5. The lips are somewhat more pursed than they are for the first degree. The lower lip is pulled slightly inward, so that its interior edge touches the sharp edge of the upper teeth, leaving a small, almost longitudinal opening in the middle.

If air is expelled in this position with a modicum of force, the result is a sound similar to that of running or boiling water. To produce such a sound with the mouth or with an instrument, it is absolutely essential that the opening through which air is forced be shaped in such a manner that one of its two edges is flat or thick, and the other sharp. We shall elaborate with figures.

---

22. In Hungary I knew a salt tax collector who could pronounce neither D nor T, and by a singular substitution used a G for the first and a K for the second. However, I have never found such a bizarre substitution in anyone else in all my life.

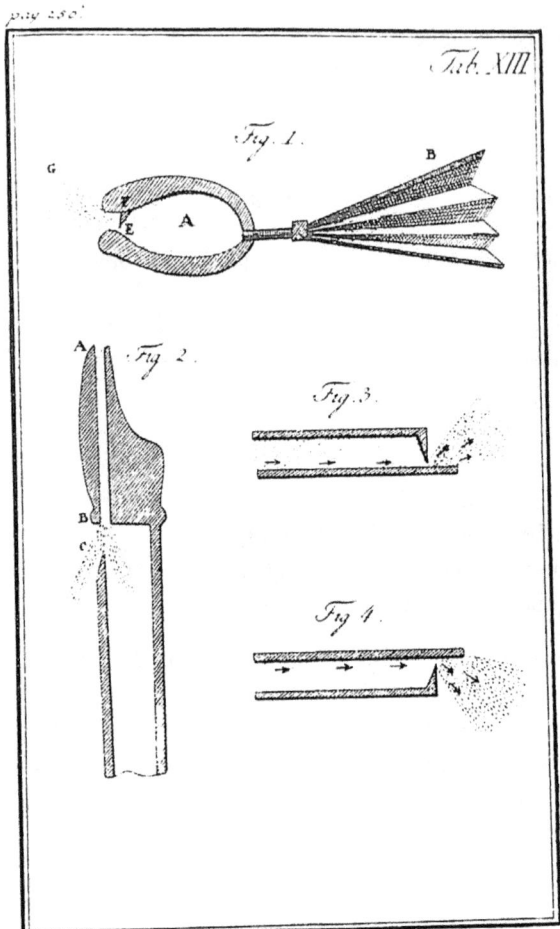

§ 145

When the bellows B in Fig. 1 of Tab. XIII are compressed, air contained within space A is forced out through the small opening E. Since the upper edge, F, is sharp, the air flows in the direction indicated by the dotted lines at G. In other words, the air must bend over the sharp edge, which hones it and creates this noise.

Everyone knows that the tone of a recorder is produced when air flowing through a channel is cut or split by the sharp edge it encounters as it exits (see Fig. 2, A, B, and C).[23] Since in the pronunciation of the letter F

23. We would be digressing too far from our objective if we endeavored to delve

the air is not split as shown in Fig. 2, but is only honed by its sharp edge as shown in Fig. 3, the result is not a whistling tone but a bubbling noise. Thus, the teeth are essential in giving F its sharp, bubbling tone. For this reason, children and elderly people who have lost their upper teeth cannot produce a sharp clear F. These people make use of their lips instead, pursing them into a small opening as if they wanted to cool their hot soup by blowing on it. This produces a sound somewhat similar to an F, but lacks the bubbling noise that characterizes this letter.

Flaws in the pronunciation of F

§ 146

The letter F is rarely confused with other letters, and thus hardly any mistakes are made in its pronunciation. I have, however, encountered a few people who err in the following manner. Instead of using the upper teeth and lower lip, they do the opposite, placing their lower teeth against their upper lip. A perfect F can, in fact, be produced in this manner, since following the laws of physics it does not matter if the air is honed by a sharp edge above (as in Fig. 3) or below (as in Fig. 4). Nevertheless, a trained ear can always detect the difference solely from the air taking a downward path, indicated by the dotted lines in Fig. 4. Although this difference cannot always be detected in a single F, it can always be discerned in a syllable where F is linked with another letter (as in *affut* and *fronde*). The transition from this F to another letter and vice versa always has a jarring and annoying quality to the ear.[24]

Another less common flaw comes about due to a defect in dental configuration. If the upper incisors are too far apart, they allow too much

---

more deeply into the source of sound for a fife or a flute. What we have already said is sufficient relative to the comparison that we have used.

24. I knew two young boys who, when they lost their upper incisors, fell into the habit of pronouncing an F in this inverted manner, that is to say with their lower teeth. Gradually their new upper teeth grew in, but they continued to keep the flawed pronunciation they had developed through necessity and had become ingrained with practice and habit. They had completely forgotten the use of their upper teeth. They kept this defective pronunciation as they grew older, and would have probably kept it into their old age if I had not tried to correct it a few years ago when I was involved with my experiments in speech. I explained to them how this letter was formed, almost exactly as I have described it here, and in a few moments had the satisfaction of seeing them on the right road. The younger one, who was somewhat more vivacious and ambitious, was cured within the first hour and only rarely fell into the old habit. It took a few months with the older one, but he now pronounces F like everyone else.

air to pass through them. Consequently, they cannot sharpen the breath. Such people have no other recourse than to pronounce F with their lower teeth as we said earlier, or, if they do form the letter with their upper teeth, they can make use of the adjacent canines. However, in this manner, the F is no longer pronounced at the center of the mouth. This not only results in an obviously incorrect sound, but also contorts the face.

G

§ 147

This letter is pronounced differently in almost every language. The French call it <jé>, the Italians <dje> or <dche>, the Germans at times name it <ié>, at others <gue>, the Hungarians call it <dié>, the English <dchi>, the Greeks <gamma>, and the Hebrews <gimel>.[25]

In several languages, when G is linked with another letter, it loses its primitive sound depending on the ensuing vowel. In French, if it is followed by an E or an I, it keeps its first pronunciation, but if it is preceded by A, O, U, L, R, etc., it becomes the letter it would have been in the alphabet. In *genie* and *magie* it has a completely different pronunciation than it has with *gout*, *galere*, *glace* and *grace*.

Before we discuss the foundation of this quite variable letter, we must agree on which of its sounds we wish to adopt. All of the examples cited are merely transpositions and superpositions of other letters of the alphabet, rather than distinctly new letters. It cannot just be a question of the Greek *gamma*, which differs from all other letters, or the G as it is pronounced by all nations in the Latin word *gallina*. Thus, it is a consonant of the third class, that is to say a voiced consonant, for which the position of the organs is the following:

1. The glottis resonates.
2. The nose is blocked.
3. The tip of the tongue is pushed against the lower teeth and its posterior portion against the soft palate in such a manner that no air can escape.
4. The teeth take no part at all.

---

25. In Latin, each nation gives this letter the sound it has in its own language. Thus, each pronounces the common word *geographie* with a different G.

5. The lips, preparing for the vowel to follow, are open to varying degrees depending on the vowel.

This letter, like B, is a compound voiced consonant because it cannot be heard in its first position, but only through its transition to another. In addition, it does not become intelligible except by the passage of the voice to another vowel or consonant.

§ 148

The G has the same affinity with the letter K as that which exists between B and P, and D and T. To transform a K into a G, it is necessary only to make the voice resonate in a muted and confined manner. The K has its origin in the tongue, which in its natural position lies horizontally and touches the lower teeth with its edges (see Table XIV, Fig. 3). It contracts its two lateral edges towards the center, thus straightening and taking on the oval form shown in Fig. 4. The anterior portion, the tip of the tongue, remains pushed against the lower teeth, while the posterior portion pushes against the soft palate and covers the entire back of the mouth, preventing the escape of air. The rest of the theory is identical to that for the letters P and T, save that for P, the air must fill the entire space within the mouth because the lips prevent its escape (see Table XII, Fig. 1). For the T, the air has a narrower space to fill because the tongue cuts off half the mouth like a partition (see Fig. 3). For a G, on the other hand, the posterior portion of the tongue first seals the entrance to the throat. Consequently, the air has a much smaller space to fill, that is, the space in the throat (see Table XIV, Fig. 1, where the valve A represents the tongue).[26] Thus, if air is compressed slightly by the pressure from the lungs, when the tongue separates itself abruptly from the soft part of the palate, air is released with a noise. This noise is the K, which becomes even more intelligible when it is followed by another letter, such as <ka>, <ke>, <ki>, <kr>, <kl>, etc.

---

26. One must not neglect to note the diverse directions air takes as it issues from each of the aforementioned cases.

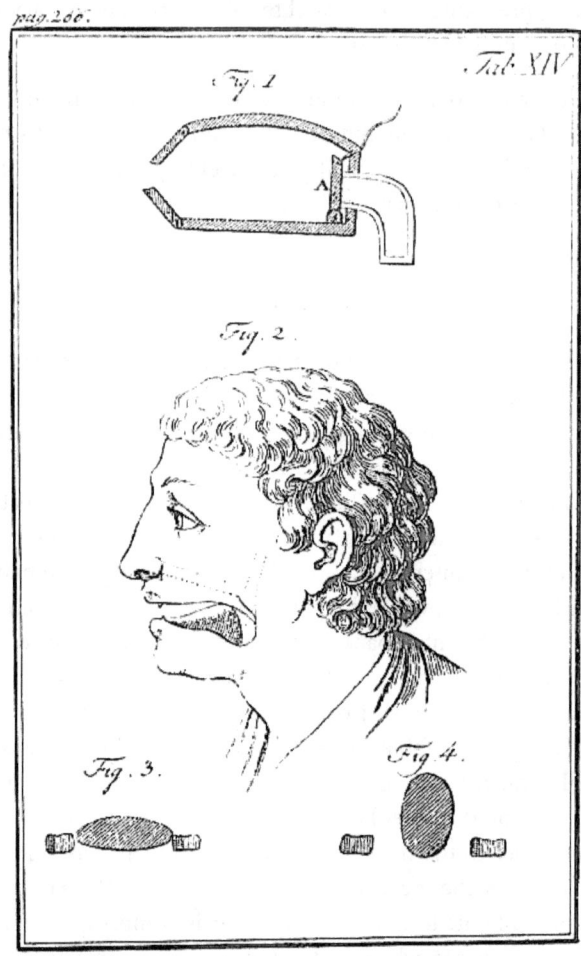

Let us now return to the letter G, which is nothing but a soft K. To form a G directly from a K, nothing is changed except that in the position for a K, the voice is made to resonate in a confined manner, as was explained in detail in discussing B. In this manner, a perfect *gamma* or *gue* is formed.[27]

> 27. Dionysius of Halicarnassus was content to say the following about this letter:
> *Nec ullo modo habituve sibi invicem differunt, nisi quod tenuiter k pronunciatur; x dense, g mediocriter ac media inter eas ratione. Sunt autem præstantissimæ, quæ spiritu copioso proferuntur, quibus proximæ sunt, quæ medio, quæ vero tenuissimo, cæ omnium deterrimæ. Vol. V de Comp. verbor.*
>
> [Nor do they differ from one another in any way or manner except that K is pronounced thinly, x thickly, g moderately and in a manner intermediate to these. Those [letters] are pre-eminent that are produced with a copious breath, next to which are those that are produced with a moderate breath, those produced with a very thin breath

§ 149

It was stated earlier, in discussing the organs of speech, that the lips open to different degrees. This can be understood to mean the following. Since the throat is completely covered by the posterior portion of the tongue, what occurs in front of that partition is absolutely irrelevant. It is of little importance whether the two rows of teeth are closer together or further apart, and whether the lips are closed or open, since the sound of the G cannot be heard until after the tongue has left the soft part of the palate. Therefore, everything depends on the opening the voice encounters: whether it is made for an A, an O, or an I, the G becomes intelligible only through the transition to any other letter. Nature[28] makes use of this opportunity and, for the duration of the G, prepares the lips for the following letter, to avoid in this, as in all her actions, a violent jump from one state to another. For example, when we wish to say *gout*, the lips are already in the position necessary for an <ou>, even as the G is being pronounced. It is open to the first degree, and once the tongue leaves the soft part of the palate, we hear the <ou> without any other movement of the mouth. In pronouncing *gant*, the lips are much more open, etc.[29]

§ 150

Another observation regarding the G remains to be made. When it occurs at the end of a word after an N, as in *long, sang,* and *étang*, the N as well as the G lose their principal quality and unite in such a way that they produce a third sound. The ordinary N is pronounced by pressing the flattened tongue against the front of the palate behind the upper teeth, thus forcing the voice to issue through the open nose. But when it is followed by a G, an N is produced by the tongue, which is pressed against the soft palate with its posterior portion as is required for a G. This allows the voice to issue through the nose, which produces a sound similar to that of an N, but which differs from it nonetheless. The G changes its principal quality, because in this case, the nose remains open. Consequently, the voice, which should have a confined sound, issues freely through this channel. Thus, since the N

---

are worst of all. Vol. V. On Literary Composition.]

28. I say *nature*, as this is probably not done deliberately and on purpose. I do not think anyone ever consciously thought about it as he spoke.

29. As anyone will easily perceive, this paragraph is also applicable to D, T, K, L and several other letters. I made this observation in discussing G because I discovered it at the time I was writing about that letter.

assumes the position of the tongue for a G, and the G adopts the open nose of the N, the two letters meld to produce a third sound.

Flaws in the pronunciation of G

§ 151

Flaws in the pronunciation of G, as it is pronounced in *gamma*, are difficult to find. However, exchanges with other letters do occur, of which we have already cited a few. The people in Austria, for example, rarely pronounce the gamma at the beginning of words. They usually replace it with a K, saying <kros>, <klas>, and <krau> instead of *gros, glas,* and *grau*. At the end of words, especially when it is followed by an E or an L, they pronounce the letter correctly, saying *orgl, spargl,* and *wagen* instead of <orkl>, <sparkl>, and <waken>.

H

§ 152

The letter H, as it is pronounced in German, English, and the French exclamation *Ha!* (the aspirated H), is a consonant of the second class, or a spirant consonant. It consists only of the expulsion of breath, or a strong voiceless puff of air. It may be heard without the accompaniment of another letter, but only weakly and only up to a distance of a few feet. I intentionally say "a strong breath", because one can breathe and not be heard at all. But what is a breath? A breath is produced when the glottis opens more than is necessary for the voice and consequently leaves a free passage for the air that comes from the lungs. If the lungs are only weakly compressed such that the air issuing from them is in proportion with the glottis, and thus it does not issue in such a great quantity that this opening cannot allow it to flow without restraint, then it is only a soft breath that cannot be heard. But, if the lungs are compressed suddenly and violently such that the air contained therein is forced to exit all at once and is no longer in proportion with the opening of the glottis, then that air, compressed by the overly narrow edges of the glottis, creates audible friction. This is the strong breath that forms the H.[30] We may easily prove this with an experiment. If one

---

30. Perhaps air, striking against the palate and the other organs of speech, and the direction it takes because of that, also contributes something to the formation of this breath.

takes a pair of bellows equipped with a rather large duct and compresses them slowly, the escaping air will not be heard. However, if the bellows are then compressed quickly, the opening will be too small and the escaping air will sound like a breath or sigh.

§ 153

This letter has a particular characteristic that distinguishes it from all others. Namely, it does not have a special position, but takes the position of the vowel that is to follow it. When the soft palate, the tongue, and the lips have taken the position necessary for the formation of a vowel, the voice that should animate that vowel cannot be heard immediately. However, with the organs in position, the lungs first push forth a breath, after which the glottis contracts and begins to resonate. If, for example, we say *heros* 'hero', the tongue and the lips are in position for an E before the H begins. If we say *hazard* 'chance', the parts will be in position for an A. For *Holland*, they will be in the position for an O, etc. To prove what we have just stated, place the tongue and the lips in the position required to pronounce an A, hold the palm of the hand in front of the mouth, a thumb's distance away, and slowly pronounce *Ha*. As <ha> is slowly pronounced, a puff will be felt on the hand for the duration of the H, and will cease when the A begins, that is, when the ligaments of the glottis draw closer and make the voice resonate.

§ 154

In writing, Germans make double use of this letter. Sometimes they pronounce it, and at other times it serves only to indicate that the syllable is long. The first case occurs only at the beginning of words, as in *hand*, *herz*, and *hinter*, and in compound words such as *verhasst*, *abhalten*, and *umhangen*. However, when the H is in the middle or end of a word, the breath is not heard. Only the vowel is stretched, as in *Mühle*, *Mühe*, *Stroh*, and *Vieh*.

In German, when the H is to be heard, it must always be followed by a vowel. There is not a single word that begins with an H which is immediately followed by a consonant. However, in the Illyrian language and all the others derived from it this is very common, for example in *Hlava*, *Hruda*, *Hlubocina*, *Hnew*, *Hladky*, and *Hrmot*.

§ 155

All European nations have this letter in their alphabet, but there are some that do not make use of it in pronunciation. Conversely, the Greeks did not have it in their alphabet, but pronounced it nevertheless. To mark it in their writing they placed an accent, *Signum aspirationis*, over the vowel as in ὑπερ (*huper* 'above') and ὕδωρ (*hudor* 'water').

The Italians never pronounce the H.[31] The French rarely do, and in a less marked manner than the Germans, as for example in *honte* 'shame'. The pronunciation of this letter is so foreign to these two nations that they do not have a proper name for it when it is by itself. The Italians say *akka*, and the French say *ache*. When native Italian and French speakers begin to learn a foreign language, this letter gives them a great deal of difficulty. Usually they omit it entirely and say <erz> for Herz, or if they wish to imitate aspiration, they try too hard.

Flaws in the pronunciation of H

§ 156

H is the sole letter for which I have never found a real flaw in pronunciation or an exchange with another letter. This observation refers to the Germans, since foreigners do sometimes make exchanges.

CH

§ 157

Some people have thought that the CH, as it is pronounced by the Germans, was nothing but an H pushed with greater force. However, when I have defined its position more exactly and have given additional details, it will become obvious that the CH is a true letter as different from H as SCH is from S. I place it in the second class, as a true *spirant consonant*. To begin, the CH is unique in that it has two different positions. When it is preceded by, or followed by, an E or an I, its position is absolutely the same as that for an I, and there is no other difference except that it is the air that acts and not the voice. We know that air creates a sound when it has to force a passage through a narrow opening. For the vowel I, the channel of the tongue is very

---

31. Except for the Florentines, who, as one knows, use H altogether too often, even instead of other letters.

narrow, thus when air is pressed with force through this narrow space, the CH sound is produced. If, for example, one wanted to pronounce the German word *ich*, one would make the voice stop when the I ought to end, and in the same position push the breath through without allowing the voice to be heard. One will then have pronounced a perfect *ich*.

Here again Nature takes the shortest route to accomplish its aim. We know, from §58, that the voice can be silenced in several ways. In this case, the glottis opens too far after the I and the continued pressure from the lungs produces the CH; in other words, the soundless current of air. The narrow opening that should restrain the air as it flows through is already in position for an I, and consequently the CH is produced as if by itself, Nature having done nothing more than widen the glottis. If we take an E instead of an I and say *pech*, we will find the same CH as in *ich*. However, it should be noted that the transition from an E to a CH is not as simple as that from an I to a CH, since in the case of the former, the channel of the tongue is open to the second degree and is consequently too wide for the issuing air to encounter an obstacle and create a sound. Therefore, after the E, the channel of the tongue must first contract to the first degree, taking the position for an I, and only then will the CH be heard. If the tongue remained in the position for an E, it would be impossible to produce a CH, even if the air were forced through with great violence. At most one could say <peh>, but never *pech*. Since there is only one degree between the tongue making an E and making an I, and it moves to this position with a very small movement, it keeps the same CH to which it is so close.

§ 158

As has been discussed, the vowels I and E seem to be higher than the others. Since the CH is produced in the position of the I, it seems to also take on some of the qualities of this vowel, and is somewhat higher than the other CH, which we shall discuss first. I will henceforth refer to this as the *high CH*, and the other (CH following an A, O, or <ou>) as the *low CH*. The latter is produced in a different position than the former. The tongue, and all the other organs of speech, are in the position for a K, save that the tongue does not block the channel with its posterior portion as completely as it does for a K, instead leaving a small opening in the center through which air may noisily issue. If one attempts to pronounce a German *ach* and sustains the CH, he will discover that the tongue is in an entirely different position than when he pronounces *ich*. Its posterior portion will be elevated and its tip will be lowered. To convince oneself even more clearly of the difference between the two CHs, one should pronounce *ich* and *ach* alternately, sustaining the CH each time. It is hard to deny the marked difference. I even believe that anyone who has not heard the vowel but only the CH would be able to state whether it was preceded by an E or an I, or by an A, O, or <ou>.

The reason that Nature formed these two CHs and why the vowels A, O, and <ou> always use the lower of these could well be because the transition from an A, O, or <ou> to an I, that is, from the third, fourth or fifth degrees of the tongue channel opening to the first, would be too jarring. Indeed, when should the tongue take the position for an I? While the voice is resonating? One would then hear <aïche>, <oïche>, and <ouïche>. If it were to occur while CH sounded it would be too late, since the CH must have its position when the I begins to resonate. If one wished to have a short pause between A and CH in order to place the tongue into position, the <ach> would no longer be linked, and one would hear <a-ch>. Moreover, the high CH always retains something of the I, which is always pronounced <aich>.[32] How do we avoid this? To avoid the I that it would have formed with its middle portion, the tongue in this case uses its posterior portion to contract its channel. The soft palate also drops a little towards the tongue, and thus the position for a *deep CH* is ready the moment the voice stops resonating.

§ 159

Both CH and H have in common that they keep the same mouth opening as that of the vowel that precedes or follows them. This, however, does not mean that H and CH are the same letter. Even if we had not said all of the above, one can easily prove that the H has an entirely different position because it requires a great deal of air, and because the lungs empty so quickly that it can barely be sustained for a second, whereas the CH may be sustained for ten seconds.

The French, Italians and English also have CH, but they pronounce it differently from the Germans. It becomes a completely different letter in their mouths. The French turn it into a <sch>, as in *chien*, the Italians turn it into a K, as in *che*, and finally the English pronounce it like <tsch>, as in *child*. They do not have words of German origin that begin with a CH: *Christ*, *Cho[i]r*, *China*, etc. are foreign words.

---

32. The people of this country generally use the high CH. To do this they ascend through an I and say *tuich* for *tuch*, *buich* for *buch*. The Jews, on the other hand, use the deep CH when they should use the high, and descending through an A say *iach* instead of *ich*.

4: ON THE SOUNDS AND LETTERS OF EUROPEAN LANGUAGES   117

Flaws in the pronunciation of this letter

§ 160

There are rarely flaws in the pronunciation of CH, except for those already mentioned in the preceding note. However, when Italians learn German, they usually replace the CH with a K, and since they add an E, they say <ike> and <dike> instead of *ich* and *dich*.

Some Germans also make the low CH resonate too deeply because they enlarge the opening of the tongue channel too far. Consequently, to fill this space they must expel too great a quantity of air with too much force. When the CH follows a vocal consonant such as L, N, or R, it is always higher, because it is very easy for the tongue, forming these three letters with its tip, to place itself in the position for an I, having only to lower itself. Some people make the mistake of not stopping the voice in time, so that it still resonates when the position for an I is ready. For this reason, they often allow an I to escape in spite of themselves, and say <milich>, zwilich>, and <mönich> instead of *Milch, Zwilch*, etc. I know of only one person who changed a CH into a <sch>. She would say <isch> instead of *ich*, <rescht> instead of *recht*, <nischt> instead of *nicht*. However, she did not wish to take the trouble to correct this flaw according to my instructions because she could not be convinced that this flaw was noticeable by others. Many a lame person imagines that he walks as upright as other men.

K

§ 161

The letter K is a consonant of the first class, namely a mute consonant that cannot be heard without the help of another letter. The position of the organs of speech for its pronunciation is the same as that of a G, except that in the case of the G the voice resonates, whereas it is silent for a K. Since I described this letter earlier while discussing G in § 148, I refer the reader to that section to avoid repetitions, and will only add a few thoughts to what has already been said.

Although the pronunciation of this letter is identical in all nations, some use a different symbol or character to denote it. The Romans, French, Italians, and Spanish replace it with a C or a Q, as in *canis, cour, qui*, and *questo*, which could be written equally well with a K, as *kanis, kour, ki*, and *kuesto*. The Greeks did not feel the necessity of including a C and a Q in their alphabet in addition to their K. These two letters, borrowed from foreign languages, contribute nothing to the richness of the German language. Rather, they overload it with useless encumbrances. Could we not equally well write *bekwem*, *Kwaal*, and *Kwelle* instead of *bequem*, *Quaal*, and *Quelle*? Would this not be the same to pronounce? Do the five or six German words still written with a Q justify the conservation of this useless letter in the alphabet any longer?

§ 162

The Germans instead have two different Ks. The first, which we are discussing here, is pronounced like the Latin C in *caput*, or the French C in *car*. The second is always followed by an H in pronunciation. In other words, it is accompanied by aspiration and sounds like <kha>.[33] Whenever K is the first letter of a word and is immediately followed by a vowel, this second K, or <kh>, is used, for example in *Khatz*, *Khind*, and *Khunst*, and similarly in compound words like *unkheusch*, *verkhürzt*, and *aufkheimen*. Conversely, if a K is immediately followed by a consonant, the first K, without aspiration, is used. For example, Germans say *klein*, *Kraft*, and *Knecht*, not *khlein*, *Khraft*, and *Khnecht*. In order to avoid confusing the first K with a <kh> when it occurs in the middle of a word and is followed by a vowel, the precaution of adding a C was taken to indicate that it should be pronounced like a C, as in *Ancker* and *Wirckung*, and not as *Ankher* or *Wirkhung*. It has however been recognized for some time that this C is superfluous. It shall probably soon be banished from the German language entirely, but it will be more difficult to remove from [the German] alphabet. It will take a long time before schools pass a resolution to recite A, B, D.

One could also consider the K in a simple way and say that the Germans, like all the other nations, have only one K. If they sometimes add an H, which is also a letter, this would not change the K in any way. If we consider K from this point of view, I must myself admit that the preceding observation is useless, and that the K is always the first K, pronounced as <ca>. However, it would always be necessary to add an H when one wants to pronounce it as <kha>, and one would have to write, as well as pronounce, *Khunst*.

---

33. One could name this the German K, since it is unknown in other languages. Nevertheless, several German provinces do not make use of it.

Flaws in the pronunciation of K

§ 163

When children first begin to speak, they usually say T instead of K, for example, <thaiser> instead of *Kaiser*, <thalt> instead of *Kalt*. Sometimes they keep this flaw into their later years. Although this rarely occurs, I have nevertheless noticed it in some adolescents, and I have even corrected a young lady who was over twenty years old. She confirmed the very close affinity between K and G for me when, immediately after I had explained clearly the position of the organs for the first of these letters, she produced a *gamma*, and she pronounced it <gaiser> instead of *Kaiser*. Nevertheless, she did finally learn how to pronounce it perfectly. Some people pronounce K with too much precision, and turn it into a KCH. The Swiss say <kchlar>, <kchnecht>, and <wolckchen>, but the error lies in the CH that they add and not in the K.

L

§ 164

L is one of the principal sounds of the voice. It belongs to the third class of consonants, which are the simple vocal consonants, because it maintains the same position of the organs throughout its duration. When pronouncing an L:

1. The glottis resonates.
2. The nose is blocked.
3. The tip of the tongue is pressed against the palate behind the upper incisors, and the rest of the tongue is at rest (see Fig. 1, Table XV).
4. The teeth have no function to perform.
5. The mouth is open.

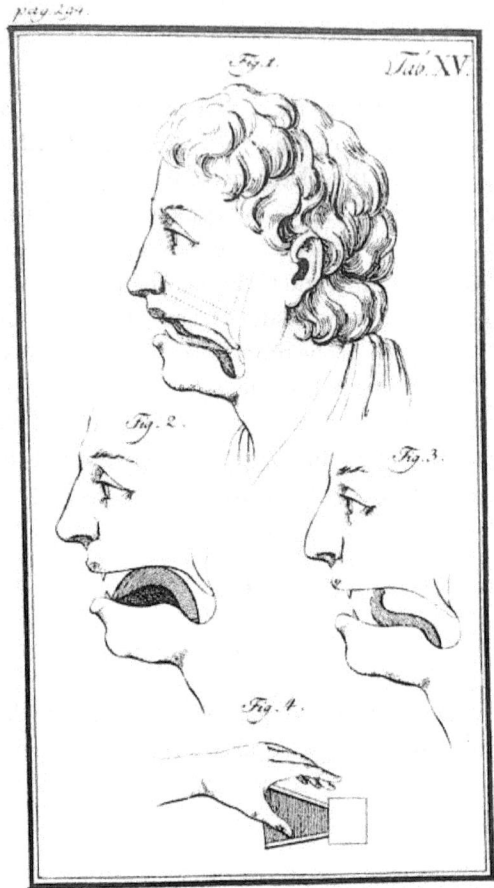

§ 165

There are three different Ls:

1. The common L; in French it is pronounced as in *vol*, and in German as in *licht* and *oehl*.
2. The palatal French L, as in *fille*.
3. The Turkish or Polish L, as in *bol*.

All three Ls are based on the same principle, namely that the tongue divides the voice into two parts. This is done by the flattened tongue pressing its tip against the palate, behind the upper incisors, and leaving its posterior portion in its natural position. From this position, a small opening is formed on both sides of the tongue, near the back molars, through which the voice can issue. This, in a few words, is the complete description of the letter L. We shall now examine this description to evaluate its accuracy. Earlier, in discussing the letter B, we said that when all the exits for the voice are blocked, it can still resonate for almost a second. However, L can be easily made to resonate for more than ten seconds. This, then, is one definite proof that the voice has an exit somewhere. It is not through the nose, because it is blocked (as one can easily prove by pressing it with the fingers). Neither can the voice issue through the regular channel directly over the tongue, since by looking into a mirror we can see that the tongue is tightly pressed in front and also as far as we can see into the mouth. Therefore, the only available exit is the very far end of the tongue. To clear any doubts on the subject, one has only to place the tongue into the position for an L and blow air through with some force without allowing the voice to resonate. That air flow will be felt at the posterior edges of the tongue and the interior sides of the cheek against which it strikes. If this experiment is repeated many times, those parts of the tongue's edges over which the air passes will become dry and will feel dry for some time afterwards. In my speaking machine I produce the L sound by holding my thumb vertically, from top to bottom, within the cavity representing the mouth, thus placing an obstacle for the voice over which it will have to split (see Table XV, Fig. 4).

§ 166

The palatal French L does not differ from the common L, except that the tongue does not block the channel with its tip, but with its middle section (see Table XV, Fig. 2). The tongue is curled into an arc, its point lowered and pressed against the lower front teeth. The middle portion presses hard against the palate, and thus blocks the channel of the tongue in such a manner that the necessary openings on both sides remain nevertheless, as for the common L.

§ 167

The deep Turkish or Polish L differs from the ordinary L solely in the position of the tip of the tongue. Being somewhat curved, it does not press as close to the teeth, but towards the middle of the palate (see Table XV, Fig. 3).

If one compares these three figures, one first notices that in each case, the voice has a larger or smaller space to fill, which, according to the principles we have adopted, must produce different sounds.

§ 168

L is one of the letters which at the beginning of a word is not followed by a consonant. There is not a single word in any of the European languages known to me that begins with an L and is immediately followed by a consonant. R, N, and M have the same characteristic, although there are some examples to the contrary in the Slavic languages for the last of these three letters such as *mnoho*, *mliko*, etc. It is obvious that L and R are not vowels, as some people claim, because one of the principal characteristics of vowels is that they can be linked to all consonants.

Flaws in the pronunciation of L

§ 169

Many people cannot pronounce an L when it follows a vowel, in which case they insert a D before it. They say <bidld>, <zodll>, and <madler> for *Bild*, *Zoll*, and *Maler*. At the beginning of words, or when it is preceded by a consonant, they pronounce it well, for example in *Land*, *Schlau*, and *Karl*. In the first instance, the flaw is due to the fact that the tip of the tongue is always at rest for vowels. Thus, when these people want to transition from a vowel to an L, they know from habit that the tongue should be arched towards the palate. However, not content with the tip alone, they press almost half the tongue against the palate as if they wished to say D. Because they do not hear an L in this position, they promptly correct the error by lowering the posterior portion of the tongue, thus providing the voice with the necessary exit on both sides which, as we said earlier, form an L. However, the voice has already sounded during the position for D, and they say <wedlt> for *Welt*. The flaw and the remedy become habit so that one never occurs without the other, and they can no longer perceive that they are deforming the L.

The reason why these people do not commit this error when the L is at the beginning of a word could well be due to the fact that they have more time to put the tongue into the required position before a sound is heard, which could not occur when L is in the middle of a word, due to the promptness with which it must be pronounced. Often, they do not pronounce it well even at the beginning of words, because they link it with other words, and they together form a single word. In this case the same error will surely be committed. They will say <sodleicht> for *so leicht* and <zudlange> for *zu lange* even though they pronounce it easily and very well when it is at the beginning of a sentence (as in *Lange genug stand ich im Fedlde*). If they pronounce L correctly after a consonant, it is only because that consonant is normally one that comes close to the position for an L. For example, in pronouncing *schlau*, the tongue is already prepared for an L while pronouncing <sch>, and the position is attained merely by closing the small opening for the SCH with its tip. Similarly with the R in *Kerl*, they do not pronounce it <kerdl> because the position for an R comes close to that of an L as much as it does with<sch>. One can easily prove for himself that R and SCH are not too different in their pronunciation with the following experiment. Pronounce *Hirsch* and observe how little the tongue changes its position in going from an R to a SCH. It only stops fluttering and the SCH is ready to be pronounced.

There are cases in which people who otherwise pronounce everything correctly must be on their guard to avoid this superfluous D. If an N occurs before an L at the end of a word, almost everyone will slip in a D between these two letters (as in <ndl>). This is where the Austrian diminutives *Pfandl* from *Pfanne* and *Hendl* from *Henne* come from.

To form a diminutive, an L is usually added to the end of a noun, or the final E is changed to an L. Thus, *Hirschel* is formed from *Hirsch*, *Bachel* from *Bach*, *Häuble* or *Häubl* from *Häube*, etc. Therefore, Henne and Pfanne should only form *Hennl* and *Pfannl*, and not <hendl> and <pfandl>. However, the D inserts itself against the speaker's will, and this happens for the following reason. To form an N, the tongue is already in position for a D, with the sole difference that the nose is unblocked. For an L, the tongue is also in position for a D, except that the nose must be blocked and two small openings have to be made on both sides of the tongue in its posterior portion. Therefore, if one wishes to go from an N to an L, two events have to occur simultaneously: the nose must be blocked, and the lateral openings must be formed by the tongue. If the nose is blocked only for an instant before the tongue has formed those openings, a D will be heard first. This may also be due to the fact that the nose is blocked sooner for convenience, so that the pressure of the confined air may help the muscles of the tongue and facilitate the formation of the lateral openings, because the tongue is accustomed to this assistance, especially in forming D, T, G, and K.

I have heard L changed into another letter only once in my life, and in a very bizarre manner at that. One of my friends in Vienna had a daughter of seven or eight who used precisely the most difficult letter, the R, instead of an L. She said <grand> for *gland*, <roup> for *loup*, and <r'isre> for *l'isle*.

I did not have much difficulty in correcting this singular error. Once I had shown her my tongue's position for an L she imitated me and immediately mastered the L. Full of joy, for hours on end she sought words to display her new-found skill to me.

M

§ 170

The letter M, like the preceding letter, is a consonant of the third class, or a simple vocal consonant. Just as A is the easiest vowel to pronounce, M is the easiest consonant. It is the first to be pronounced by children, in *Mama*. This letter is common to all European languages and is always the same. The organs of speech are in the following position:

1. The glottis resonates.
2. The nose is unblocked.
3. The tongue lies in its natural state.
4. The two rows of teeth are slightly separated.
5. The lips are closed.

§ 171

M and N are the only two letters for which the voice issues through the nose and not through the mouth as it does for all the other letters. M is consequently a nasal sound. There are those who place it among the labial sounds, but I do not believe that it belongs to this class, because if one wishes to name a letter after one of the organs of speech it must be after the dominant organ, that is the organ that contributes most to its formation. In this case however the lips are in a relaxed and natural state, just as they are when one is silent. Therefore, they cannot be regarded as active organs, but as passive ones. We cannot ignore them completely because they have to close the mouth, but just as the eyes are indispensable to drawing, we would not say that drawing is done with the eyes. True labial sounds are something else entirely. The lips are in motion and consequently active, as in B and P, or they place limits on the opening through which the sound must pass, as in W and V. For M, however, it is a completely different organ that acts. If I want to pronounce the French word *mon* when I am quietly seated with my mouth closed, what do I do to produce an M? I keep my lips closed, just as they already are, unblock my nose and make my voice sound. Unblocking the nose and allowing the voice to issue through it are actions that belong solely to the nose, and thus the nose is the active organ for the formation of an M. Therefore, M should be named after that organ and labeled a nasal sound. Why are people in accord when it comes to designating N as a nasal sound? Does the voice not issue through the nose for an M as well? By the same token, should N not be labelled a lingual sound because the channel of the tongue is blocked by the tongue, and label M a labial sound because the channel is blocked by the lips? The contradiction is obvious.

§ 172

The prevailing opinion that M is a labial sound may have been the basis for what Mr. Adelung (1793) says about this letter in his dictionary. "Many grammarians," he says, "exclude the M from the number of primitive letters. With some modifications they are not wrong, because the sound that expresses M is not always so clearly determined in nature that the other labial letters cannot express it with equal precision."

I cannot understand the meaning of these words exactly. If there is a particular sound expressed by M, it must be determined in nature, because M is such a simple, primitive, and invariable letter that there can be no modifications in its determination. Once this sound exists, it is a definite sound that cannot be imitated by any other labial sound, let alone be expressed with such precision. It can be replaced by another sound, but then all traces of an M will disappear. A principal and essential characteristic of labial sounds is that when the nose is blocked, the voice or voiceless air must issue through an opening in the mouth that is smaller at times and larger at others. On the other hand, it is impossible to pronounce an M if the mouth is not completely closed and the nose open. Just as we cannot reconcile the ideas of *being open* and *being closed*, similarly a labial sound cannot produce an M or anything that comes close to it. We shall try to substitute the labial sounds one after the other for an M to see if it can be imitated by any of them. Adelung, in his system for the German language (1793), adopts five labial sounds, W, B, F, P, and M. Substituting them for M in the word *mein*, we will have <wein>, <bein>, <fein>, and <pein>. Placing them at the end of the word *Leim*, we will have <leiw>, <leib>, <leif>, and <leip>. We find no trace of an M in any of these words.

It is only with respect to B that we might agree that there is some similarity with M, if we wish to assume that the air, which for this letter resonates in a confined manner, issues through the nose. In fact, some people with a congested nose do use a B instead of an M. They will say <banger> for *manger*, but not on purpose. By habit, they close their mouth as if for an M and try to make the air issue through their nose, but, finding the exit blocked, the air resonates as if it were enclosed, which, according to our theory, is one of the principal characteristics of a B. Nevertheless, an attentive ear will not allow the perception of an error and will always hear <banger>. However, one usually allows that he has understood the speaker. This could have provided a basis for the idea that an M can sometimes be replaced by another letter.

Flaws in the pronunciation of the letter M

§ 173

Since M is so simple and so easily formed, any defect in its pronunciation or exchange with another letter will rarely be noted. One defect may be found in people who, as we have said, have a congested nose and say <barbontel> instead of *Marmontel*.

N

§ 174

There are four different Ns, which, though they are represented by the same symbol in writing, are however pronounced differently. We shall begin with the universal N, as it is pronounced in the alphabet of all nations. The other three are only derivations, the explanation of which will follow. The natural sound of the N, as it is pronounced in the Latin word *nemini*, is a consonant of the third class, a *simple voiced consonant*, which is also called a *nasal sound*. The position of the organs is as follows:

1. The glottis resonates.
2. The nose is unblocked.
3. The tongue, with its tip flattened, is pressed against the palate immediately behind the upper incisor teeth and completely blocks the channel of the tongue.
4. The teeth play no part at all.
5. The mouth is open at will.

4: ON THE SOUNDS AND LETTERS OF EUROPEAN LANGUAGES 127

With the organs of speech in this position, it will first be noted that the N does not differ from the preceding letter, M, save that for M the channel of the tongue is closed by the lips, and for N the channel is closed by the tongue itself. For both, the voice issues through the nose (see Table XVI, Fig. 1)

The position of the tongue for an N is the same as that for a D or a T. Thus, if one wished to pronounce *Aente* in German, the position of the tongue would not change from the N to the T. One must only block the nose in the position for an N, and the start of a T is already at hand. The T itself is realized when the point of the tongue detaches itself from the palate. This letter is one of those which, at the beginning of a word, cannot be followed by another consonant.

The three derivations or deviations from this true common N are the following:

1. The French N as it is pronounced in *an*, and in German in *Anker*.
2. The <gn>, belonging to the French language and several others, as in *seigneur* and *campagne*.
3. The French N as it is pronounced in *en*, *enlever*, and *ainsi*.

The tongue is in a different position in each of these cases. The one thing they all have in common with the ordinary N is that the nose is unblocked in every case. We will consider each one individually.

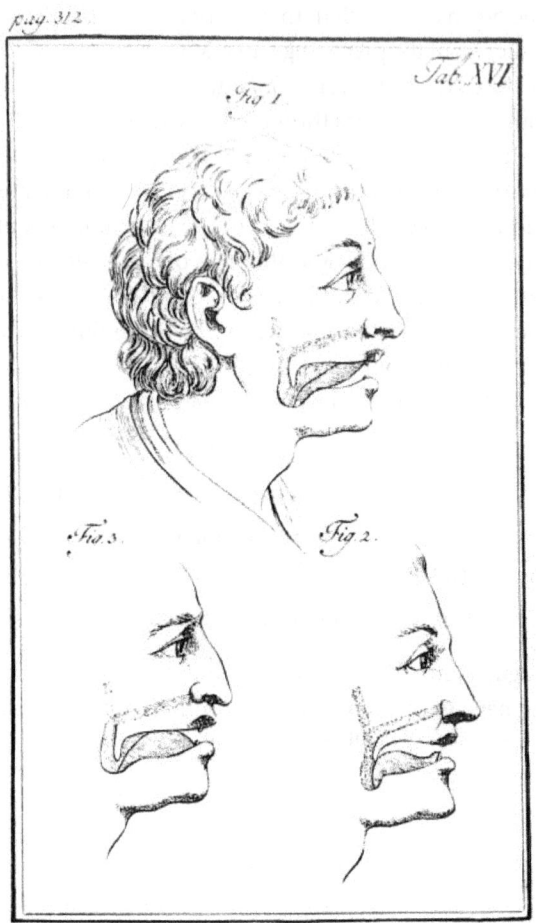

§ 175

The French N in *an* and the German N in *Anker* are formed when the tongue blocks its channel with its posterior portion, that is to say, when it sets its back portion upright and takes the position required for a *gamma* (see Table XVI, Fig. 2). This N is used in all languages when it is followed by a G or a K. In German, take for example *lang, Dank, eng, denken, schwung,* and *Prunk,* or in Latin take *fingo, tinctura, Hungaria,* and *Sanctus,* and so on in all other languages derived from these. The reason for this is obvious. Since N does not require anything other than that the channel of the tongue be blocked and the nose unblocked, Nature here takes the shortest path. Since the ensuing letter also requires that the channel of the tongue be blocked, it takes advantage of the situation and prepares for the letter to follow, having nothing to do then but to unblock the nose and re-block when a <ga> or a K must sound. Conversely, if Nature wanted to use the ordinary N, it would first have had to raise the tip of the tongue against the palate (as in Fig. 1). Then, after the N, it would have had to lower the tip of the tongue promptly and raise its posterior portion in order to form the <ga> or K (as in Fig. 2). This movement of the tongue would always require some time so that such an N would never be linked to a <ga> or a K. For, if Nature repressed the voice during the transition from an N to a K, an interval would be observed and the French words <en-core> and <en-gager> would be heard, but if it allowed the voice to resonate, we would hear <enecore> and <enegager>.

§ 176

Secondly, the <gn>, as it is pronounced in the French word *campagne*, is common to many languages. In Italian it is used in *signore*, *segno* and *impegno*. In Hungarian it is written as *ny*, as in *nyar* and *hany*, and in the Slavic language, as in *Panye* and *Swinye*. The Germans do not have it except in a few borrowed foreign words such as *Schampagner* and *Compagnie*. However, many people unfamiliar with the <gn> sound pronounce it as a common N, as in <schampanier> and <companie>.

The difference between this sound and the two preceding ones does not consist of anything more than a change in the position of the tongue, which in this case is not lifted by its tip or by its posterior portion, but by its center. It blocks the channel of the tongue by pushing against the palate (as in Fig. 3). The theory we have adopted, namely that the difference in tones very much depends on the size of the space within the mouth to be filled by air, is clearly confirmed here. Let us compare the three figures. The first, which represents the common N, has the largest space, and the second, which represents N as it is pronounced in <gn>, has the smallest.[34]

---

34. Valis [Wallis] must have already observed that the space within the nose, through which the voice passes, is of great importance, because he says "Si vero spiritus totus ad nares dirigatur, aërem in oris concavo manentem solummodo in transitu concutiens. De sonorum formatione" [If indeed all breath is sent toward the nostrils, striking the air remaining in the hollow of the mouth only in passing]. *On the formation of sounds.* (Wallis and Kemp, 1972)

§ 177

For the third N, it is generally agreed that the N as it is pronounced by the French in *enlever* or *enfin* is the one that resonates through the nose the most. However, in studying the matter more thoroughly, we will find that precisely the opposite is true. During its pronunciation less voice issues through the nose than for all the others, even though the nose is completely unblocked.

To explain more clearly, the two exits, the nose and the channel of the tongue, as well as the mouth, are completely open. Thus, the voice, which for the other letters only issues through one of these exits, in this case encounters both openings. Consequently, the part of the voice that exits through the nose must be weaker than it is for all the other Ns, where the undivided current of air issues only through the nose.

The reason why the N in *en*, in spite of this, still seems to resonate through the nose more than all the other Ns will become immediately obvious if we reconsider the matter from another point of view, and think of it as nothing but a vowel for which the nose is simultaneously open. When I want to pronounce <en> in French, as in the word *enlever*, I sound an A whilst leaving the nose open, which is what produces the true sound of an <en>. It is true for all other vowels, such as the <on> in *bonté*, and the <ain> in *ainsi*. For, as we said earlier, the nose must be blocked for all the vowels. If it is not, the vowel is distorted, and the ear, hearing a nasal sound where it should not be, is so offended that one is led to believe that he is hearing nothing but a louder than normal nasal sound.

We experience the same thing with other senses. With the sense of taste, when we find a dish too salty, we exaggerate and say that the dish is pure salt, even though it is far from saturated.[35]

§ 178

One other observation to be made is that when a vowel is followed by an N, it is always pronounced with an unblocked nose, as if it were to be followed by an N of the third class. Take for example the Latin words *ante*, *ens*, *inde* and *unde*, the French words *animer* and *bonnet*, and the German words *Anstand*, *binden* and *ohne*. This probably takes place in order to save a detour and to

---

35. Valis [see Wallis and Kemp 1972] made some excellent observations on the first two Ns, but he said nothing about the origin of the last two. And perhaps he could say nothing about them, especially the last one, because no one, as yet, has pointed out the existence of such an N in human speech in spite of the fact that it is frequently encountered in the French language.

avoid competition between several movements that would be too difficult to execute accurately. For, if the nose is already unblocked for the preceding vowel, one needs no other movement for the N than pressing the tip of the tongue against the palate. Conversely, if the nose were blocked during the pronunciation of the vowel, as it must be in all other cases, and only had to open for the N, this would have to come about at the very moment the tongue pushed against the palate. If this were not done with the greatest exactitude, an intermediate and foreign sound would always be heard, for example a D as in <edns> for *ens*, <udnde> for *unde*, and <adnstadnd> for *Anstand*.

Flaws in the pronunciation of N

§ 179

The majority of the errors committed in the pronunciation of N are the interchanges between its four different qualities, namely when one is used where the other should be. This rarely happens when someone is speaking in his mother tongue, but quite commonly when one is learning a foreign language. Thus, an Italian will transpose the N he uses in *bonta*, *vendere*, and *pensare* into the French words *bonté*, *vendre*, and *penser* and will thereby immediately reveal that he is not a Frenchman. Similarly, a German student will use the same N in the French word *sonder* as he would use in the German word *sonder*. The Frenchman will do the opposite.

Another very noticeable bad habit is due to a natural defect or a disease of the organs. Those people whose noses are completely blocked usually use an L instead of an N and will say <lourir> instead of *nourir*. They do place their tongue in position for an N, but cannot produce that sound because they cannot force air through their nose. They try to find another exit for the air without changing the principal position of the N, and consequently, they forcefully push the point of the tongue against the palate, as if for an N , but lower the middle of the tongue just enough to allow the air to escape from both sides, which, according to our principles, should produce an L.

P

§ 180

The letter P is a mute consonant of the first class. Children learn it easily, pronouncing it as well as a B, saying *baba* or *papa*. It is also called a hard labial sound or a hard *P*. Since we already spoke of its origin and its characteristics in discussing B because of its analogy with that letter, we have nothing further to add here.

Flaws in the pronunciation of P

§ 181

No flaws in the pronunciation of this letter have been observed.

R

§ 182

R is a consonant of the fourth class, that is to say a consonant that is spirant and voiced at the same time. It is the most difficult letter to pronounce. There are entire nations that do not know it and adults can rarely learn how to pronounce it.[36]

Its position is the following:

1. The voice resonates.
2. The nose is blocked.
3. The flattened and fluttering tip of the tongue is placed against the palate, initially behind the upper incisors.
4. The teeth take no part in the pronunciation.
5. The lips are open to the third or fourth degree.

This sound is produced by a very rapid movement of the tip of the tongue that strikes the palate. This movement is not produced by the muscles of the tongue,[37] but solely by the air that rushes between the tip of the tongue and the palate. The tongue, which is almost in the position for a T, always strives to remain attached to the palate, while the air strives to detach it. Thus, the alternative triumphs of these two forces follow one another with the greatest

---

36. R, being the most difficult letter to pronounce, becomes even more difficult when it is preceded by a B, P, or W. There are, however, no difficulties at all with D and T. The inhabitants of Otaheite could never learn how to pronounce *pr, br*, etc., although they pronounced R very well when it fell between two vowels. There are entire nations that do not have this letter in their language and for whom it is, consequently, impossible to pronounce. *Adelung's Critical Dictionary. The Letter R* [1793].

37. No other part of the human body has muscles that can produce such a rapid movement. The most rapid trill of the best trained singer is very slow in comparison with the rapid vibrations of the tongue when R is being pronounced.

rapidity, resulting in a vibration of the tongue comparable to the vibration of the glottis. However, in the latter case there are two vibrating membranes, while the tip of the tongue vibrates alone and has more extended vibrations or oscillations. The embouchure of a clarinet can serve as an example here; its reed is certainly not made to vibrate by any muscles, but by the introduction of air, and an alternating resistance due to the natural elasticity of the bamboo from which the reed is made. It should also be noted that there must be a fixed ratio between the force of the air trying to push its way through and the resistance from the tongue seeking to impede it, without one or the other gaining the dominance. Otherwise, the tongue would either remain attached to the palate, or the dominance of the air would always keep it at a distance. Once again, the clarinet can serve as an example. If the reed is compressed harder by the lips, one must blow with greater force to produce a sound. On the other hand, if the reed is compressed too little and the air is blown in with too much force, no sound will be produced.

The lack of this equilibrium, which many people never in their life succeed in attaining, is the reason why the R is so often mutilated and mangled in various ways.

§ 183

One very singular observation to be made is that to pronounce the R, air forced out of the lungs is made to vibrate twice: once by the glottis in the larynx, where it becomes voiced, and a second time near the tip of the tongue, where it encounters resistance and becomes an R.[38]

When one speaks loudly, the voice must always be made to sound, which is what makes R a vocal consonant. But when one speaks softly, the air, devoid of sound, only produces a slight trembling at the tip of the tongue which resembles the noise a butterfly makes with its wings when it is held between the fingers. In ordinary conversation, when R is not linked to other letters, the tongue will not vibrate much more than three times. However, when it is pronounced distinctly and on its own, it may require one or two more. If it is allowed to vibrate as much, or more, when it is linked with other letters, a double RR will result. In *repos*, there will be three vibrations,

---

38. We can go further and make the air vibrate three times during the same interval if, in maintaining or prolonging the R, the mouth is closed to the degree it is closed for a U. The lips will then follow the same movement by exactly imitating every vibration of the tongue. However, this movement of the lips is not necessary for speech, and only occurs only when one is enunciating in a vicious manner.

in *narré* there may be six or more, the number being very difficult to determine exactly because of the great speed.

The Bohemian RSCH

§ 184

Although R is one of the most difficult letters to pronounce, the Bohemians make it even more difficult by adding or incorporating a SCH. It is impossible to give an exact idea of this sound to someone who has never heard the Bohemian language. A SCH and an R are heard simultaneously, but both are heard imperfectly. This cannot be described except by saying that the tongue is in the position for SCH and does not touch the palate completely during its vibrations, but always leaves a small opening through which the hissing tone, accompanied by the voice, can pass without interruption.

Flaws in the pronunciation of R

§ 185

Without a doubt this letter is subject to a number of especially diverse flaws. If neglected in childhood, these flaws are very difficult—often impossible—to correct at an older age. R is sometimes pronounced in a manner completely contrary to the way it should be. Some pronounce it too vigorously and the sound is stretched too long, while others omit it entirely. The former use the same R in *rose* as they use in *charriage*, the latter say <ose> and <chaiage>.

The most common error is burring. Since children often do not know how to go about forming this very difficult letter, they try different positions of the tongue. If they find one that produces vibrations similar to those of an R, they keep it. Satisfied with having found the rumbling sound and being understood, they do not worry about any other R. But where does burring come from? It is due to the fact that the soft part of the palate performs the functions of the tongue. The posterior portion of the tongue lifts itself, almost as if for a K, until it lightly touches the soft part of the palate or the outer surface of the soft palate that keeps the nose blocked. If the air then forces its way through, the tongue will actually oppose it, but the soft part of the palate, which rests lightly against the tongue, yields by alternately rising and falling, which creates vibrations similar to those of the true R.³⁹ In this manner the organs are used in reverse. Here the tongue performs the function of the palate for the true R, that is to say it is the immobile part, while the soft part of the palate performs the functions of the tongue and becomes the oscillating part. But, as already stated, it is not easy to substitute one organ for the other during speech and not have the ear immediately perceive the difference. There are also different degrees of burring. Some people burr their R excessively while others know how to moderate it so expertly and imitate the true R so well that one cannot tell the difference without very close attention.⁴⁰

While some people make R resonate by vibrating their lips, as we said earlier, others replace it with another letter: for example, they pronounce *bravo* with a W <bwavo>. Others use a T and say <btavo> while still others replace R with L or H <blavo> or <bahavo>. I cannot confirm that all these flaws can be corrected; I have not corrected anyone, but it is also true that I have never seriously tried.

S

§ 186

The letter S is a consonant of the second class, a spirant consonant. The position of the organs for its pronunciation is as follows:

1. The voice is silent.
2. The nose is blocked.
3. The anterior portion of the tongue is pressed against the palate so that its curved point still touches the base of the lower teeth (see Table VI. Fig. 5).

---

39. Amman [1694] thought that many people were unable to pronounce an R because the tip of their tongue was too thick and consequently heavier than its posterior portion, rendering the formation of this letter very difficult for them, even in the throat. But let the tip of the tongue be as thick as it wishes, its posterior portion will always be proportionally thicker and always incapable of vibrating. It is therefore only the soft part of the palate that vibrates. It is in this manner that Amman sometimes made errors in his observations. Nevertheless, I prefer him to all the other authors who have discussed this subject, because his observations, on the whole, are the most exact and the most carefully determined.

40. It seemed to me that in Paris at least a quarter of the population burred their R not because they could not pronounce a true R but because they liked it and have made it fashionable. Unfortunately, this fashion will not end as other fashions do because entire families have forgotten how to form the lingual R and trilling will be transmitted from generation to generation.

4. The teeth are not absolutely necessary, but they serve to sharpen the sound of the S.

5. The lips are open at will.

Since we described this letter at length in § 86 during the discussion of the organs of speech, I refer readers to that section.

This letter is identical in all languages and is also written in the same manner. Only the Germans have several forms ſ, s, ſz, but they almost always pronounce it in the same manner. The Hungarians, who make use of the Latin characters in their writing, give S the SCH sound, for example they pronounce *sas* as <schasch>. If it should be pronounced like a Latin S, they add a Z as in *szo*, and *szent*. We have already mentioned that the French use a C instead of an S.

When S is at the beginning of a word and is followed by a vowel, it is pronounced as was explained here. In the middle of words, however, it is often pronounced like the French Z: the French *rosée* and *misere*, and the German *Wiese* and *Mäuse* are pronounced *rozée, mizere, Wieze,* and *Mäuze*.[41]

In German, when a word begins with an S and is immediately followed by a consonant, it is always written with a *sch* and is pronounced in the same manner. If the second letter is a mute consonant, only the S is used in writing, but it is still pronounced as a SCH, for example in *Span* and *Stein*. For all the other consonants the hissing tone of the SCH is formed first, as *Schlaf, Schmaus, Schnee, Schrift*. In English, S combines with almost all the consonants like *scarp, skin, slave, smoke, snow, spoon, stone,* and *sweet*. Only the R forms an exception. There is not a single word in Latin, or in the French language derived from it, nor in the German or English languages that begins with *Sr*. In Latin, a C is always placed between them as in *scribo, scrotum,* or *scrutor*. The Germans and the English prefer to use the hissing tone rather than the S and say *Schraube, Schrecken, Schrift, shrimp,* and *shroud*.

This is probably due to the fact that the tip of the tongue is pressed against the lower teeth for an S as we said earlier, and has to contract slightly and press against the palate in order to make the transition into an R. However if a SCH is used, the tip of the tongue is already against the palate, almost exactly where it should be for an R. Consequently, the

---

41. It must be noted that we are not discussing the German Z (tset) here, otherwise we would hear *Wietse, Mäutse*. We are assuming a Z as it is pronounced in *mazette, horizon*. Since in German we have an S accompanied by a Z (sz), we could be more precise and use it when the S should be pronounced like the French Z. We would then write *Speiszen, raszen, reiszen*. Where *sz* is now used instead of a double *s*, we would always use *ss* and write *Ross* instead of *Rosz*, and *Strauss* instead of *Strausz*. How is a foreigner to know that the S in *sagen* is different from the S in *rasen*? However, these are all grammatical observations that fall outside the scope of this work.

transition from SCH to R is easier than it is from S to R and it is for this reason that the shortest and most convenient route would be favored.[42]

Flaws in the formation of S

§ 187

Since the tone of this letter has a quality something like whistling, it requires great precision. If the tongue is not firmly pressed at the appropriate point, the whistling quality immediately becomes either too strong or weak. This is why one finds such a variety of flaws in pronunciation in so many people.

Some push the tip of the tongue forwards against the incisors and thus produce a more obtuse sound, similar to an F.

Some push the middle of the tongue against the palate and so produce a sound similar to a SCH.

Others replace the S with an F and say <la faifon est faine> instead of *la saison est saine*.

In forming S and SCH, some people place their tongues in the position for an L, but, instead of the voice necessary to form the L, they produce voiceless air which gives a warbling tone far from the true sound of an S or SCH.

People who dwell too long on each S also produce a unique effect by sounding a double S where only a single one should be heard. For example, they say <ssoyés ssatisfait de ssavoir ssaigner>.

A very comical manner of pronouncing S is found in those people who substitute a perfect SCH for an S and say <Esch ischt schon die schönschte tscheit verfloschen>.

Many people think that changing all the Ss into the French Z we discussed earlier will give their elocution more zest and energy. I have heard a few of the more skilful actors say on stage: <Zo tief zind zie gezunken> instead of *So tief sind sie gesunken*.

---

42. De Brosses [1765] was very much mistaken when in his treatise on the mechanics of language formation he named this consonant a *nasal consonant*. He says: "The nose forms the second duct for the instrument. Its hiss, or the nasal letter *se*, is used frequently and ubiquitously because of the habit people have of pushing the sound from their mouth into their nose, or of redirecting it from the nose into the mouth. It differs from Z only in that it has a *rough path* along the nostrils while the Z has a *smooth path* along the palate." It is inconceivable how they could have sought the S sound in the nose, which is completely blocked and cannot have the slightest role in its formation, as we have already said. One cannot understand what De Brosses wants to say in this passage.

SCH

§ 188

In German, these three letters taken together denote the hissing tone that the Hebrews mark with ש, the French with *ch*, the English with *sh*, the Italians with *sc*, and the Hungarians with an S.[43] It is closer to a hiss than to the common S and differs fundamentally from the latter because the tongue has an entirely different position. It is pushed against the palate with its tip curved upwards, thus forming the small opening which, for the ordinary S, is formed by the middle of the tongue (see Tab. VI. Fig. 5). The rest of the position is identical to that for an S. It should be noted here that the air has different spaces to fill, namely that space situated before the narrow passage of the channel of the tongue, and later, the space it encounters beyond this passage, as can be seen in Figures *a* and *b* of the same table. The direction that the air takes in this position also contributes much to render the sound more whistle-like because, for an S it is driven through an arched channel whereas, in this case, it must bend over a more cutting edge which here is the tip of the tongue. This creates the sharp hissing, so to speak.[44] This letter is of the second class, that is to say a spirant consonant.

§ 189

In some Italian provinces they have a distinctive S that falls halfway between the common S and the SCH. This is due to the fact that the tip of the tongue is curved upward as for a SCH, but it is pressed against the palate further forward, almost against the upper teeth.

---

43. "It is certainly very inconvenient to have to express this simple sound with three different letters S, C, and H, and most irksome in spelling. Many scholars, most recently Mr. Mazke, have proposed using a special symbol for this sound. Especially since the Hebrews, among others, have already given us an example with their *schin*, the idea should be even more acceptable." *Adelung's Critical Dictionary* [1793].

44. Here again Amman [1694] was mistaken when he said *Si spiritui transitus, ob linguam depressiorem, amplior est, S, fit obtusius, quod Germani reddunt per sch, Galli per ch* [If the passageway for the breath is more ample because of a more depressed tongue, the S becomes thicker, which the Germans render as *sch*, the French a *ch*.

Flaws in the pronunciation of SCH

§ 190

The most repulsive flaw, at least to my ear, is when people, instead of pronouncing a SCH, push voiceless air through their nose with the channel of the tongue blocked. They might as well be about to blow their nose in the middle of a conversation.

Those who do not have a SCH in their own language but replace it with an S seem to have something effeminate about them. In Germany this is not too noticeable, because there are entire provinces that speak in this manner. However, it becomes insufferable in English, French, and Hungarian and leads to a thousand *quid pro quos*. If, for example, one hears <saux>, one might think it is a question of *sceau* and not of *chaux*, <santre> could be mistaken for *centre* and not *chantre*, <sant> for *sang* and not *chant*. Similarly, many misunderstandings can occur in German if one says <er hat sie gehasst> instead of *er hat sie gehascht*, or <sie vermisst alle Speisen> instead of *sie vermischt alle Speisen*. There are many Italians who, while speaking French, use the intermediate sound between an S and an SCH that was discussed above, and say <s'ai santé une sanson> instead of *j'ai chanté une chanson*.

It is not difficult to correct these mistakes, if one has a serious desire to do so. I have put many people on the right path in a few minutes simply by demonstrating the correct position of the tongue to them.

There are people who sustain the SCH as well as the S for too long—they double them, so to speak—saying <Waschschen>, <Umschschtand> and <Schschtunden>. The best advice in this case is moderation.

Finally, there are some people who pronounce SCH like the French J as it is pronounced in *jamais*. They say <jweige von deiner Jande> instead of *schweige von deiner Schande*. These people only have to be told to suppress the voice and they will have a correct SCH. This will become even clearer in the discussion of the next letter.

J

§ 191

I did not place this letter after the vowel I, but rather here after the SCH because it does not have a single connection to I and is similar to it in form only, the tail added to its extremity being the only distinction. On the other hand, this letter is very close to the SCH in pronunciation. The sound we shall discuss here is that of the J produced in the French words *jamais*, *jurer*, and *déjà*, or the G in *genie*, and *venger*. It is a consonant of the fourth class: spirant and voiced at the same time.

Its position is the same as that for an SCH, and differs only in that the SCH consists of air alone, while the voice also takes part in sounding a J. If one wishes to pronounce this sound perfectly, one only has to prolong the SCH and allow the voice to sound. Air is then reunited with the voice, to form a true J. J can be defined, in a few words, as a SCH accompanied by the voice. The German language does not have this sound. The Italians have it in *gia, oggi*, and *giorno*, and many other words that they always write with a G but pronounce as if a D were inserted before the G and the words were written as <dja>, <oddji>, <djorno>.

The English, like the French, have it in both forms, sometimes as a G and at other times as a J. In pronunciation, however, they always place a D before it, as in *German, gently, join*, and *judge*, which they pronounce as <djerman>, <djently>, <djoin>, <djudge>. The reason for this can again be derived from nature and the economy of speech. A comparison will serve us best.

§ 192

If one wishes to remove dust or tobacco from a piece of paper by blowing on it, one will need more air and blow with greater force than for ordinary speech. Some purse their lips into a small opening, as if they want to pronounce W, and will push their lips and blow air through with force. Others will close their mouth tightly, compress the air in their lungs and let it escape all at once through a small opening of the lips. Both are successful methods in achieving their aim of removing the dust. It should be noted that J is the letter that demands the greatest effort from the air and the voice. Some make this effort immediately and produce a J on the spot like the French. Others, who do not believe they can do this directly, have another method. They first completely block the channel of the tongue with the tongue, expanding the air in the mouth to prepare in advance for the burst which must follow. They then slightly detach the tip of the tongue from the palate, thus the voice gains space and bursts into a <dj>, as we said earlier in discussing breath. Therefore, this last J is not a true J, but a J accompanied by another sound. It is this J that the Italians and English use.

Flaws in the pronunciation of J

§ 193

No flaws are committed in the pronunciation of this sound other than exchanges with other letters. There are entire provinces in France and in Italy where it is not given its true sound. Many Frenchmen say <déscha> and <schamais> for *déjà* and *jamais*; the Italians say <dia> and <diorno> for *gia* and *giorno*. Germans have a difficult time with Js when they learn foreign languages because they do not have it in their own. One can find Germans who speak French well and fluently, but with the flaw of changing all the Js into SCHs. For example, they say <sche ne schure schamais> for *je ne jure jamais*. In order to teach them how to pronounce a J, they should be directed to prolong their SCH for a while, and then make their voice sound at the same time; they will be astonished to find how easily they can produce this sound that they thought so difficult. They will master the Italian *gia* even more easily by inserting a D before it and pronouncing <dscha>. Here we have assumed that they have mastered the D, and can make the distinction between D and T, otherwise they might say <tscha>. In that case one would have to begin by teaching them the D, following the method specified earlier.

T

§ 194

T is a consonant of the first class, a mute consonant. Its position is exactly the same as for D and therefore unnecessary to repeat. The only difference between these two letters is that for D the voice resonates, whereas it is completely silent for T. T also differs in the compressed air that bursts out when the tongue is pulled away from the palate. The T, therefore, has no sound of its own, and becomes intelligible through the subsequent sound, or solely by the eruption of air, which creates some noise. In order to be heard, the immediately following sound can never be a consonant of the first class, or a mute consonant, and must always be from one of the three other classes. Moreover, even among these there are some that do not combine with a T. B, D, G, CH, M, J, and Z cannot be linked to this letter. If, for example, *entbinden* is pronounced, a slight breath will be heard between the T and the B as it is in *mitgehen, entmannet*, etc. On the other hand, F, H, N, R, S, SCH, V, and W combine very well with a T, as in *entführen, That*, and *Zunge*, which are pronounced <Tsunge>, <entstehen>, and <quetschen>[45]; the English words *twelve, twenty* etc. [show that W combines well with T][46]. Very often, even the T at the end of a word is linked to the first letter of the following word; *mit seiner Hand* is pronounced as if it were written <mitseiner Hand>, and *mit Ruhm, mit Schimpf* are pronounced as <Mitruhm> and <Mitschimpf>.

§ 195

To avoid becoming tedious, I shall give only a couple of examples for each of the two aforementioned cases. The reason why the T does not link itself to a B or a G is the following: to pronounce a T, the tip of the tongue must block the exit for the air, and in order to be heard, the air must burst out at the very moment the tongue leaves the palate. For a B, the mouth is closed by the lips, while for a G, the channel of the tongue is closed by the posterior portion of the tongue. It is therefore impossible for the air to issue when another obstacle opposes it. Thus, to render the T intelligible, <enthbinden> and <mithgehen> will always be heard, the H here being regarded as nothing but a short aspiration. If one were to omit it, <enbinden> and <migehen> would be heard.

In the second case, where T is followed by F, S or SCH, the channel of the tongue or of the mouth is not completely closed for any of these letters. The lips are set for an F at same time that the T should burst out. The air is thus confronted with the position for an F, through which it issues together with the sound of a T. The same is true for S or SCH. If the tongue drops only slightly from the palate, the position for an S or SCH is formed, and while the air for T escapes, it hisses in the manner that these letters require. Consequently, the intermediate aspiration is no longer necessary, and we do not hear *enthführen, Thsunge,* and *enthstehen*. All of the above, with the necessary modifications, is easily applicable to the two other mute consonants, K and P.

§ 196

In addition to the ordinary T, the English have another T that they write as TH.[47] In pronunciation, however, it has no connection with either the T

---

45. The mismatches between the two sets of words are present in the original text. –the eds.

46. We have added the section in square brackets so that this clause makes sense. –the eds.

47. This is probably the sound the Greeks denote with their θ or ϑ, which in their

or the H of which it is composed. This sound belongs rather to the category of Fs. Recall what was said earlier about F in §§ 144 and 145. Just as the upper teeth press over the lower lip and allow the air to escape through a small opening to produce an F, here they press against the tip of the tongue instead of the lips to produce a TH. All the rest is the same as for an F, but the TH is not always pronounced in the same manner. Sometimes it is formed by air alone as in *thought* and *third*. At other times it is accompanied by the voice as in *they are*. Thus, these two methods of pronunciation have the same affinity between them as that between F and V, which we shall discuss more amply when describing V.[48]

Flaws in the pronunciation of T

§ 197

T, being one of the easiest letters, and the one that children first learn to pronounce after P, is rarely mispronounced. There will be some people in the population who, instead of pushing the tip of their tongue against the palate, rest it against the lower teeth and use its midsection to form the T. However, these people are either simple or partially deaf, and their language has something primitive about it in general.

V

§ 198

The letter V is a consonant of the fourth class, *spirant and vocal at the same time*. Its true sound is the one it has in Latin, French, Italian and almost all the other European languages, for example in *vivo, verité,* and *voglio*. Only in German is it pronounced as a true F when it occurs at the beginning of words. When it falls between two vowels it is sometimes given its true sound, as in *Sclave*.

---

language is an intermediate sound between δ and τ.

48. Adelung says: "The hissed Θ or *th* of the Greeks, Anglo-Saxons and Modern English does not exist in our language at present, and it has not been proven that it has ever existed."

§ 199

The position of V is exactly the same as that for an F and differs only in that to pronounce it, the voice sounds, making it a spirant and vocal consonant at the same time. An experiment using the pronunciation of *ferus* will demonstrate this. Prolong the spirant sound of the F for some time, and then let the voice resonate in the same position without any change. The F will first change into a V and, if *erus* is pronounced afterwards, *verus* will be heard. Thus, these two [Latin] words, which according to German pronunciation should have the same meaning, will denote two different ideas, namely *ferus*, meaning 'savage', and *verus*, meaning 'true'.

§ 200

Some people are of the opinion that V is only a reinforced or sharper W, and in a sense they are correct. If the upper teeth are used for the first of these letters, the sound should be sharper than it is for the second, which is formed with the lips. However, if the matter is examined in depth, one will find that V is fundamentally different from W, because different organs are used for the two, as we shall soon see.

This letter has been badly confused with U in dictionaries, tables of contents, indices, etc. in spite of the fact that it fundamentally differs from U.[49] The Germans call it *Vau* or *Fau* to distinguish it, probably after the Hebrew Vav.

Flaws in the pronunciation of V

§ 201

This letter is not subject to any difficulties other than the exchange with F and W which happens, above all, in the German language wherein they say <Larfe>, <Pulfer>, <Falentin>, and <Fagabund>. The Germans, not content with having changed the V into an F at the beginning of words in their own language, also transpose this erroneous pronunciation into foreign languages they learn. They say <focatifus, feni, fidi, fici, and Brafo>, or, if they wish to avoid the F, they will use the softest sound of a W, and they will say <weni,

---

49. Adelung, in his Critical Dictionary [1793], was right in separating these two letters and treating them as two different sounds. He also made very beautiful and persuasive observations about V. Nevertheless, I do not agree with him that the V was pronounced as a W when it was a consonant in Latin.

widi, wici> instead of *veni, vidi, vici.* Above all, the F creates many mistranslations when, for example, they say <fel> for *vel,* <fere> for *vere,* and <fas> for *vas,* etc. However, this does not all happen because the Germans do not have this sound in their pronunciation; on the contrary, they very frequently use it instead of a W, which we shall see when we discuss W.

W

§ 202

W is also a consonant of the fourth class, a spirant and vocal consonant at the same time. The position is as follows:

1. The voice sounds.
2. The nose is blocked.
3. The tongue expands or contracts its channel according to the requirements of the vowel that follows.
4. The teeth take no part in the process.
5. The lips are closed except for a very small, almost longitudinal, opening.

For a W, the edges of both lips are contracted as if for a B without, however, closing them entirely, and leaving enough of an opening so that the air can pass through. The voice resonates as for a B, with the difference in this case that it is not completely confined, but has an exit between the lips. However, since this exit is very small, there are two consequences: firstly, the partially confined voice can resonate only softly; and secondly, the air must issue with force and thus create a sound similar to that of the wind. It is the combination of these two actions that forms a W. To render the definition more precise, the W is nothing but a breath accompanied by the voice. If one holds his hand in front of his mouth while saying *wo*, he will feel the flow of air during the W, which ends when O begins.

§ 203

The channel of the tongue does not always keep the same width: this depends on the vowel that follows. The tongue prepares itself in advance, expanding or contracting its channel according to the requirements of each vowel that follows. If, for example, someone says *wille*, the tongue will be in the position for an I at the start of the W: the tongue will only be open to the first degree. If on the other hand one wishes to say *wunde*, which is pronounced <wounde>, the tongue lowers significantly during the W, and the channel of the tongue will widen to the fifth degree, so that the <ou> that follows does not require any further movement of the tongue. This characteristic is common to all other consonants where the lips are the principal organs and are, for this reason, named labial consonants, such as B, F, M, P, V, and W.

This is yet another example of the economy of Nature, who here, as on all other occasions, seizes the moment when the tongue is not engaged and uses it to prepare for the positions of the letter to follow, even as the lips are forming the first letter. It is the same process *vice versa* when the tongue is the principal organ in forming a letter: the lips, instead of remaining idle, prepare for the sound to follow. If, for example, we say *libre* or *labirinthe*, the lips have already taken the position for an I or an A during the pronunciation of the L. All of this happens instinctively, without any self-direction, or even any conscious thought.

§ 204

The [ancient] Romans, French, Italians, and Hungarians do not have a W. The English use it in writing, but in pronouncing it they open their lips farther than the Germans. In this manner the sound resembles the wind less and becomes almost identical to the <ou>, or they pronounce W like a V, as in *Wool*.

It must be noted that in German the two letters V and W never have a consonant either before or after them, except in compound words such as *Wahnwitz, entweder, umwenden, Grossvater, unvollendet*, etc. The Slavic people, on the other hand, have many words where the *V* is linked with other consonants, such as *Vlassi*, etc.

Flaws in the pronunciation of W

§ 205

The W is far too simple a letter to be subject to incorrect pronunciations. Children say *wehweh* at a very early age but labial sounds have always been subject to many changes, and one is often used in place of the other. The same is also true of this letter; there are many people, principally in Germany, who frequently change W into a V or a B. They will say vird dem Vind viderstehen>, and by doing so think that they are giving a great deal of energy to their speech. Others, especially the inhabitants of the Carniole and the Italian Tyrol, say <Bei barmen Better trink ich benig Bein, aber viel Basser>.

Z

§ 206

In the general discussion of the alphabet in § 103 I mentioned that by this letter we do not mean the German Z, which is nothing but a combination of T and S, but the French Z, as pronounced in *zêle* and *gazon*; it is therefore a spirant and vocal consonant at the same time. It has exactly the same position as an S, the only difference being that it is accompanied by the voice, which changes the hissing of the S into a buzzing sound. Thus, when one begins to say S, and allows the voice to resonate in this position, one will have a true Z.

§ 207

This sound is also used in the German language. In writing, however, it is denoted by an S, and only usage teaches when S should be pronounced as Z. Normally, and I even believe always, it requires this pronunciation when it falls between two vowels in a word, as in *Lesen*, *Wiese*, and *Rasen*. At the beginning and end of words, it keeps its natural sound, as in *sein* and *Haus*.[50]

Flaws in the pronunciation of Z

§ 208

This Z is often transformed into the German Z as in *Horizon*, *zona*, and *Zodiacus*, which many Germans pronounce as *Horitson*, *tsona*, and *Tsodiacus*; or into S, as in the words *Zemire* and *Azor* which many pronounce as *Semire* and *Asor*. These individuals will never pronounce it any other way in their lives, unless their attention is drawn to the fact and they are reminded to make the voice resonate when they pronounce S. This flaw can be easily corrected if the speaker wishes to make a small amount of effort.

---

50. One can refer to what was said in the first footnote of § 186 in discussing S.

Supplement to the Consonants

§ 209

Every consonant can be linked with every vowel that can precede or follow it. The same is not true of linking one consonant with another. There are many that can only be linked at the beginning or end of a syllable, or both conditions simultaneously. On the other hand, we have a far greater number of consonants that do not allow any linkages at all, or at least we do not have any examples of such linkages in the European languages. In order to indicate the consonants that have this characteristic, I shall include as complete a table as possible for each consonant, where I shall demonstrate, with examples, those consonants that can be linked together. In the first column of the table, the two different consonants are at the beginning of a syllable, and in the second they are at the end. Blank lines indicate that I have been unable to find a single example in any of the languages I know. If any are discovered, space is allowed for their inclusion. These tables can be very useful in shortening the task of those who might wish to build a speaking machine with a keyboard that can be played like a harpsichord, because by using the tables they can omit the mechanisms required for combining consonants that are not linked.

Examples

B

	At the beginning of a syllable	At the end of a syllable
Bd	βδάλλω, bdellion	mobb'd (English)
Bf		
Bg		
Bh		
Bch		
Bk		
Bl	bleu, blanc, blame	table, foible, by omitting the e
Bm		
Bn		schreib'n (German)
Br	brun, brouillard	arbre, marbre (French)
Bs		
Bsch		
Bj		
Bt		([51])
Bv		
Bw		
Bz	Bezançon, since the e is not pronounced	limbs as limbz (English)

---

51. *Gehabt* and *geraubt* cannot be used here, for example, because even though these words are written with a B, they are pronounced *gehapt* and *geraupt*.

D

	At the beginning of a syllable	*At the end of a syllable*
Db		
Df		
Dg		
Dh		
Dch		
Dk		
Dl	dlho (Slavic)	Handl (German), fiddle (English)
Dm	δμωὴ	
Dn	Dnieper (the river)	Haydn (proper name)
Dp		
Dr	drame, dresser	
Ds		stands, finds (English)
Dsch		
Dj	giuro as djuro (Italian)	age, pronounced edj (English)
Dt		Stadt (German)
Dv		
Dw	dwell (English)	
Dz	zia, as dzia (Italian)	rids (English)

F

	At the beginning of a syllable	*At the end of a syllable*
Fb		
Fd		
Fg		
Fh		
Fch		
Fk		
Fl	flute, flanc	Tafl (German), ruffle (English)
Fm		
Fn		
Fp		
Fr	franc, froid	coffre, souffre
Fs		Erschufs (German)
Fsch	Fschahno (Bohemian)	
Fj		
Ft		Kraft, oft, Luft (German)
Fv		
Fw		
Fz		

G

	At the beginning of a syllable	*At the end of a syllable*
Gb		
Gd		Vàgd (Hungarian), hang[e]d
Gf		(English)
Gh		
Gch		
Gk		
Gl	gloire, gland	
Gm	Gmunden (proper name)	
Gn	Gnome	
Gp		
Gr	gratter, gros	tigre
Gs		Flugs (German)
Gsch		
Gj		
Gt		gesagt, gesiegt (German)
Gv		
Gw		
Gz	Xavier, which is pronounced gzavier in French	legs, pronounced legz (English)

H

	At the beginning of a syllable	At the end of a syllable
Hb		
Hd		
Hf		
Hg		
Hch		
Hk		
Hl	hledat (Slavic)	Wahl[52]
Hm		Ruhm[52]
Hn	hnet (Slavic)	Lohn[52]
Hp		
Hr	hrat (Slavic)	Fuhr[52]
Hs		
Hsch		
Hj		
Ht	hzem, pronounced htzem (Slavic)	
Hv		
Hw	whip, pronounced hwip (English)	
Hz		

52. *Wahl, Ruhm, Lohn,* and *Fuhr* are written with an H, but this is not pronounced and only serves as an indication that the vowels should be longer. Consequently this example can't be applied here.

CH

	At the beginning of a syllable	*At the end of a syllable*
Chb		
Chd		
Chf		
Chh		
Chg		
Chk		
Chl	Chlari (Swiss), instead of Klari	
Chm	Chmel (proper name)	
Chp		
Chr	χρυσὸς	
Chs		Friedrichs, Reichs (German)
Chsch		
Chj		
Cht		Acht, Recht, Sucht (German)
Chw		
Chz		

K

	At the beginning of a syllable	At the end of a syllable
Kb		
Kd	kdo (Slavic)	
Kf	Kfahr (Austrian German)	
Kh	Khind (German)	
Kch	kchlein (Swiss German)	
Kl	klein, Klotz (German)	fickle (English)
Km	kmischt (Austrian German)	
Kn	Knabe, Knopf (German)	denkn
Kp		
Kr	Kranz, Krieg (German)	acre, sacre
Ks	Xerxes, ξίφος ([53])	pax, stocks (English), ἄναξ
Ksch	Kschir (Austrian German)	
Kj		
Kt	kteri (Slavic), κτάω	Markt, welkt (German)
Kv		
Kw	Kwal, Kwelle (German)	
Kz		

---

53. In pronunciation *ks* is always the composite sound represented by X.

L

	At the beginning of a syllable	At the end of a syllable
Lb		Kalb, gelb (German)
Ld		Wald, Feld (German)
Lf		Wolf, Hülf (German)
Lg		Balg, Gefolg (German)
Lh		
Lch		Kelch, Milch (German)
Lk		Schalk, welk (German)
Lm		Halm, Schelm (German)
Lm		Zähl'n (German)
Lp		Alp (German), to help (English)
Lr		
Ls		Fels, Hals (German)
Lsch		falsch, wälsch (German)
Lj		
Lt		alt, Welt (German)
Lv		
Lw		
Lz		tails, nails (English)

M

	At the beginning of a syllable	*At the end of a syllable*
Mb		il tombe
Md		Hemd, Fremd (German)
Mf		
Mg		
Mh		
Mch		
Mk		
Ml	mlieko (Slavic)	Taum'l (German)
Mn	μνάομαι, mnoho (Slavic)	
Mp		Plump, Dampf (German)
Mr	Mraf (proper name, Bohemian)	
Ms		Adams, Wamms (German)
Msch		Nimsch (proper name, German)
Mj		
Mt		Amt, nimmt (German)
Mv		
Mw		
Mz		beams (English)

N

At the beginning of a syllable	At the end of a syllable
Nb	
Nd	Hand, Kind (German)
Nf	Hanf, Senf (German)
Ng	Klang (German), thing (English)[54]
Nh	
Nch	Mönch (German)
Nk	Dank, Wink (German)
Nm	
Nn	
Nr	
Ns	Hans, Zins (German)
Nsch	Mensch, Wunsch (German)[55]
Nj	
Nt	beka[n]nt, Testament (German)
Nv	
Nw	
Nz[56]	beams, pronounced beemz (English)

54. This is used here not in the pronunciation of the common N, but the N that is formed by the posterior portion of the tongue (see the description of the letter N, §174 to 179).

55. These are normally pronounced as *mendsch* and *wundsch*, or as *mentsch* and *wuntsch*.

56. *Kranz*, *Lenz*, and *Prinz* do not belong here as they are pronounced *Krants*, *Lents*, and *Prints*.

P

	At the beginning of a syllable	*At the end of a syllable*
Pb		
Pd		
Pf	Pfand, Pferd (German)	Kopf, Tropf (German)
Pg		
Ph		
Pch		
Pk		
Pl	place, plaine	apple (English)
Pm		
Pn	πνεῦμα	
Pr	prince, projet	apre
Ps	Psalmus[57]	lips, ships (English)
Psch	Pshaw (English)	hübsch, pronounced hüpsch (German)
Pj		
Pt	πτερὸν, πτόλεμος	haupt, geschupt (German)
Py		
Pw		
Pz		

---

57. The Greeks combined the two letters P and S into one letter, with the sign ψ; many words begin and end with this, such as ψιλὸς and μὰψ.

R

	At the beginning of a syllable	*At the end of a syllable*
Rb		starb, derb, Korb (German)
Rd		Pferd, Mord (German)
Rf		Dorf, Wurf (German)
Rg		Sarg, Berg (German)
Rh		
Rch		durch, Furcht (German)
Rl		Kerl, perl (German)
Rm		Arm, Sturm (German)
Rn		Kern, Horn (German)
Rp		stirp, sharp (English)
Rs		ars, mors (Latin)
Rsch		Hirsch, Bursch (German)
Rj[58]		large
Rt		Art, Hirt (German)
Rv		nerve (English)
Rw		
Rz		

---

58. R and J jointly form the Bohemian RSCH, which is almost impossible for foreigners to pronounce.

S

	At the beginning of a syllable	*At the end of a syllable*
Sb		
Sd		slic'd, minc'd (English)
Sf	sforzato (Italian), σφαῖρα, σφάλμα	
Sg		
Sh		
Sch	σχέτλιος	
Sk	scherzo (Italian), scandalum (Latin), sky (English)	ask, brisk (English)
Sl	slight (English)	
Sm	small, smelt (English), σμῆνος	Friesl (German)
Sn	snap, snuff (English)	
Sp	spes (Latin), spell (English)	
Sr	srezo (Slavic)	wisp, rasp (English)
Sch		
Sj		
St	status (Latin), steam (English)	
Sy		Last, Kost (German)
Sw	swear, sweet (English)	
Sz		

SCH

	At the beginning of a syllable	At the end of a syllable
Schb		
Schd		lasd, pronounced laschd (Hungarian)
Schf		
Schg		
Schh		
Schch		
Schk	scala, pronounced Schkala (Hungarian)	
Schl	Schlaf, schlau (German)	Hörschl (proper name)
Schm	Schmidt, Schmerz (German)	
Schn	Schnee, Schnur (German)	
Schp	Spatz, pronounced Schpatz (German)	
Schr	Schrift (German)	
Schs		
Schj		
Scht	Stall, pronounced Schtall (German)	durscht instead of durst (German)
Schv		
Schw	schwarz (German)	
Schz		

J

I only know a single word in which J is linked to the consonant that follows it, and it is *Zrat*, in the Slavic language, which is pronounced <jrat>.

T

	At the beginning of a syllable	At the end of a syllable
Tb		
Td		
Tf		
Tg		
Th	thin, thrift (English)	Spath, Nath (German)[59]
Tch		
Tk		
Tm		
Tn		tret'n, leist'n (German)
Tp		
Tr	trancher, trois	Mart'r, weit'r (German)
Ts	Zahn, Zinn (using the German Z)	Schatz, Sitz (German)
Tsch	csak, csont, pronounced tschak and tschont (Hungarian); chalk, chest, pronounced tschak etc. (English)	acs, pronounced atsch (Hungarian), fetch, match, pronounced fetsch and matsch (English)
Tj		
Tv		
Tw	twenty, twin (English)	
Tz		

V and W

These two consonants are very rarely linked to other consonants and are never found at the end of syllables. They are found at the beginning of syllables in a few words, such as *vrai* in French, and *Vlassi* and *Vsal* in Bohemian.

Z

At the end of syllables Z does not allow any following consonants, but it does at the beginning of syllables, especially in Italian. For example, *sbaglio*, *sdegno*, *sventura*, and *smania* are pronounced <zbaglio>, <zdegno>, etc. The Slavic language has *zdravy*, *zlato*, *zlomit*, etc.[60]

---

59. We do not know of any such words in German, nor if they existed would they involve the same sound as English *thin* and *thrift*. –the eds.

60. According to the Doric and Aeolian dialects of Greek, Z was not formed of *ds*, but rather of *sd*, and was probably pronounced <zd>. As a result, σδευς was pronounced and written instead of Ζευς. Because the Romans usually followed the Aeolian dialect, they formed their word *Deus* from σδευς, leaving out the σ for harmony.

5: On the speaking machine

§ 210

Inventing a speaking machine and attempting to build it according to a deliberate plan could certainly qualify as one of the most daring of human projects. Before describing my speaking machine I must, in all honesty, admit to my readers that I did not start out with the idea of working on such a machine. When I began my experiments, my intention was at most to imitate a few vowels with instruments, in other words to mimic a few sounds of the human voice. I dared not think about consonants, which seemed too difficult to me, and I believed that combining them with vowels would be absolutely impossible. I had for several years already mastered the most important sounds and letters individually, but the possibility of joining them and forming syllables and words seemed remote. Later, it will become obvious that even the possibility of building a speaking machine that could pronounce everything came to me very gradually and quite late.

Every invention, every machine, particularly one as complicated as this, proceeds at its own pace that allows for progress in very slow steps, especially when it is a question of imitating living organs. Since the path I followed might be of interest to several of my readers, I present here the story—or rather an abridged history—of this invention.

The story of the invention of a speaking machine

I do not remember exactly what first gave me the idea of imitating human speech. I only remember that in 1769, while I was working on my chess playing machine, I began to examine a variety of musical instruments in the hope of finding the one that came closest to human speech. I did not omit any that produced only one sound. I even experimented with a trumpet, a hunting horn, and even a bugle, and whatever else I could think of, but I found nothing that resembled human speech in any of them. Nevertheless, I owe these instruments some important secondary discoveries relevant to speech.

5: ON THE SPEAKING MACHINE

I knew as well as everyone else that the reed in oboes, clarinets, bassoons, etc. came closest to resembling the human voice because its functions are similar to those of the glottis. I also knew that for quite some time, especially in France, pipe organs had been fitted with a so-called *vox humana* in the form of reeds for large and small clarinets. However, since they imitated the human voice very imperfectly and also produced a most disagreeable noise I did not think them appropriate for my undertaking. After having reviewed all of the familiar instruments, I finally found one that came passably close to fulfilling my requirements. It was an instrument rarely seen in towns that was brought to my attention during a chance visit to the country. I had often heard similar instruments and should not have excluded them from my experiments; I do not remember why I did. It was just a country walk that led me unexpectedly to a tavern where some villagers were dancing. As we approached they took a break, during which the musician tuned his instrument. From a distance I could hear something I could not quite make out. It seemed to me that I could hear a child singing, alternating between two or three tones, and seemingly intertwining them. When we finally reached the tavern, it turned out to be none other than a musette, or bagpipe. My joy was extraordinary at having so unexpectedly come upon the very thing which I had been searching for so arduously. That tone, out of everything I had tried, best imitated the human voice to my ear. No music in my whole life had given me as much pleasure as the pitiful braying of that bagpipe. Here was the very thing I had so long been searching for, and seizing the instrument, I tried to create some sounds without letting the bass pipe rumble. The moment I saw that I had succeeded, I immediately wanted to buy the bagpipe from the musician, at any price. But no matter what I offered, he would not part with it, saying that it was his means of livelihood and that it could not be easily replaced. Nevertheless, he promised to send me the man who had made his instrument when he ran into him at the next fair. When one has made such a discovery one does not have the equanimity to wait while weeks and months go by. I insisted, but in spite of all the compliments and persuasions I used all he would give me was a small, shrill reed flute, used with the bagpipe he played, which he had in reserve.

I quickly returned to the city with my acquisition and began experimenting that very evening. I took a pair of ordinary leather bellows from the kitchen, fitted my reed flute to its iron tip, and made it sound by pushing the handle. I then placed the iron tip of the bellows, with the reed flute still attached, into a transverse flute, the upper stopper of which I had previously removed. However, the iron tip did not completely fill the opening of the transverse flute, so I wound some cloth around it and covered it with a moist cow bladder in order to prevent air loss.

I then covered the top three holes of the flute with one hand as I forced air in with the bellows. Lifting my fingers by degrees, I found I could produce higher or lower sounds, but no distinct vowels. Realizing that I could not make great progress in this fashion, I thought of fitting a wide section of pipe to the bellows, representing an open mouth in some way. I found an oboe at my disposal, and I took its funnel-shaped lower end and used it instead of the flute. By covering the wooden funnel with my left hand, sometimes completely, halfway, or only partially, I could, as I pressed the bellows with my right hand, produce different vowels by varying how far I opened my left hand. However, this would not happen unless I subsequently made various rapid movements with my hand and fingers. Conversely if I held any hand position for some time, it seemed to me that all I could hear was an A. From this, I soon drew the conclusion that speech sounds only become distinct through the relationships that exist between them, and they only achieve perfect clarity when linked in complete words and phrases.[1] I realized that this was at least the case with my machine, and thus I could only attain clarity separately, when I opened my hand to the exact degree required to produce a vowel.

I was convinced that my machine, pitiful though it was, could produce different vowels as well as some consonants distinctly, but not at will or in any prescribed order. The next day, as I continued my experiments, my wife and children ran in from the third room, and with great curiosity asked what was going on, because they thought they had heard a voice praying loudly and with great zeal, without being able to tell what language it was.

Here, then, is the first foundation upon which I later built my entire machine and upon which a complete system for human speech might eventually be constructed—if, as I have stated elsewhere, talented observers wish to take the trouble to pursue the discoveries I have made thus far and improve upon them.

Therefore, in order to continue with my work, it was above all necessary to understand perfectly what it was that I was trying to imitate. I had to study speech, and constantly observe Nature as I pursued my experiments. Thus my speaking machine and my speech theory made equal progress, and one served to guide the other. The first conclusions I was led to by my observations were the following: like all musical instruments, or rather like anything that produces sound, human speech cannot consist of anything other than the disturbance of air. It is clear that during speech the lungs draw in and expel air,

---

1. This is the same as with musical notes. If one plays only a single note on a harpsichord that is lower than normal, one cannot tell whether it should be a *re*; one will believe that it is a *mi* or an *ut*, but when some fragment of a piece of music is played, it is possible to recognise the tone through its links with, and relationships to, other notes.

and it is equally clear that this air is disturbed by the glottis, as if by a reed, and that it resonates, producing sound. It is also clear that the mouth and tongue change position for each sound, thus creating different obstacles in the path of the resonating air, that is to say they meet with variously formed openings, large at times and small at others. From this it can be established that speech, or articulation, is nothing but the voice passing through different openings. My daily experiments and discoveries confirmed this until finally, in my eyes, it became a mathematical certainty.

Thus, I told myself that for a speaking machine one only needs lungs, a glottis, and a mouth. I had the lungs in my bellows, the glottis in my reed flute, and the mouth in the funnel-shaped piece of the oboe. My ear confirmed that my bellows and reed flute perfectly duplicated the action of the lungs and the glottis in speech. To improve my machine, it was only a question of adding a cavity that more closely resembled the mouth than my funnel, to which various precisely-shaped openings with valves could be attached. Once this cavity was found, complete speech would not be too far from being realized. I was even convinced by my imperfect experiments, which had already provided me with a few somewhat weak vowels, that finding such a cavity was possible, and that consequently my efforts should be entirely devoted to discovering it. Little did I know how far I was from realizing this goal. I carried out my experiments with inconceivable patience. Even now I cannot understand how I could have persevered for months on end without a single step forward. The certainty with which I knew that speech had to be imitable encouraged me to persevere, and some lucky discoveries in the course of the work made me think that I could occasionally count on Fortune to aid in my efforts.

By chance I went one day to see an organ manufacturer so that I might order an organ bellows to replace my pitiful kitchen bellows. I found him working on a small project called *vox humana*. The tones of this instrument were supposed to imitate the human voice singing. The keys were not yet in place, but by opening one valve after another with the fingers while compressing the instrument's bellows, each tone could be heard separately. The intermediate tones were quite good, but the high and low tones were too loud, and more reminiscent of a trumpet's blare. This was an important discovery for me. I thought I could easily eliminate the roughness of the pipes, or rather the roughness of their reeds, and later I proved to be right. I immediately bargained for and bought the unfinished machine, and had it delivered to my home. It consisted of bellows with four ribs and a wind trunk into which, instead of organ pipes, thirteen wooden reeds of different size were set, decorated with ivory and of different sizes. The wind trunk (Table XVII, Fig. 1 *a* and *b*) was provided with valves at the bottom and thirteen holes (see *c* and *d*), one for each of the pipe reeds. Two of the pipes (*e*), were left in their original state. The others (*f*), were altered according to my instructions.

I now thought that I would definitely find the five vowels amid the thirteen tones, since I was still under the false impression that height and depth were the major factors in the formation of vowels, and that it was among the principal contributors to the marked differences between them. For example, the letter I always seemed much sharper to me than O or <ou>. However, to my great disappointment, things turned out to be entirely different. Each pipe, large or small, that I made sound would only give me an A. Depending on the size of the pipe it produced a higher or lower sound, but nevertheless the sound always remained an A.

Undaunted, I continued to try to discover how I could change this eternal and obstinate A into another vowel, but for a long time did not succeed. I very quickly realized that since each pipe represented an open mouth, and since the vowel A is pronounced with the mouth completely open, this instrument could produce no other tone. I also knew, from my first experiments, that the pipes had to be partially closed. Therefore, I held my hand or something else like a small board or card in front of the pipes at various distances and in different configurations, thus blocking them by different degrees. This was done in vain, however: the A was always distinctly present. At least it seemed so to my ear, probably for the reason cited earlier that without a link to other tones I would always hear only one tone. For several months this discouraged me completely. Finally, I could find no means of realizing this linkage of sounds other than providing my machine with keys (see Table XVII, Fig 1 g), so that I could make the tones sound promptly by using my fingers as with a harpsichord. I also positioned the bellows in such a manner that they could be operated by foot (XVII, Fig 1 h and i). To eliminate errors due to differently tuned high and low pipes, I tried as much as possible to tune the four or five middle pipes to the same tone.[2] I still had to provide the pipes with different openings, since my right hand was busy pressing the keys, the left hand could not move quickly enough from one pipe to the other and form the correct opening. The simplest method was to glue the board to the opening of each pipe, and depending on the situation, cut a larger or smaller opening in each board. However, this was not quite enough. I did find a significant difference between an A and the other vowels, but I could not find an exact enough opening to produce a definite O or <ou> in any pipe. All I could get was an intermediate sound.

Therefore, in order to be able to enlarge the opening instantaneously and at will, I made small slides for the pipes (see XVII, Fig. 2 a). This was equally inadequate for my purposes since the interior of the funnel, as well as the opening of the slide, was square. The human mouth had to be better imitated so that the voice could bounce against a vaulted inner surface as it does with the palate. I therefore had a turner make some round and oblong boxes, which I cut longitudinally through the middle such that they represented both jaws (see XVII, Fig. 3). I fastened a leather hinge to the posterior end of the lower piece, (*a*), or rather a leather bag (*b*), such that its front end (*c*) could be raised and lowered. So that I could instantly enlarge or constrict the opening, I passed a gut cord through the bottom of the lower jaw (*d*), then through a very small hole in the upper cover (*e*), with which I could raise the lower jaw or hold it at a level I judged appropriate. This was possible because

---

2. I will show below how to tune the pipes and to eliminate their rough tone.

the cord was constricted in this narrow hole (*e*), and had to be pulled with some force. In this manner I saw my plans adequately accomplished as I was soon able to produce the vowels A, O, and <ou>, as well as an imperfect E. However, I could never find the slightest trace of an I or Ü, regardless of how wide or narrow I made the opening of the wooden mouth.

I therefore had to be satisfied with my three vowels, and then started to think about some consonants, in order to quickly be able to produce a few syllables. My first successes were with P, M and L, but I am almost ashamed to admit that their discovery took the better part of two years. In order to avoid repetition, I shall not here cite how and through which experiments I finally succeeded, because I will later relate the origin of each letter, as well as the way in which I use it in my speaking machine.

I therefore had three vowels, A, O, and <ou>, and three consonants, L, M, and P, with which a few syllables and even words could be composed, such as *Mama, Papa, Mappa, aula, lama, mola, poma, mulo*, etc. Each letter had its own key, which, when struck, would make it sound. However, when I wished to link several letters into syllables and words, two quite disagreeable things happened. First of all, the first letter had to stop sounding when the second was about to begin. As a result, a pause always occurred between the two letters which, although short, was perceptible to the ear. If this pause was not long, the two sounds would blend and sound together. If the pause was too long, the sounds became too disconnected. For example, if I wished to say *papa*, I sounded <p-a-p-a>. Secondly, once the valve of a letter opened into the wind trunk, air suddenly rushed out with too much force together with the sound and added a certain *je ne sais quoi* to the beginning of each sound. This is a quality I cannot exactly define, but which sounded like a weak K. *Aula* sounded a bit like <ka-ku-kl-ka>. Finally, a puff of air or aspiration would always be heard after a P. *Papa* sounded like <ph-a-ph-a>. None of the great pains I took or the changes I made advanced my work by a single step.

At that point, I began to realize that by using the method I had developed it was only possible to produce single letters that could never be combined into syllables. I also realized that I had to follow Nature absolutely with a single glottis and a single mouth through which all the sounds issued and it was this that linked them together. I therefore had to throw out nearly two years of work and begin again. I did not regret the cost or the effort, however, as I thought myself richly rewarded by the six letters I had acquired, which later provided much clarification along the obscure route I had taken. However, the problems did not end there, and I faced many difficulties later and had to reject a large amount, which I shall not recount to my readers. I will only mention the successes that remain part of my machine. Had I wished to include a detailed description of everything I rejected in the same manner I used to describe my first experiments, I could have easily added another volume to this work, something which suits neither my intentions nor those of the reader. Suffice it to say that only a strong horse might, with great difficulty, pull the cart loaded with all the equipment I had to discard.

The speaking machine

§ 211

It is natural for a machine designed to produce articulated words and pronounce everything to be very complex, but almost [all] of my machine's merit [is] precisely in its lack of complexity. Although it is still very far from being perfect, the fact that it fulfills its purpose in spite of the simplicity of its construction is amazing. I firmly believe that if, in time, its improvement is carried as far as possible, it will be as easy to play as a harpsichord or a pianoforte. Anyone wishing to build a speaking machine based on my description and to conduct further experiments with it should not be discouraged by the amount of work involved. I will do everything I can to describe all parts of its structure as clearly as possible, so that it may be duplicated easily. I shall treat each part separately and describe it with the aid of diagrams. I shall also indicate its remaining shortcomings and occasionally add suggestions for improvements I have not yet had the time to make myself. I will then indicate how each letter is produced and, finally, I shall include an abridged set of instructions to facilitate the operation of the machine.

§ 212

The principal parts of the machine consist of the following pieces:

1. The mouthpiece, or reed, which represents the human glottis
2. The wind trunk, with its internal valves
3. The bellows, or the lungs
4. The mouth with its constituent parts
5. The nostrils

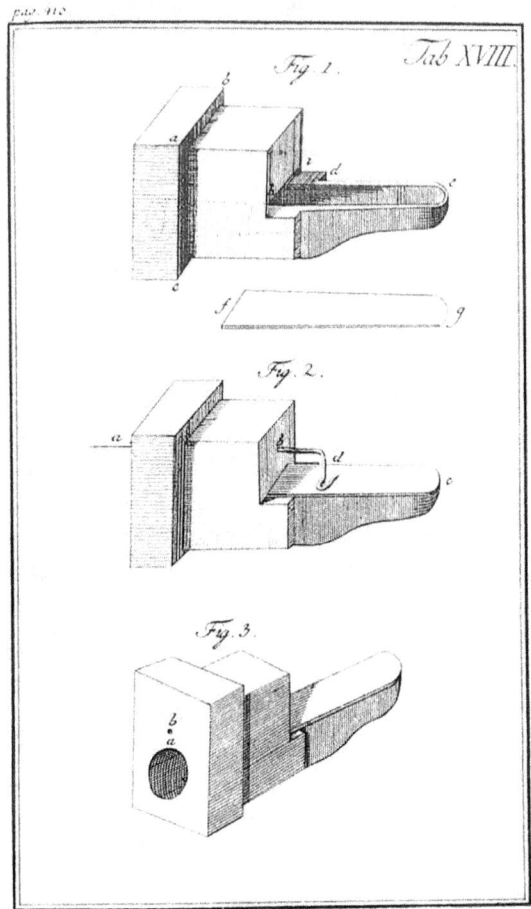

The mouthpiece, or the reed

§ 213

Table XVIII Fig. 1 represents the reed in actual size. It is made from a single piece of wood and fits exactly into the opening of the wind trunk, into which it is pushed up to points *a*, *b*, and *c*. The edge of the channel (see *d* and *e*) is almost half a line wide. It extends from *e* to *d*, widening as it approaches *d*, in order to provide the languette with a more solid support.

The languette, or tongue (see Tab. XVIII Fig. 1 *f* and *g*), consists of a very thin sheet of ivory that is about the thickness of a playing card. It must cover the edges of the channel exactly without extending beyond them. However, it has to be cut slightly longer than the channel, so that its posterior end can be slid into the opening (*see h* and *i*), where it is glued and fixed firmly in place with small wooden corners.

§ 214

To eliminate the harshness of the reed and the wooden sound it produces, and to give it a softer, more pleasing tone, I lined the edges of the channel and the underside of the ivory sheet with dog skin. A piece of skin is simply attached to the tongue with a thin glue, such that the smooth side of the skin is on the outside. The excess is trimmed as close to the ivory as possible. Lining the edges of the channel demands a little more care and precision. Glue is spread on the edges and a piece of skin is then placed over the entire channel, rough side down. A heavy object is then placed on top. When the glue is dry, the inner section of the skin is trimmed close to the edge with a sharp penknife so that the channel is open on the inside. The piece is then turned over onto a smooth board and the excess skin on the outside is trimmed off, so that the entire edge is covered with skin. The tongue is then attached as described above, and the complete mouthpiece appears as illustrated in Fig. 2.

§ 215

To tune this duct, a small hole (see *a* and *b*) is pierced into the wood, through which a brass wire is passed. The wire is bent as shown in Fig. 2, such that its end lies flat across the tongue. The farther the drawn brass wire is pushed towards the point of the tongue (*c*), the shorter is the end that is free to vibrate when air is forced through. Earlier, we showed how the shorter this free end is, the more rapid the vibrations, and how more rapid vibrations mean a sharper sound.[3] It should also be noted that the

---

3. I have often wondered whether one could, using a precisely built instrument, realize this lengthening and shortening at will, thus raising and lowering the voice to produce, if not a tune or rhythm, at least a variation in tune during speech. This would add a true embellishment to my machine, which until now pronounces everything in a monotone. I even tried changing the position of the thin brass wire as I operated the machine. The result was a very perceptible change in tone. However, I was only rarely able to capture the exact tone I wanted, since I could not always extend the thin brass wire by the exact amount. In the meantime, I note this down and leave it as a clue for others to explore. What seems certain to me is that such an instrument cannot be realized in precisely calculated degrees; these amounts must be found empirically

ivory tongue does not rest on *c* completely, but is slightly raised so that air can enter the channel or duct. If the tongue covered the channel exactly, external air pressure would not only prevent it from being lifted open, but would also close it more firmly, and thus sound would never be produced. When the tongue is pushed hard by the drawn brass wire at point *d*, its end (*c*) will normally bend by itself and will always remain curved. If, however, this does not happen naturally, it only has to be bent manually from time to time, and eventually it will keep this curvature.

In the first figure, the dotted lines mark the opening that goes through the wood and leads into the channel from the outside. It can be seen more clearly at *a* in the third figure, where the small hole for the drawn brass wire at *b* can also be seen.

The wind trunk

§ 216

The wind trunk is a small box with an interior length of three and a half inches, a width of two and a half inches, and a height of an inch and a half. The pipe for the voice, seen in Fig. 2 of the preceding table, is placed inside and fitted into the square opening from the anterior wall to the end. To ensure a tight seal, a piece of leather is glued around the opening (*a*). The posterior wall (*b*) is an inch and a half thick, with a round hole at point *c* into which the tip of the bellows is placed from the outside. This wall is deliberately made thick because it is the only point where the bellows are connected to the box. Otherwise it is completely free.

---

since the ivory sheet can never be rendered so even that it does not have a weaker or stronger spot. It will require very fine tuning at times and less at others. Obviously, I am leaving the reader a vast field to explore.

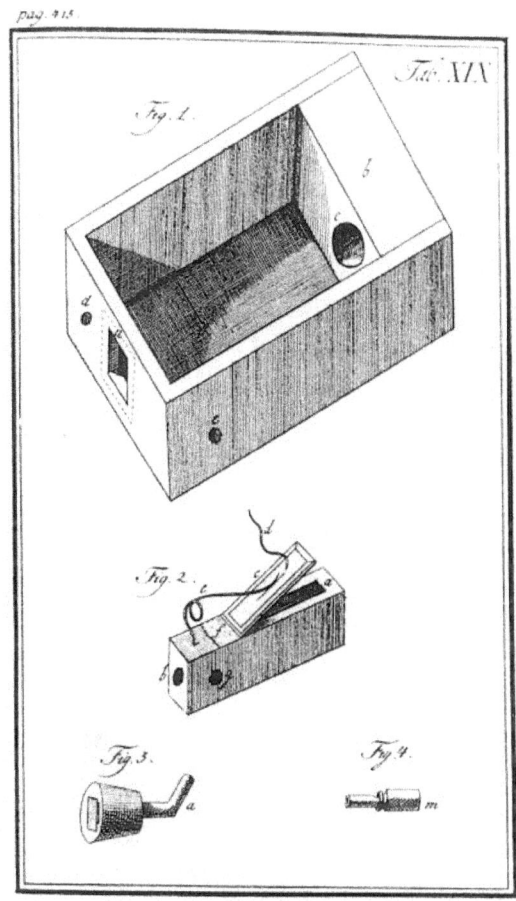

§ 217

Two smaller boxes (see Table XIX, Fig. 2) are placed inside the wind trunk such that one joins exactly against the right wall and the other against the left, while the reed, when placed into the opening a, lies between them. Each of these boxes is made from a single piece of wood. From the top to just beyond the center, they are pierced by a rectangular opening (a), which in one of the boxes is connected to a round opening b, cut into the front of the box from the exterior, to allow for the passage of air. A cover or valve (c) that can be raised by the drawn brass wire (d) and lowered by the spring in the wire at c is placed over the opening a. The leather covering the underside of the valve must extend slightly beyond the back end of the valve so that it forms a hinge when glued to the box at f.

As we stated earlier, one of the small boxes *a* has a small round hole at *b*, and in the other the opening of this hole is sealed, and another hole is pierced on the side at *g*. When these small boxes are positioned and secured inside the large box (Fig. 1), they must be pushed completely against the anterior wall, so that their openings *b* and *g* line up perfectly with those in the larger box at *d* and *e*. A brass pipe, shown in the third figure, is then placed in the hole *d* of the larger box. The mouthpiece *m* of the wooden duct in Fig. 4 is glued into the hole *e*. Later, the significance of the two pieces shown in Figs. 3 and 4 will be explained more clearly, where they will be depicted in actual size and will consequently be better defined and described. Here we will only say that they are destined for the hissing sounds, Fig. 3 for S and Z and Fig. 4 for SCH and J.

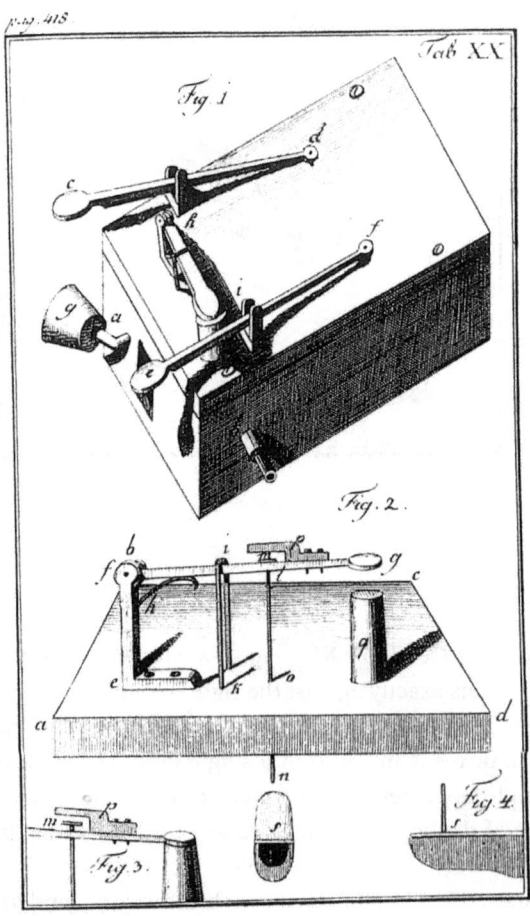

§ 218

Here, then, is the complete interior arrangement of the wind trunk. We shall now put its cover in place and consider the pieces fitted onto its exterior. Table XX Fig. 1 represents the exterior of the wind trunk. The wooden funnel depicted in Fig. 3 of Table XIX can be seen in the hole *a*. The other duct marked *m* in Fig. 4 of the same Table is glued to *b*. *c* and *d*, and *e* and *f* are two levers, or brass keys, the ends of which (*d* and *f*) are attached to the valves of the two small boxes within the wind trunk by means of a thin brass wire threaded through the cover. If the key *c* is pressed, its other end (*d*) will lift the cover or valve of the small concealed box through which air enters the funnel *g* and allows an S to be heard. The same sequence of events occurs with the other lever where *e* and *f* are attached to the duct *b*. The lever (*i* and *h*) serves the letter R, as we shall see in the following.

§ 219

Fig. 2, *a-b-c-d*, is an actual-size front view of the wind trunk cover onto which the brass piece (*e* and *f*) is fastened perpendicularly with screws. The brass piece has a mortise at *f* into which the tenon of the lever (*f* and *g*) is placed. This lever can be raised and lowered at the peg that traverses it. The steel spring *h* holds the lever in an elevated position. A bent piece of drawn brass wire (*i* and *k*) keeps the lever from rising beyond its height at *i*. At *l* a drawn brass wire, the thickness of a medium pin, traverses the lever. A small brass disc (*m*) is welded to the top end of this wire in order to keep the lever from slipping off. The entire length of the wire from *m* to *n* goes through the hole *o*, which must be large enough to allow for some play. A small piece of wood *p* is screwed onto the lever to prevent the drawn brass wire from jumping any higher. This piece is deliberately made of wood; the reason will be evident later. Another piece of wood (*q*) prevents the lever from falling further than it should. The profile of the reed, which should be shown as if it were inside the wind trunk and viewed from the side, below the brass wire, appears as in *s* in Fig. 4.

R

§ 220

When the brass lever *g* is pushed down until it reaches the piece of wood *q*, it also lowers the drawn brass wire (*l* to *n*) onto the ivory tongue of the reed.

When the lever is held down with a finger, the upper end of the brass wire, that is to say the disc *m*, will be halfway between the arm of the lever and the wooden bridge *p* in Fig. 3. If air is blown into the reed in this position and the ivory tongue begins to vibrate, its movements will throw the brass wire resting on it as high as the wooden bridge *p*, which will then push it away in such a manner that it is rapidly flung from one side to the other. This creates a noise, which, while it does not exactly resemble the fluttering made by our tongue does nevertheless approximate the R very closely and produces the R that is formed by the soft palate. I was satisfied with this, considering that thousands of people cannot produce it any better.

In the beginning my intention was to classify these letters in alphabetical order. However, I had to abandon that scheme because the letters were not realized in that order during the construction of the machine. The original plan would have created confusion and repetitious descriptions. Therefore, contrary to my expectations, R became the first letter. Since we are discussing the wind trunk, other letters such as S and SCH that have their direct origin there will also be discussed here.

S

§ 221

Earlier, in Table XIX Figs. 3 and 4, the two instruments pertaining to S and SCH were illustrated, reduced in scale, to indicate where they should be fitted into the wind trunk, also illustrated, on an even smaller scale. Here they are shown in their actual size. Table XXI Fig. 1 is a round, funnel-shaped box fitted with a slightly bent latten duct at its front end. The second figure more clearly depicts the cover which goes over its back end. This cover must be a quarter of an inch thick, and have a square opening in the middle. A thin piece of cardboard is glued over the opening, as indicated by the dotted line, in such a manner, however, that the opening is not completely covered but has a longitudinal opening half a line wide, as shown in Fig. 1 *a* and *b*. When this has been done on one side, that is to say on the exterior, the cover is turned over and the process is repeated on the interior, so that the two longitudinal openings are aligned exactly opposite each other. The cover is then fitted to the box, Fig. 1, and after inserting a piece of leather between them, it is firmly fastened to the box with wooden screws.

5: ON THE SPEAKING MACHINE

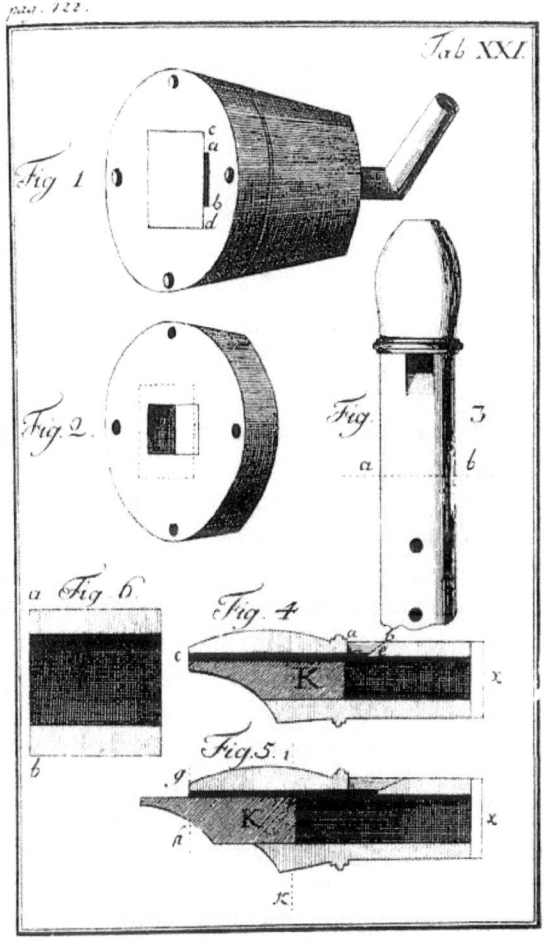

The reader should now recall what we explained at length above about whistling, and what was explained in Table IV, Figs. 2 and 3. I could not, however, make use of the box with the round hole that I described earlier, since it produced a perfect hiss and not the near-hissing tone required by S. After many attempts, I finally discovered that the two openings facing each other had to be longitudinal and only have a single sharp edge, in this case the edge of the cardboard (*c* to *d*). The other edge (*a* to *b*) had to be a consistent partition in the thickness of the wood, so that at least on one side air could pass in a direct line from one opening to the other, while on the other it could, upon entering, be first bent by the edge of the cardboard and then enter the space between the two pieces of cardboard. This produces a half whistling sound, that is to say the sound required for an S.

Thus, when the lever *c* Table XX, Fig. 1, is pressed, its other end *d* lifts the valve cover which is inside the wind trunk and belongs to *g*. Air enters the instrument we have just described through this valve and allows a perfect S to be heard.

SCH

§ 222

It is with the same theory that I found SCH. However, since it requires a deeper sound than S, I tried, according to my principle adopted in § 79, to greatly enlarge the interior space into which the air must enter. I took a small recorder, Fig. 3, and cut it at *a* and *b*. I then glued a small board over the hole at the bottom, as shown in the side views Fig. 4 and 5. By blowing softly into *x* in Fig. 4, I first obtained a sound that made me expect a SCH, but it still hissed too much. I therefore wanted to enlarge the space, and so I removed the small board *x* and inserted a latten duct into the opening. The duct was two and a half inches long and sealed at the bottom. However, there was no difference and the hissing tone persisted. I lengthened the hole from *a* to *b*, as illustrated in Fig. 5, but still found no improvement. Finally, I noticed that the air blown in at *c* emerged at *d*, much too close to the sharp edge *e*, and that consequently it was bent too much by this edge, and this could have been the reason for the strong hissing tone. I therefore pulled the stopper *k* out a little so that the air could not first issue at *a-b*, but would have to bend over the cutting edge *f* at a greater distance from *e*. This worked fairly well, but left me with the opposite problem. Since I had to enlarge the hole *a-b*, the sound whistled too little. This was soon remedied by placing some wax on the sharp edge until the hole was as small as indicated in Fig. 4, and I finally had the satisfaction of hearing a perfect SCH. I immediately discarded the latten duct, sealed the opening *x* as it had been before, cut off the excess length of the duct beyond *g-h*, and placed everything, up to the dotted line *i* to *k*, inside the wooden duct in Fig. 6. I sealed it with wax and put the duct in Fig. 6, with its end *a-b* in place (see Table XX, Fig. 1 *b*), where the lever *e-f*, when pressed at *e*, makes the SCH resonate.

Z, J

§ 223

The letters Z and J are produced like the S and the SCH, the only difference being that for the latter the mouth is absolutely closed, while for the former it is not as completely closed, so that the voice can accompany these letters somewhat.

The Bellows

§ 224

The boards of my bellows are ten inches wide at their posterior end, four inches wide at their anterior end, and one foot six and a half inches long. The bellows have three whole folds and two half folds. Like all common bellows the bottom board has a ventilator, or valve, through which air is drawn in but cannot escape. This valve should be entirely omitted if one wanted to, or rather could, imitate nature. As with humans, air should enter through the same opening from which the voice issues. However, this cannot be easily done, since the opening that the ivory tongue leaves for the reed is much too small to allow the amount of air necessary to fill the bellows to be drawn in fast enough, whereas in man the glottis can be enlarged, and consequently air can fill the lungs very quickly. It must be taken into consideration that my machine, it in its present state, requires perhaps six times as much air as a human speaker. The reason why will be seen later. Furthermore, it is irrelevant how air enters the bellows, just as nothing would change in human speech if man had a hole, with a concealed inner valve, in his chest through which he could draw in air.

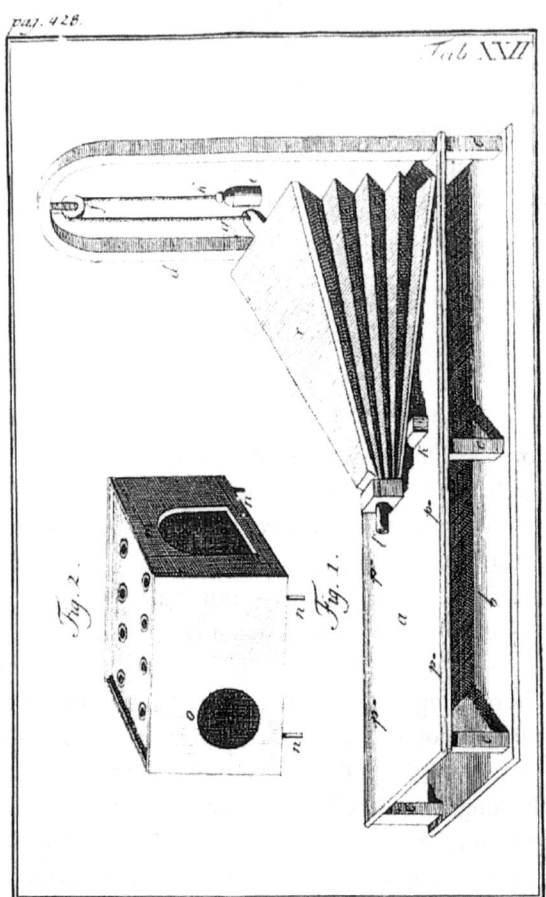

Table XXII, Fig. 1 depicts the bellows with its pedestal. The latter consists of two long tables, *a* and *b*, placed horizontally on top of each other and held together by the columns at *c*. These have no purpose other than convenience, so that when the machine is placed on a table in order to be played, it will be somewhat elevated and one does not have to bend down too much. The two columns *d* and *e* are connected at the top by an arc from which a small pulley *f* is suspended. A cord passing through *g*, *f*, and *h*, passes over the pulley and has the weight *i* at one end. This weight serves to raise the upper board after it has been pushed down. The weight consists of a latten box filled with bullets and lead shot which can be increased or decreased, depending on the requirements of the situation. As with the upper board of the bellows at *g*, the lower board also has a small tab projecting beyond the end of the board, which is fastened to the base (*a*) with screws. In front, at *k*, the bellows rest on a support so that the duct at *l* is somewhat elevated and can be easily slotted into the wind trunk.

§ 225

Fig. 2 is a box that is placed on the base *a* such that its posterior opening *m* is opposite the duct *l*, and completely encloses the wind trunk at the point where it is fitted to the duct. The pegs at *n*, when placed into the holes at *p*, anchor the box so that it cannot be disarranged. The covering of the box is made of taffeta and has several openings embellished with ivory rings. It also has a second cover, made of wood, which goes over the taffeta. The two large openings *m* and *o* have cloth curtains. This box does not contribute to speech, but I have chosen to use it for two reasons, primarily to keep dust from entering the interior of the machine, and secondly to reduce the loss of voice, forcing it to issue from one side only, namely from the top side that is pierced with holes.

§ 226

When the bellows are thus prepared, with the wind trunk connected to the duct and the box placed on top, I stand at the machine, rest my right arm on the bellows so that my elbow is approximately at *r*, while my hand, up to the wrist, is in the opening *m* and is held suspended over the wind trunk. I place my left hand in the hole at *o* and thus use both hands to manipulate the various holes and keys. As soon as I press the top board of the bellows with my right elbow, the voice sounds. The moment I stop pressing, the voice stops because the weight *i* immediately lifts the bellows and draws in air. These, then, are all the functions of the bellows.

The mouth

§ 227

The part of my machine which represents the mouth and is therefore its most important aspect, is actually also the most incomplete and still requires many improvements. It has no teeth, no tongue, and also no soft palate. Earlier, when discussing the theory of speech, we saw how essential these last two in particular were. Given the fact that they are missing, it follows that the machine will pronounce some letters in an indistinct manner. This shortcoming is limited to four letters; it pronounces the rest very well. We shall discuss all this later, but first we should describe what the mouth consists of.

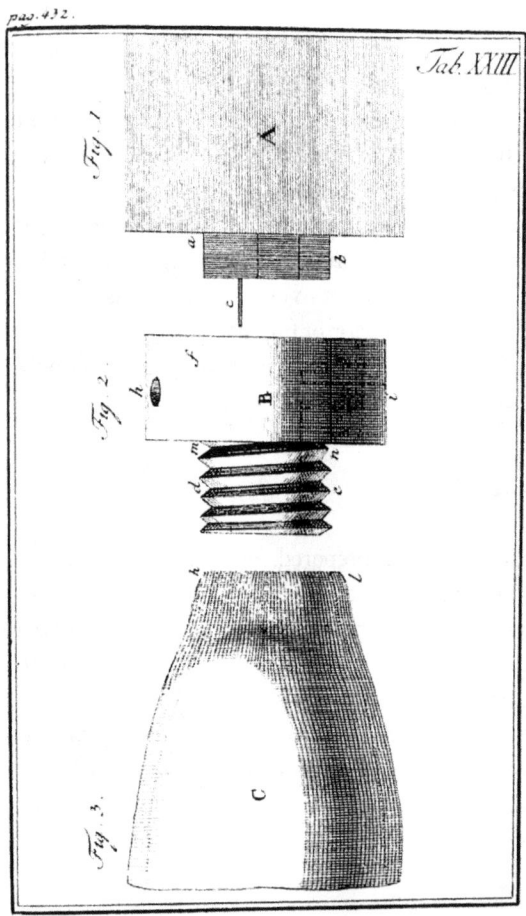

§ 228

In Table XXIII Fig. 1, *A* (actual size) is a section of the wind trunk already fitted with the reed. The tip of the reed (*a* to *b*) and the drawn brass wire *c* extend beyond a round piece of wood *B* with a threaded portion (*d* and *e*).

5: ON THE SPEAKING MACHINE

The dotted lines indicate how its interior is hollowed out (see Fig. 2). The end (*a* and *b*) in Fig. 1 is fitted into the square cavity (*f* and *g*). One of the holes, *h*, is pierced from the top, and this belongs to the nose. The opening leading to the small bellows, *i*, can be seen in Fig. 3 of the next Table. *C* is an implement made of elastic rubber that resembles a small bottle, the lower half and narrow neck of which have been cut off. At its narrowest part (*k* to *l*) it is screwed onto the threads at *d* and *e* of Fig. 2, as far as points *m* and *n*. The neck of this implement must be quite narrow in order to grip the screw tightly so that no air may enter. Since the rubber stretches, it grips quite easily once one has succeeded in getting over the first turn of the screw. It can be removed equally easily when detaching it. I preferred to use elastic rubber rather than any other material available because it remains uniformly supple and soft, despite being temperature dependent, and this imitates the human mouth in which the voice always strikes soft surfaces.

§ 229

When the three parts A, B, and C are joined together, they appear as illustrated in Table XXIV, Fig. 1. There are still a few comments to add, which are the following: some letters, such as P, T, and K, require an explosion of air. In nature, this explosion is attained by enlarging the glottis, allowing a large amount of air to rush into the mouth, and then expelling it all at once. This cannot be accomplished by my machine because its glottis, the reed, keeps a constant opening that cannot be enlarged when speaking to such a degree that a large quantity of air can flow through freely and without vibration. Here, therefore, I needed another expedient. To keep the mouth constantly full of air, I took a small brass pipe (a to b), though a feather may serve the same purpose. I then made a hole c in the wind trunk A, and another hole, a, opposite it in the elastic bottle C. I had to cut a groove (from a to z) in piece B because it blocked my path. I then placed the duct into the aforementioned holes and thereby connected the mouth to the wind trunk. By doing this I gained two advantages. Firstly, by closing the opening of the elastic bottle (e to f) with my hand and pressing the bellows, I could compress the air as much as I wished, and create a burst with the abrupt removal of my hand and produce a perfect P. Secondly, this device gave me an important benefit in that I could use it to silence the voice for those letters where it is not used, namely for the spirant consonants such as F, S, and SCH. This can be done in the following manner. When the hand covers the opening of the mouth and the air inside is compressed, it tries to return to the wind trunk through the posterior opening of the reed. However, because air is also forced into the reed from the inside by the very same pressure from the bellows, these two airflows meet and confront each other with equal resistance. Consequently, equilibrium is re-established and the ivory tongue of the reed cannot be made to vibrate since, as has already been proven, the flow of air is absolutely indispensable for the voice. Here, again, the principle we adopted in our theory of language while discussing the letters B and D should be recalled, namely that the air contained in the mouth is compressible and that it can always resonate within the mouth until it is entirely compressed. If the pipe, a to b, were omitted here, the reed would vibrate for some time after the mouth was already closed, thoroughly marring speech. Although this pipe may seem unimportant and of little consequence, it is one of the essential parts of this machine, and I cannot imagine how a speaking machine can exist without it, or without some other means of direct communication between the mouth and the wind trunk.

P

§ 230

To increase the explosive quality of the mute consonants, I made an important addition to my machine. Under the piece B, I fitted a small bellows (*g-h-i*) consisting of two small square boards, two and a half inches wide, joined by an ordinary piece of leather, *k*. These bellows have no aperture other than the one indicated by the dotted line (*m* to *n*). This aperture leads to the principal opening of the reed, as indicated by the dotted line *l-m-q-o*. This can be better seen in Fig. 2, which is a profile view of Fig. 1. Thus, when the mouth and nose are closed and the larger bellows are pressed, the compressed air also inflates the small bellows. If the hand keeping the mouth closed is abruptly pulled away, the small bellows, compressed by the drawn brass spring *p* to *q* that is attached to the wind trunk, push the air strongly out, which of course makes the explosion through the mouth more forceful. It is in this manner that we have the letter P in its perfection.

The Nose

§ 231

Nothing in this machine can be simpler than the nose. Table XXIV, Fig. 2, shows a side view of the two holes, *u-v* and *x-y*, pierced through the disc B from top to bottom, and leading to the principal opening of the reed. Two brass tubes with rims, *l* and *m*, are placed into the openings from the top. These can be covered by two fingers. When these pipes are open while the mouth is closed, all of the voice issues through them, which forms a perfect M, as good as a human one. However, if only one of these pipes is covered, an N is produced. The machine's version of this organ differs from the human organ, in that for the machine the nose is blocked externally, while in man it is sealed from the inside by the soft palate. In practice, however, this difference is not noticeable. It should also be noted here that these two channels serve no other purpose than to produce M and N, and that they must remain covered for all the other letters, both vowels and consonants.

§ 232

In Table XXV we can see a reduced-scale view from above of the entire machine, and of the manner in which it is operated. The right hand is placed on the wind trunk A so that the first two fingers are placed on the small ducts *m* and *n* to cover their openings. The palm of the left hand covers the opening of the elastic funnel C from *b* to *c*. In this position, if the bellows, X, the anterior part of which can be seen in the drawing, are compressed, the machine will remain silent because the voice has nowhere to issue from.

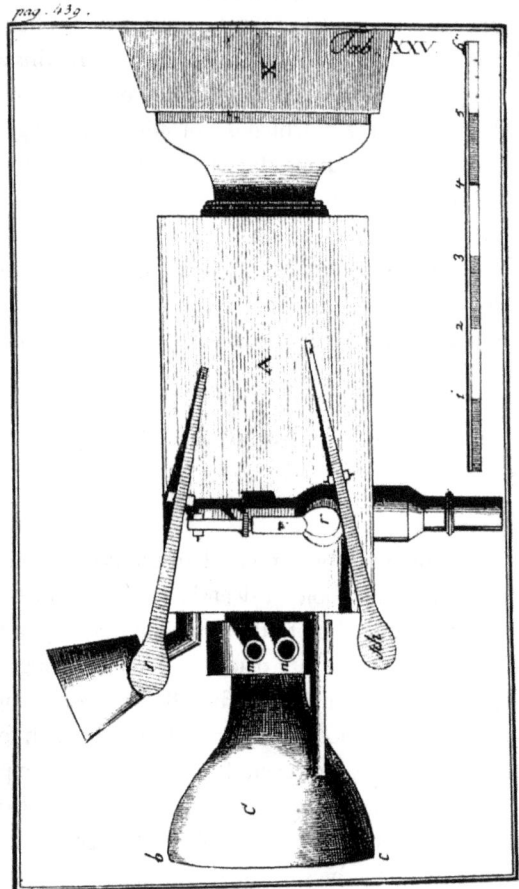

§ 233

All of the vowels are formed solely by the position of the left hand. In other words, they are determined by the greater or lesser distance between the left hand and the edge of the funnel. I cannot give instructions as to exactly how far the left hand must be pulled away for each vowel, since this very much depends on the diameter of the elastic bottle. However, these distances can be easily found through experience and by ear. I will only indicate approximately where to look for each vowel, and in which order they can be found, in decreasing order of opening size.

> **A:** For the A sound, which I always consider the fundamental sound of speech, the hand is entirely removed from the mouth opening, so that the voice has a free outlet.
>
> **E:** E is next. For this sound, the slightly cupped hand rests completely against the lower edge of the mouth, while it is held almost an inch away from its upper edge.
>
> **O:** For O, the cupped hand is brought closer to the upper edge of the mouth.
>
> **U:** For U, the palm of the hand is held very near the opening of the mouth in such a manner that it is not entirely covered, and the voice can still sound.
>
> **I:** For I, the flattened palm of the hand is pressed against the entire edge of the mouth and only the first finger is held far enough away to create a small opening, near its lower joint, through which air must be pushed out with slightly more force than for the other vowels. The other vowels, Ä, Ö, Ü, and É, are formed by modifying the distances for the principal vowels, and can be easily found with practice.

§ 234

As for the consonants, we have already shown how some of them are formed, namely P, R, S, SCH, M, and N. Only B, D, F, H, K, L, T, W, and Z remain to be discussed. I must first admit that four of them, D, G, K, and T, cannot yet be distinctly produced by my machine, and I substitute them with a P. With practice, I have learned to form them by pulling my hand away more or less abruptly, and by adding such a small difference it deceives the ear. For example, one may hear a K or a T, even though the sound is basically a P. It is particularly easy to be led into error when the word to be uttered by my machine is known in advance. When the machine actually pronounces it, one believes to have heard it distinctly. If a well-trained ear recognizes the difference, the childlike voice of the machine becomes as asset. A child who occasionally stammers and erroneously substitutes one letter for another is readily forgiven, and the listener contents himself with the fact that he has understood what the child wished to say. Nevertheless, I believe that this drawback can be easily remedied, but not having had the time to carry out my ideas on this subject using my machine, I present them here as propositions whose execution I leave to those who would like to assume the task.

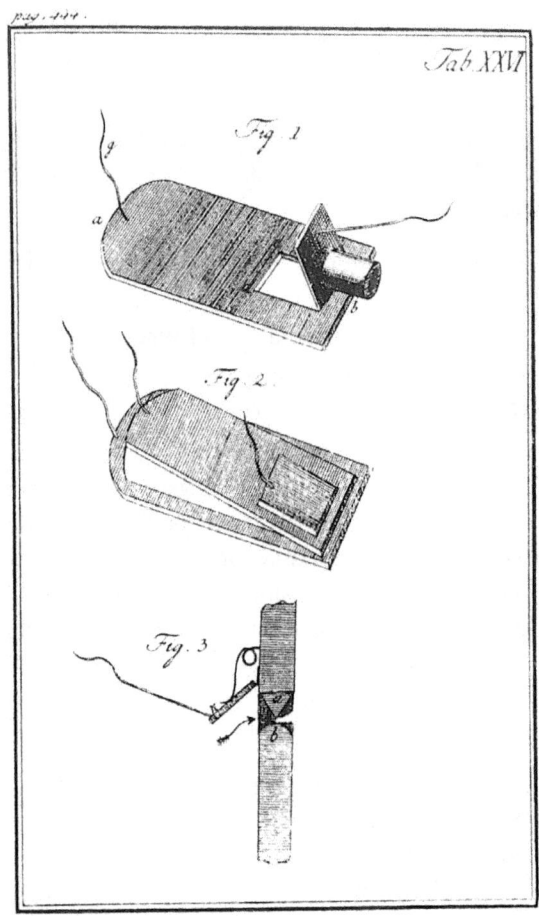

§ 235

We know from the theory of human speech that the following letters are formed by the tongue: D and T by its tip, and G and K by its posterior portion. Accordingly, a tongue made from a small board can be fitted in the mouth, as shown in Table XII Fig. 3, *B* and *C* and Table XIV Fig. 1 *A*.

The first table would produce D and T, and the second table would produce K and G. However, since this would mean two tongues, one short and the other long, they can be combined in the following manner. One would have to begin by making a larger board, seen in Table XXVI, Fig. 1 *a-b*, into which a hole, *d-e*, would have to be cut. A cover *f*, attached with a leather hinge, would then be fitted onto the hole. When the cover is closed and the front end of the larger board (*a*) is pulled against the palate by a string or a drawn brass wire, *g*, it will have the configuration shown in Table XII, Fig. 3 *B*, and will block the outlet of the voice.

> **T and K:** If the wire is released abruptly the tongue will fall, as illustrated in Fig. 2, and the issuing voice will produce a T. Conversely, if one wished to pronounce K or a G, the larger board would have to remain recumbent and only its small cover *F* would be lifted. This cover is also provided with a wire (see Table XIV Fig. 1, *A*, where it is shown holding the main opening of the reed closed). When the wire is released, the issuing voice produces a K. The greatest difficulty lies in forming good seals between the inner walls and the raised tongue, so that no air can escape. The small tongue will present fewer difficulties because it need only cover one round opening.
>
> **D and G:** For the letters D and G, the only thing to note is that the small boards do not have to be as tightly sealed as for T and K, since the voice should resonate a little. This arrangement leads to another important change, without which everything would fail. The tube *a-b* depicted in Table XXIV Fig. 1 can no longer remain in the space it occupies, but has to be moved from the wind trunk, below the reed, into the principal opening of the voice, so that the air can flow through it and gather within the two tongues just described, as it does for a P, and a sudden explosion can be produced.

§ 236

> **B:** B differs from P only in that the voice resonates. In the machine, one only has to close the mouth exactly as for the P, allowing the voice to resonate a little. When the hand is withdrawn, that is to say, when the hand is held in the position to form the vowel following it, a <ba>, <be>, <bi>, etc. will be heard.

§ 237

F: For this spirant consonant, I first made a square opening in the wall of the wind trunk, which I then covered on the inside with an adjustable valve (as can be seen in Table XXVI. Fig. 3). Into this opening I then glued a wooden prism (*a*), the same width as the upper piece of wood, with a point only slightly less wide than the somewhat rounded lower piece of wood. I left a very narrow opening through which, when the valve *K* was lifted, air would issue with the whistling that is characteristic of this letter. Thus, nature is perfectly imitated, since the thickness of the wood at *b* represents the lower lip, and the wooden prism represents the upper teeth. Later, finding that too much air escaped through the small openings for the wires, the internal valves and the drawn brass wire designated for R, and that I could obtain the same whistling sound if I pressed harder on the bellows, I decided that the arrangement was too impractical. Always very glad to avoid complications, I resealed the opening and sounded the F by pressing the bellows harder and leaving everything else closed.

§ 238

V: Having much affinity with the F, V is also formed by the same means in the machine, with the exception that the voice is made to resonate by opening the left hand very slightly.

W: For W, less air and more voice should be heard. The position is the same as that of an F.

§ 239

H: The H and the CH are self-generated, and I have no special mechanism for these letters in my machine. However, when I press the bellows more gently, that is to say not hard enough to make the ivory tongue of the reed vibrate, air issues from both the reed and the wind trunk *a-b*, and is similar to the breath necessary for an H.

CH: If I press the bellows harder, I get a CH. If I cover the exit of the voice slightly, the small tongue I have proposed for K and G will contribute much to the improvement of the CH.

§ 240

L: L is one of the easiest letters to produce. Just as in natural speech, it consists of nothing more than lifting the tongue so that it stands in the way of the voice, dividing it into two parts, and allowing it to flow on both sides. Similarly, in the machine I must only thrust the thumb of my left hand as deeply as possible into the mouth, as I have already indicated in Table XV, Fig. 4, and a perfect L is immediately produced. It would be equally easy to produce this letter in a machine equipped with keys, where there would, of course, be no thumb. One would only have to fit a smaller, somewhat narrower, and slightly shorter board to the projecting wooden tongue (see Table XXVI Fig. 1) and connect it to the tongue with a hinge added to its back end in such a way that its front end can be elevated as far as the palate. This arrangement would serve the same purpose as the thumb serves, but the small tongue, designated for K and G, would also have to be added. Thus, there would be three tongues lying over each other, as shown in Fig. 2.

Abridged directions for finding each letter in the machine in alphabetical order

Preliminary observations

§ 241

1. I observed above that the right hand must be extended over the wind trunk *A* in Table XXV, such that the first two fingers exactly cover the two nostrils *m* and *n*. The thumb should be over the lever, or key, for the sound SCH, and the little finger over the S. The palm of the left hand should cover the mouth opening at *b* and *c*.

2. When one wishes to sound a letter, the right elbow, which always rests on the bellows, must push them with greater or lesser force. This pressure should be maintained until the completion of the word being pronounced, otherwise the letters and syllables will not be linked. Once the elbow is lifted, the voice stops.

3. The nose must be blocked for all the letters except M and N.

4. The mouth must be closed for all the mute and spirant consonants.

5. For all simultaneously voiced and spirant consonants, the mouth should not be completely closed. However, a little opening will allow

the voice to sound a little. Thus, when in discussing a letter it is stated that the voice sounds, this will always mean that the mouth will not be as open as it is for a vowel, but that it will be so slightly closed, that the voice can barely be heard.

§ 242

A: Left hand held away from the mouth entirely.

B: Mouth closed slightly, allowing the voice to resonate.

D: Until now similar to a B.[4]

E: Palm of the hand held against the edge of the mouth, about an inch away at the top.

F: Everything is closed. Pressure from the bellows slightly increased.

G: Like D.

H: Bellows pressed gently, mouth open.

CH: Somewhat greater pressure on the bellows, yet in such a manner that the voice is not heard.

I: Everything is closed, with the exception of a small opening at the third joint of the left index finger. Hard pressure on the bellows.

K: Imperfect, like D (see footnote 162).

L: The left thumb in the middle of the mouth (see Table XV Fig. 4).

M: Mouth closed, both nostrils open.

N: Mouth closed, only one of the nostrils open.

O: Cupped hand held against the base of the mouth, an inch and a half away at the top.

P: Everything is closed. The hand is abruptly pulled away from the mouth and placed in the position required for the vowel to follow.

R: Mouth open for the vowel to follow and the "r" key is pressed by the thumb (see Table XXV).

S: The "s" key is pressed with the little finger. Everything else is closed.

SCH: Mouth closed; thumb presses the "sch" key.

---

4. Through practice one can acquire a certain promptness in retracting the hand and applying just the right amount of pressure in the bellows that is not possible to describe but can give an adequate D, especially if it is linked to other letters.

J: Like SCH, but the voice resonates.

T: Imperfect, like D (see footnote 162).

U: Left hand held against the mouth, less than for I, but more than for O. The exact size of the opening will be learned by experience.

V: Similar to F, but the voice resonates. Pressure on the bellows is somewhat higher.

W: Like V, but less air and more voice.

Z: The "s" key is pressed with the little finger and some voice.

§ 243

One might become incredibly adept at operating the speaking machine in as little as three weeks, especially if one concentrates on Latin, French or Italian. The German language is much more difficult because of its frequent consonants, spirant sounds, and silent letters that appear at the end of many of its words. I can immediately pronounce each French and Italian word that is requested of me, but a somewhat long German word gives me a great deal of trouble, and only in rare cases do I succeed perfectly. As for complete phrases, I can only produce a few, but again they have to be short, since the bellows are not large enough to supply the necessary amount of air. For example: *Vous êtes mon ami. Je vous aime de tout mon cœur.* Or in Latin, *Leopoldus secundus. Romanorum Imperator. Semper Augustus.*

As for the rest, I am convinced that equipping the machine with keys, like a harpsichord or an organ, so that it is easier to play than it is now, will not require too much skill. However, this is an additional step towards perfection that I leave to those among my readers who might devote some attention to this new invention, still in its infancy, and who might like to carry it further with their ideas and care. If time will ever allow me to perfect it myself, I will not fail to continue its description.

References

Adelung, Johann C. *Grammatisch-kritisches Wörterbuch der Hochdeutschen Mundart.* Breitkopf, 1793.
Amman, Jean Coenrad. *The talking deaf man.* London: Thomas Hawkins, 1694.
Anonymous. Ueber Herrn von Kempelens Schach-Spieler und Sprach-Maschine. Zweeter Brief. *Der Teutsche Merkur,* Part 1, 1784a, pp. 178–182.
Anonymous. Schreiben über die Kempelische Schachspiel- und Redemaschine. *Hessische Beyträge zur Gelehrsamkeit und Kunst.* Vol. 1, No. 3. 1784b, pp. 475–487.
Biester, Johann E. *Schreiben über die Kempelischen Schachspiel- und Redemaschinen.* Berlinische Monatsschrift. Vol. 4, 1784, pp. 495–514.
Bougeant, Guillaume-Hyacinthe. *Amusement philosophique sur le langage des bestes.* Chez Gissey, Bordelet, Ganeau, 1739.
Brackhane, Fabian. "Die Sprechmaschine Wolfgang von Kempelens-Von den Originalen bis zu den Nachbauten". *Phonus 16 Forschungsberichte des Instituts für Phonetik der Universität des Saarlandes.* Saarbrücken, 2011. pp. 49–148.
Brackhane, Fabian. "Kann was natürlicher, als Vox humana, klingen?"–Ein Beitrag zur Geschichte der mechanischen Sprachsynthese." Dissertation. *Phonus 18 Forschungsberichte des Instituts für Phonetik der Universität des Saarlandes.* Saarbrücken, 2015.
Brackhane, Fabian and J. Trouvain. "What makes 'mama' and 'papa' acceptable? Experiments with a replica of von Kempelen's speaking machine". *Proc. 8th International Seminar on Speech Production (ISSP '08).* Strasbourg, 2008, pp. 328–332.
Brackhane, Fabian, et al. "Editing Kempelen's 'Mechanismus der menschlichen Sprache': experiences and findings." *Proc. 2nd Workshop on History of Speech Communication Research.* Helsinki, 2017. pp. 16–24.
Camper, Peter. "Account of the organs of speech of the orang outang." *Philosophical Transactions of the Royal Society of London 69.* 1779. pp. 139–159.
Comte de Buffon, Georges-Louis L. *Histoire Naturelle, générale et particulière, avec la description du Cabinet du Roi.* Imprimerie Royale, 1749–1804.
Court de Gébelin, Antoine. *Monde primitif, analysé et comparé avec le monde moderne, consideré Dans divers Objets concernant l'Histoire, le Blason, les Monnoies, les Jeux, Les Voyages des Phéniciens autour du Monde, les Langues Américaines, &c. 9 volumes* [The primitive world, analysed and compared with the modern world]. Chez L'Auteur, 1773–1782.
de Bomare, Jaques-Christophe Valmont. *Dictionnaire raisonné universel d'histoire naturelle, Tome Second.* Chez Didot, 1764a.
de Bomare, Jacques-Christophe Valmont. *Dictionnaire raisonné universel d'histoire naturelle, Tome Cinquième.* Chez Didot. 1764b.

de Brosses, Charles. *Traité de la formation méchanique des langues : et des principes physiques de l'étymologie*. Saillant, Vincent, Desaint, 1765.

Diodorus Siculus. *Delphi Complete Works of Diodorus Siculus* (Delphi Ancient Classics). Delphi Publishing Limited, 2011.

Dionysius of Halicarnassus & J. Singer. *Dionysius of Halicarnassus On literary composition: being the Greek text of the De compositione verborum*. AMS Press, 1976.

Dodart, Denis. "Mémoire Sur les Causes de la Voix de l'Homme, & de ses différens Tons". *Mémoires de l'Académie royale des sciences*. 1700. pp. 244–293.

Dudley, H. and T. H. Tarnoczy. "The Speaking Machine of Wolfgang Von Kempelen". *The Journal of the Acoustical Society of America* 22.2. 1950. pp. 151–166.

Ebert, Johann J. *Nachricht von dem berühmten Schachspieler und der Sprechmaschine des K. K. Hofkammeraths Herrn von Kempelen*. Müllersche Buchhandlung, 1785.

Ferrein, Antoine. "De la formation de la voix de l'homme". *Histoire de l'académie royale des sciences de Paris 51*. L'Imprimerie Royale, 1741. pp. 409–432.

Garland, Alex. "Alex Garland of 'Ex Machina' Talks About Artificial Intelligence". *New York Times*, 22 April 2015. Accessed on 17 November 2017 from https://goo.gl/csU8ac.

Herder, Johann. *Ideen zur Philosophie der Geschichte der Menschenheit, I. Theil*. Johann Friedrich Hartknoch, 1784.

Herder, Johann. *Abhandlung über den Ursprung der Sprache [Treatise on the Origin of Language]*. C.F. Voss, 1789.

Hindenburg, Carl F. *Ueber den Schachspieler des Herrn von Kempelen. Nebst einer Abbildung und Beschreibung seiner Sprachmaschine*. Müllersche Buchhandlung, 1784.

Kratzenstein, Christian G. *Tentamen resolvendi problema ab Acad. Petropolit. 1780 propositum qualis sit natura litterarum vocalium a, e, i, o, u*. Typis Academia Scientiarum, 1781.

Kratzenstein, Christian G. *Essai sur la naissance & la formation des Voyelles. Observations sur la physique, sur l'histoire naturelle et sur les arts*. 1782. Vol. 21. pp 359–380.

Kraus, Joh. Paul. "Ankündigung eines Werks unter dem Titel: Wolfgangs von Kempelen k. k. wirklichen Hofraths bey der k. Hungarischen und Siebenbürgischen Hofkanzley". *Mechanismus der menschlichen Sprache; nebst der Beschreibung seiner sprechenden Maschine. Intelligenzblatt der Allgemeinen Literatur-Zeitung*. Nr. 17, 3. February 1790. pp. 129–132.

Lichtenberg, Georg C. "Etwas über den Schachspieler, und die Sprachmaschine des Hrn. Hof-Cammerraths von Kempelen". *Lichtenberg, Georg Christoph (Ed.), Magazin für das neueste aus Physik und Naturgeschichte*. Vol. 3, Part 2. 1785. pp. 183–192.

Lieutaud, Joseph. *Anatomie historique et pratique, Nouvelle édition, augmentée de diverses Remarques historiques & critiques, & de nouvelles Planches, par M. Portal*. Chez Vincent, 1776–1777.

Lieutaud, Joseph. *Zergliederungskunst*. Junius, 1782. Translation of Lieutaud 1776–1777.

Miller, James D. "Auditory-perceptual interpretation of the vowel." *The journal of the Acoustical society of America* 85.5. 1989. pp. 2114–2134.

Monboddo, James. *Des Lord Monboddo Werk vom dem Ursprunge und Fortgange der Sprache*. J. F. Hareknoch, 1785. [Translation by Ernst Schmid of Monboddo, James. *Of the Origin and Progress of Language*. Kincaid, 1773.]

Nicolai, F. "Die Schachspielende Figur des Hrn. von Kempelen. Beschreibung einer Reise durch Deutschland und die Schweiz im Jahre 1781". *Nebst Bemerkungen über Gelehrsamkeit, Industrie, Religion und Sitten*. Vol. 6. Self-published, 1785. pp. 420–436.

Reimarus, Hermann Samuel. *Allgemeine Betrachtungen über die Triebe der Thiere, hauptsächlich über ihre Kunsttriebe. Zum Erkenntniss des Zusammenhanges der Welt, des Schöpfers und unser selbst*, 2nd ed. Johann Carl Bohn, 1762.

Rouse, W. H. D., translator. Lucretius. *On the Nature of Things*. Revised by Martin F. Smith. Loeb Classical Library 181. Cambridge, MA: Harvard University Press, 1924.

Scaligero, Giulio Cesare. *Iulii Caesaris Scaligeri De causis linguae Latinae libri tredecim*. Apud Seb. Gryphium, 1540.

Schulze, Benjamin. *Orientalisch- und Occidentalisches A, B, C-Buch welches hundert Alphabete nebst ihrer Aussprache so bey denen meisten Europäisch-Asiatisch-Africanisch- und Americanischen Völkern und Nationen gebräuchlich sind, nebst einigen Tabulis Polyglottis verschiedener Sprachen und Zahlen vor Augen leget, von Benjamin Schulzen, Königl. Dänischen Missionarii zu Tranquebar, und mit darzu gehörigen Kupfern versehen*. Christian Friedrich Geßner, 1769.

Sproat, Richard. *Language, Technology, and Society*. Oxford, 2010.

Sproat, Richard. *List of subscribers to Wolfgang von Kempelen's Mechanismus*. http://rws.xoba.com/newindex/subscribers.html, 2013.

Sussmilch, Johan Peter. *Essay on a demonstration that the first language did not draw its origin from man, but solely from the Creator*. 1766.

Thicknesse, Philip. *The speaking figure and the automaton chess-player, exposed and detected*. Stockdale, 1784.

Trouvain, Jürgen. and F. Brackhane. "Zur heutigen Bedeutung der Sprechmaschine von Wolfgang von Kempelen." *Band 2 der Tagungsbände der 20. Konferenz Elektronische Sprachsignalverarbeitung (ESSV '09)*, Dresden, 2010. pp. 97–107.

Trouvain, Jürgen. and F. Brackhane. "Wolfgang von Kempelen's speaking machine as an instrument for demonstration and research." *Proc. 17th International Congress of Phonetic Sciences*, Hong Kong, 2011. pp. 164–167.

Trouvain, Jürgen. and F. Brackhane. "The Relevance Today of Wolfgang von Kempelen's Speaking Machine". In Trouvain, Jürgen und Barry, William (Eds.), *Phonus 16 Forschungsberichte des Instituts für Phonetik der Universität des Saarlandes*. Saarbrücken, 2011a pp. 149–166.

Vicq-d'Azyr, Félix. "Mémoire sur la voix. De la structure des organes qui servent à la formation de la voix considerés dans l'Homme & dans les differentes classes d'Animaux, & comparés entr'eux." *Mémoire de l'Academie royale des Sciences*, 1779, p. 206.

von Haller, Albrecht. *Elementa Physiologiae Corporis Humani* [Physiological Elements of the Human Body], 8 volumes and supplement. Lausannae (volumes 1–5 and 9): Sumptibus Marci-Michael Bousquet & Sociorum; Bernae (volumes 6–8). 1757–1782.

von Haller, Albrecht. Onomatologia medica completa. Ulm, Frankfurt, and Leipzig: Gaumischen Handlung, 1756. [The article Dens ['tooth'] referred to by von Kempelen is on pp. 298–307.]

von Helmont, Franciscus M. *Alphabeti vere naturalis Hebraici brevissima delineatio quae simul methodum suppediat, juxta quam qui surdi nati sunt sic informari possunt, ut non alios saltem loquentes intelligant, sed & ipsi ad sermonis usum perveniant.* Lichtenthaler, 1657.

von Helmont, Franciscus M. *Kurtzer Entwurff des Eigentlichen Natur-Alphabets der Heiligen Sprache: Nach dessen Anleitung man auch Taubgebohrne verstehend und redend machen kan. Ans Licht gegeben durch F. M. B. V. Hellmont.* Lichtenthaler, 1667.

von Kempelen, Wolfgang. *Mechanismus der menschlichen Sprache nebst Beschreibung einer sprechenden Maschine. (Faks.-Neudr. ed. H. H. Brekle & W. Wildgen).* Frommann, 1970.

von Kempelen, Wolfgang. *Mechanismus der menschlichen Sprache nebst Beschreibung einer sprechenden maschine.* J. B. Degen, 1791a.

von Kempelen, Wolfgang. *Le mécanisme de la parole, suivi de la description d'une machine parlante.* J. B. Degen., 1791b.

von Kempelen, Wolfgang, et al. *Mechanismus der menschlichen Sprache.* TUDpress, 2017.

von Windisch, Karl Gottlieb. *Karl Gottlieb von Windisch's Briefe über den Schachspieler des Herrn von Kempelen nebst drey Kupferstichen die diese berühmte Maschine vorstellen, herausgegeben von Chr. von Mechel der K. K. und anderer Akademien Mitgliede.* Mechel, 1783a.

von Windisch, Karl G. *Briefe über den Schachspieler des Herrn von Kempelen.* Löwe, 1783b.

von Windisch, Karl G. (1783c). *Lettres De M. Charles Gottlieb De Windisch Sur Le Joueur d'Echecs De M. De Kempelen. Trad. libre de l'allemand. Publ. par Chrétien de Mechel, Membre de l'Acad. Impériale & Royale de Vienne & de plusieurs autres.* Mechel, 1783c.

von Windisch, Karl G. *Inanimate reason; or a circumstantial account of that astonishing piece of mechanism, M. de Kempelen's chess-player; now exhibiting at No. 8, Savile-Row, Burlington-Gardens; illustrated with three copper-plates, exhibiting this celebrated automaton, in different points of view. Translated from the original letters of M. Charles Gottlieb de Windisch.* Bladon, 1784.

Wallis, Johannis. *Grammatica linguae anglicanae: cui praefigitur, de loquela sive sonorum formatione, tractatus grammatico-physicus. Et (nunc primum) subjungitur, praxis grammatica.* Oxford: Typis L. Lichfield, 1674. [For an English translation, see Wallis and Kemp 1972.]

Wallis, John and J. Kemp. *Grammar of the English language: with an introductory grammatico-physical Treatise on speech (or on the formation of all speech sounds).* New ed. / with translation and commentary by J.A. Kemp. Longman, 1972.

Weibel, Peter. 2007. "Preface". In *Man-[in the]-Machine*, Bernhard Serexhe and Peter Weibel, eds. Matthes und Seitz, 2007. p. 6.

Zobel, Rudolph H. *Thoughts on the different opinions on the origin of language.* Lange, 1773.

Contributors

Bert Vaux is Professor of Phonology and Morphology at Cambridge University and a fellow of King's College, Cambridge.

Rivka Brod Hyland is a Rhodes Scholar and a graduate of Harvard and Oxford Universities. She lives and works in Istanbul.

Amanda McHugh holds BA and MPhil degrees in Linguistics from King's College, Cambridge University, with specialisms in phonetics and French.

Shushan M. Teager, an alumna of Wellesley College and MIT, is a retired research associate at the Boston University School of Medicine where she worked with her late husband, Professor Herbert Teager, chief of the department of biomedical engineering, on mapping air flow in the vocal tract during phonation. She lives in Belmont, MA.

www.ingramcontent.com/pod-product-compliance
Lightning Source LLC
Chambersburg PA
CBHW071830170426
43191CB00046B/1194